MODELING CONSCIOUSNESS ACROSS THE DISCIPLINES

Edited by

J. Scott Jordan

University Press of America,® Inc.
Lanham • New York • Oxford

Copyright © 1999 by
University Press of America,® Inc.
4720 Boston Way
Lanham, Maryland 20706

12 Hid's Copse Rd.
Cumnor Hill, Oxford OX2 9JJ

Library of Congress Cataloging-in-Publication Data

Modeling consciousness across the disciplines / edited by J. Scott
Jordan
p.   cm.
Includes bibliographical references and index.
1. Consciousness. I. Jordan, J. Scott
B808.9.375   1999   126—dc21   99-045035 CIP

ISBN 0-7618-1523-6 (cloth: alk. ppr.)

♾™ The paper used in this publication meets the minimum
requirements of American National Standard for Information
Sciences—Permanence of Paper for Printed Library Materials,
ANSI Z39.48—1984

Contents

Explicit Models of Consciousness

Foreword

Explaining Consciousness:
What Questions?
What Answers?

Wolfgang Prinz

Explaining Consciousness:
Correlations Versus Foundations

During the last decade, consciousness has reached the brain. For centuries, if not millennia, it was the exclusive reserve of philosophical discourse. However, more recently, and for more than a century now, experimental and other psychologists have also joined in. And now neurobiologists are declaring this to be the decade of the brain and getting involved too. They have published book after book promising to solve the last remaining human enigma through the natural sciences: the enigma of consciousness—namely, the enigma regarding how consciousness emerges from brain activity. And psychologists, who, naturally, do not wish to be pushed aside, continue to brood over which functions *the* consciousness may possess in our mental machinery, what it achieves, what it is good for, and how we would manage without it. Complete books, journals, special issues, learned conferences, and eminent scientific societies talk about nothing other than *the* consciousness.

What for actually? Seen in the light of day, ordinary research practice in neurobiology and experimental psychology has absolutely nothing to do with these questions. Although the research programs of both disciplines have historical forerunners that started off with questions describing consciousness, this was all a long time ago, and in the 150 years since then, we could almost say that these sciences have mislaid consciousness. Modern experimental psychology studies the mechanisms underlying cognitive performance, and it does this almost exclusively on the basis of behavioral data. Cognitive neurobiology takes a very similar approach: It studies how these mechanisms are produced by brain functions, and it does this almost exclusively by experimentally observing the physics, chemistry, or physiology of brain processes. There is no trace of consciousness. To carry out their daily business, both disciplines have arranged things in order to ignore the issue.

Nonetheless, we cannot let it be, and this is certainly not just because of philosophers who, despite several centuries of philosophical discourse, have never tired of thinking about the nature of consciousness. It is also due to ourselves; to the fact that we ourselves *are* the systems we *study* scientifically. One consequence of this is that we cannot desist from thinking about how our consciousness relates to our brain processes—so to speak, weekend thoughts that we indulge in when resting from our everyday research.

Let us leaf through these books: We find a great deal on what modern neurobiology knows about brain functions; about the chemistry, the physics, the physiology, and, not least, the neuroinformational modeling of neural activity at various integration levels. Further on, we read what modern psychology knows about information processing, about functional system architectures and operations that work on them. Finally, we also find suggestions regarding which of the structures and processes described in this way *are related*, as it is always phrased, *to consciousness.*

Does this mean that we have already collected all the necessary pieces for a theory of consciousness? Haven't we got everything we need? Apparently not, because reading these books generally leaves us with an extremely empty feeling. We do not gain the impression of having gained any explanation of what is special about the phenomena of consciousness that would enable us to understand why these phenomena are the way they are; in other words, why they possess the character that defines them as being conscious. And we cannot shrug off the feeling that even if we were to have an accurate theory on what constitutes the neurobiological correlates and/or the psychological functions of consciousness, we would still be far from understanding why the neurobiological correlates produce *exactly this quality*, or why the psychological functions *require exactly this quality* and not some other. And, vice versa, we are just as far from understanding why *certain* processes at the subpersonal level elicit this quality at the personal level, whereas others, in contrast, do not. What distinguishes these subpersonal processes that possess this potential from those that do not possess it? None of the theories currently being offered can provide even a suggestion of an answer to such questions. Instead, they provide explanations in terms of formal correlations that one can acknowledge, but not in terms of *substantial foundations* that one can understand.

Against this background, I shall present a brief discussion on the two questions posed in the title. The first refers to the nature of the *explanandum*: What is it exactly that should be explained? What does *conscious* actually mean? Anyone who poses this question is walking into a minefield. All terms, all concepts, and all ideas that have ever been introduced to differentiate and isolate what is meant in this discussion have a confused history and a confusing present. Nonetheless, I shall propose an answer. It is not new, but of all those with which I am familiar, it is the most plausible as well as the most productive.

The second question refers to which types of explanation the previously determined *explanandum* has to provide in order for them to be valid. My concern here will not be to deliver my own theory on the phenomena in question, but to specify which demands such theories have to meet. Criteria can then be derived from these demands and used not only to judge existing theories but also to develop new ones. My guiding idea is simple enough: Not only must theories report (in formal terms) *under which conditions* a certain factual situation emerges; they must also provide a plausible account (in terms of content) of why it is *exactly this factual situation* that emerges under these conditions and not any other. The first question, is easy; the second, in contrast, is rather difficult.

What Questions?

Hence, what is our *explanandum*; what do we want to explain? Being awake, or conscious is expressed in the fact that we are conscious of *certain contents*. We cannot be conscious in a pure, content-free form. When we are conscious, it is always certain contents that we are conscious of—or to express it another way—of which we are aware. It is through *being aware* of these *contents* that we first recognize that it is *we* who are *conscious*.

A number of theories believe that mental contents can possess a conscious or a nonconscious character. However, mental contents that are not conscious cannot be directly observed, but only indirectly infered. This is why the properties that we attribute to them depend strongly on our prior theoretical assumptions about the conditions under which mental contents are conscious versus nonconscious, and when they can change from the one state into the other. *Unconscious, preconscious, inaccessible to consciousness, subliminal*—these are all examples of completely different, theory-dependent complementary terms. They describe classes of mental contents that are distinct from the class of conscious mental contents. For all these nonconscious contents, we believe (or the corresponding theories so claim) that they are fully capable of influencing behavior in the background, even when persons do not know anything about them and their effectiveness.

How, then, are conscious mental contents possible? What exactly is responsible for their conscious character? An answer to this question should provide us with the *explanandum* that we can then use in our search for appropriate explanations. In 1874, Franz Brentano published a study on the empirical foundations of psychology that contained a detailed discussion on the nature of mental phenomena and what distinguishes them from physical phenomena (Brentano, 1924). The theory of mental acts developed in this study is simultaneously a theory regarding the structure of the facts of consciousness.

Brentano uses an extremely simple example to discuss the nature of mental acts: What actually happens when we hear a tone? What is responsible for the conscious character of this event? According to Brentano, there are two contents interwoven in every mental act: the *tone* that we hear and the fact that we *hear* it. However, these two mental contents are not represented in the same way. The tone is the primary object of hearing; we can observe it directly in the mental act.

Hearing itself, in contrast, is—in a paradoxical formulation—the secondary object of the act of hearing. Brentano says that it cannot be observed in the mental act, but attains consciousness in another, indirect form: "We can observe the tones that we hear, but we cannot observe the hearing of the tones. This is because it is only in the hearing of the tones that the hearing itself is assessed" (1924, p. 180, translated).

Phenomena of consciousness are thus characterized by a twofold content: They contain the object toward which they are directed (the tone) and the way in which this object is given (through hearing). In modern terms, we would say that the object (the primary object) is conscious *explicitly*; the form in which it is given (the secondary object), in contrast, is conscious *implicitly*.

However, if we want a really exhaustive characterization of the structure of mental acts, we have to go one step further: If it is true that the hearing of the tone contains not only the tone itself but also, implicitly, its hearing as well, then the subject who hears must also be included in the act in *still another encapsulation*. This is because hearing is inconceivable without a subject who hears—just like a tone is scarcely conceivable without a hearing that is directed toward it.

This brings us very close to what I consider to be a convincing descriptive characterization of what determines the conscious character of mental contents: Conscious mental acts are characterized by the fact that the subject of the actor is always implicitly present in them. The mental acts of a person *differ* according to their secondary objects (the person hears, sees, thinks, believes, hopes, fears, or feels that something is the case) or even according to their primary objects (the person hears a tone, a noise, a voice)—but they *are identical* in that the same subject is present in the background of all acts. When I hear a tone, the hearing is *my* hearing; and when I think about something, it is *my* thought; and when I want to do something, it is *my* volition that I become aware of. In other words, and detached from Brentano's act terminology, the implicit presence of the *mental self* is constitutive for the conscious character of mental contents. In this sense, the mental self forms the common content-related *brace* that ties together the otherwise completely different phenomena of consciousness.

It seems as if we have reached a point at which we have sufficiently demarcated our *explanandum* and can start to look for *explanantia*. The question we pose is directed toward a certain property that mental contents can assume under certain conditions: How is their being conscious possible? How is it possible for mental contents to assume a conscious character in this sense?

What Answers?

As mentioned above, the present concern is not to discuss answers to this question, but criteria that the answers would have to meet in order to be viewed as satisfactory. What sort of explanations do theories have to offer us before we can finally say that we now *understand* how conscious mental contents are possible?

Basically, the considerations so far have led to the conclusion that the conscious character of mental contents can be explained only by theories that clarify the role of the implicitly present mental self. Were this role to have been understood—so is my premise in the following—the functional foundations of the conscious character of certain mental contents would also have been understood.

However, what does explaining the role of the mental self mean exactly? We still need to specify this task more precisely in a twofold way. First, what does it mean to explain *a role*? How can we explain, for example, the role of the liver for the organism? We do this by reporting two things: *what* the liver does for the other organs and the total organism, and *how* it does this. Complete explanations of function always require both the specification of the *performance* of an organ and the specification of the *mechanisms* by which it achieves this performance. In biology, these two types of explanation have sometimes been described as ultimate versus proximate explanations.

Second, what can it mean to explain the role of *the mental self.* Theories explaining the role of the mental self and its significance for the conscious character of mental contents are nothing more than theories about the *personal constitution* of conscious mental life. If they wish to provide an understanding of this personal constitution, they are well-advised to draw on other explanations that are nonpersonal or extrapersonal. Ultimate explanations on the suprapersonal level can be considered just as much as proximate explanations on the subpersonal level.

What theories on the conscious character of mental contents have to deliver can now be defined. In particular, they have to deliver two things: First, they have to provide a plausible account of what the mental self performs *from a suprapersonal perspective.* Second, they have to describe the mechanisms responsible for these performances *from a subpersonal perspective.* Only when we have both—performance and mechanisms—shall we have a chance to understand the personal constitution of conscious mental life and to explain the conscious character of mental contents.

Suprapersonal Stories

What is the mental self good for? Why did evolution (or human history) invent it? And when did this occur? Did it already emerge in insects, in reptiles, or in birds? Or not until the mammals, the primates, or the hominoids? Or, finally, did it appear between the Iliad and the Odyssey as Julian James has tried to convince us? The answer is crucial for our understanding of ourselves and the world—and also for our relationship to other animals.

Theories proposing answers to these questions typically take the form of suprapersonal stories—stories explaining how it came about that the mental self was invented, and which advantages this brought. In other words, these theories construct hypothetical scenarios that provide plausible accounts of how certain (groups of) life-forms, which initially do not possess a mental self, gain certain fitness advantages when they form such an element—with the consequence that they change from a *self-less into an self-shaped constitution.*

A number of stories of this kind have been told in recent years by, for example, Dennett (1992), Jaynes (1976), Lutz (1992), Metzinger (1993), and Prinz (1996). Although this is not the place to discuss their relative merits, it may be interesting to name a few points toward which they all converge despite their many differences. First, they believe that the transition from a self-less to a self-shaped state occurred at some point during the history of the human race; be it in dark, anonymous prehistoric times (Prinz) or comparatively recently between the Iliad and the Odyssey (Jaynes). Second, they emphasize different kinds of cognitive and dynamic advantages that accompany the formation of a "model of the self " (Metzinger, translated) such as the performance of the mental self as a center of cognitions and/or source of actions (Dennett, Prinz). Third, they also discuss the transition to a self-shaped state in terms of how it contributes to the social control and sanctioning of actions as well as—in a related context—the societal and political conditions that have promoted or hindered the psychohistorical process of the constitution of the self-shaped state (Jaynes, Lutz, Prinz).

Subpersonal Mechanisms

Which properties do we have to attribute to the subpersonal mechanisms underlying the effectiveness of the mental self?

What such mechanisms should look like cannot be discussed in detail here. Nonetheless, two aspects are important: First, ideas have to be developed on how the mental self is represented, and how this representation differs from that of other objects and events. Second, ideas have to be developed on which representational foundations may be responsible for the explicit representation of objects and events being supplemented by the presence of an implicit self. The theory will meet our expectations only when both are achieved: first, to provide a (correlational) understanding of why the conscious character of mental contents *occurs only when* the conditions of the implicit presence of the self are met, and, second, to simultaneously provide a (foundational) understanding of why the conscious character of mental contents *consists in the fact that* the mental self is implicitly present.

As a consequence, theories on the subpersonal mechanisms that elicit conscious mental contents have to be theories on processes and structures with a *metarepresentational character*. They have to provide at least two levels of representation: one for the mental contents (primary object), and a further one for the relationship of the contents to the self (secondary and tertiary object). Approaches toward such theories can be found in, for example, Edelman (1989), Flohr (1994) and Metzinger (1993).

The Hen and the Egg

I started with the observation that conscious contents are characterized by the implicit presence of the mental self. However, I have subjected this observation to a specific interpretation that goes further. Namely, I have assumed that the presence of the self gives rise to the conscious character of mental contents: *no consciousness without self*. This interpretation has to be accepted if we want to obtain a representational theory that derives the conscious character of mental contents from the implicit presence of the self, and the questions and answers sketched here are meaningful only within the framework of this theory.

The opposite would be a theory based on the inverse assumption that the conscious character of mental contents is primary, and that the mental self is a secondary outcome of this: *no self without consciousness*. By following this interpretation, it is naturally impossible to do what I have done and use it to derive an approach for explaining the phenomena of consciousness. If the mental self comes from *being conscious*, where *being conscious* itself comes from is still a mystery.

Who's right? Which is the hen and which is the egg? I believe that my proposal distributes the roles in such a way that several enigmas disappear while no new ones arise to replace them. This is, in any case, the yardstick against which my proposal will be measured.

References

Brentano, F. [1874] 1924. *Psychologie vom empirischen Standpunkt* [Psychology from an empirical perspective] (Vol. 1). Reprint, Leipzig, Germany: Meiner.

Dennett, D. 1992. The self as the center of narrative gravity. In *Self and consciousness: Multiple perspectives*, edited by F. S. Kessel, P. M. Cole, and D. L. Johnson. Hillsdale, NJ: Erlbaum.

Edelman, G. M. 1989. *The remembered present: A biological theory of consciousness*. New York: Basic Books.

Flohr, H. 1994. Denken und Bewusstsein [Thinking and consciousness]. In *Neuroworlds. Gehirn-Geist-Kultur* , edited by J. Fedrowitz, D. Matejovsky, and G. Kaiser. Frankfurt, Germany: Campus.

Jaynes, J. 1976. *The origin of consciousness in the breakdown of the bicameral mind*. Boston, MA: Houghton Mifflin.

Lutz, C. 1992. Culture and consciousness: A problem in the anthropology of knowledge. In *Self and consciousness: Multiple perspectives*, edited by F. S. Kessel, P. M. Cole, and D. L. Johnson. Hillsdale, NJ: Erlbaum.

Metzinger, T. 1993. *Subjekt und Selbstmodell. Die Perspektive phänomenalen Bewusstsein vor dem Hintergrund einer naturalistischen Theorie mentaler Repräsentationen* [Subject and model of the self: The perspective of phenomenal consciousness against the background of a naturalistic theory of mental representations]. Paderborn, Germany: Schöningh.

Prinz, W., Roth, G., and Maasen, S. 1996. Kognitive Leistungen und Gehirnfunktionen [Cognitive performance and brain functions]. In *Kopf-Arbeit. Gehirnfunktionen und kognitive Leistungen* , edited by G. Roth and W. Prinz. Heidelberg, Germany: Spektrum-Verlag.

Preface

In the Spring of 1994, *Scientific American* published an article entitled, "Can Science Explain Consciousness?" It was no coincidence that this article opened with a discussion of Nobeloriet Francis Crick's opinion on the topic. Crick's outspoken neurological materialism symbolizes the resurgence of consciousness as a viable topic of scientific investigation, and further serves as fair warning that the game is afoot: The race for consciousness is on.

As I read this article, and others regarding this new science of consciousness, I tried to visualize the model of consciousness being developed. Most of what I read left me with two options: (1) Consciousness is caused by the brain, or (2) Consciousness *is* the brain. The former position acknowledges that consciousness is something different than the brain, but no one seems to know just *where* this non-brain consciousness is located. The latter position claims to know both *what* consciousness is and *where* it is located. Of course I jest, and perhaps I simplify, but in all honesty I found, and continue to find, these models of consciousness much too simple. In both, consciousness is described as an *effect*. In neither model do I find room for consciousness to be the cause of its own effects, or the effect of its own causes. Consciousness is being downsized: Beethoven and Shakespeare are being laid-off from their high-paying positions as spokespersons for the human condition, and are being forced to undergo out-placement training as brain manipulators.

Concerned about the vigor with which such downsizing was being professed, I initiated, at Saint Xavier University in Chicago, what I called the Consciousness Project. I called together faculty from within the School of Arts and Sciences whom I felt would be interested in this topic, and at our first meeting I knew I had struck a vein. Within minutes, people were describing both the explicit and implicit models of consciousness being utilized within their disciplines. When I was finally able to call the meeting to order, the first question the group had for me was, "Well Scott, what do you mean by consciousness?" I felt at the time the answer would most likely reveal itself within a transdisciplinary dialogue. Thus was born, *Modeling Consciousness Across the Disciplines: A Symposium.*

The purpose of the symposium was to initiate such a transdisciplinary dialogue. This format was intended to reflect the multiple, dynamically-interrelated levels of organization that must be in place in order for the phenomenon of human consciousness to exist. These levels of organization range in scale from the atomic to the social. It was assumed that such a transdisciplinary exchange would provide a forum in which the phenomenon of consciousness might receive the sort of holistic approach its complexity warrants. It was also assumed that such an approach might provide a unifying theme for the arts and sciences by revealing their dependency upon that from which all disciplines emerged—namely, human consciousness.

This book contains chapters based on the symposium's proceedings. Larry R. Vandervert, who gave the keynote address, describes consciousness as arising from the algorithmic organization of the brain, and the implications it holds for the future form of general education. Lawrence Souder writes about the rhetoric of consciousness, and the manner in which such rhetoric serves to constrain the debate. Charlotte Stokes traces out the historical relationship between models of consciousness and art, while Michael D. Rabe deciphers artworks from the aniconic period of early Buddhism to determine what they reveal about the Buddhist approach to consciousness. E. Paul Colella invokes the writings of Giambattista Vico—a contemporary of Descartes who saw, even then, the danger incurred by the dividing of human condition into *res cogitans* and *res extensa*. Andrew Bailey proposes that William James' seemingly inconsistent approach to consciousness becomes rather coherent when conceptualized within the framework of chaos theory, and L. Andrew Coward describes a system architecture which, due to its functional complexity and lack of explicit instructions, affords a realistic means of relating the phenomena of consciousness to physiological processes. I am eternally grateful to these scholars, first for having participated in the original symposium, and second, for having inspired me to see this book through to its end. The patience and tolerance they extended to me throughout the entire process has been a model of professional congeniality.

In order to extend the book's multidisciplinary reach, I have included six additional chapters. These were contributed by scholars whose approach to consciousness had not yet been touched upon by any of the earlier contributions. These include a contribution of my own, in which I present John Dewey's century-old critique of the reflex-arc concept, and then recast it within the conceptual framework of a theory which assumes consciousness to be anticipatory in nature. Cees van Leeuwen, Ilse Verstijnen, and Paul Hekkert present a theory of the conscious and unconscious processes involved in perception and imagery, and then use this theory to account for why it is artists generate sketches during the production of modern visual art. Jochen Müsseler discusses special relativity theory and the possibility that such an account can also be given of human consciousness. Bruce K. Kirchoff addresses the social, constructive nature of consciousness, and describes the implications of assuming the primacy of any particular construction. Harald Atmanspacher and Frederick Kronz examine the concept *realism*, how it is used in theoretical physics, and what it might mean to say something is "real." Finally, Larry R. Vandervert and I describe academia's current commitment to dualist conceptualizations of truth and consciousness, and the impact such conceptualizations have upon the nature of liberal education.

As the reader will see, I have divided the book into two general sections. The first contains contributions which explicitly address the nature of consciousness, while the second contains those that examine the manner in which the term "consciousness" is utilized. The only reason for creating these general sections is to once again make explicit the purpose of this book. I am not proposing a particular theory of consciousness. To the contrary, I am attempting to bring together a collection of works that collectively clarify the immense scope of the problem. The concept "conscious" influences all of our disciplines in one way or another, and if we want to have anything to say about the nature of that influence, we need to be engaged in the debate.

Acknowledgments

I am indebted to a number of individuals and institutions for their support of this project. As regards institutions, I would like to thank Saint Xavier University, the Max Planck Institute for Psychological Research, and the Alexander von Humboldt Foundation. I would also like to thank the following journals: *Transactions of the Charles Peirce Society*, *New Ideas in Psychology* and *Acta Polytechnica Scandinavica*, for granting permission to reprint the papers of Andrew Bailey, J. Scott Jordan, and Harald Atmanspacher and Frederick Kronz, respectively. As regards individuals, I would like to extend my sincere gratitude to the Dean of the School of Arts and Science at Saint Xavier University, Dr. Lawrence Frank, for his enthusiastic support of the symposium that inspired this book. In addition, I would like to thank Ms. Alice Brosius and Mr. Richard Randol for all the help they provided to ensure the success of the symposium. Also, a special heart-felt thanks goes out to Dr. Michael D. Rabe and Ms. Jacquelyn Harrison for creating the beautiful icon that adorned the symposium's program. And last, but not least, I would like to thank my wife Linda K. Jordan for her constant support and advice.

Explicit Models of Consciousness

Chapter 1

Maximizing Consciousness Across the Disciplines: Mechanisms of Information Growth in General Education

Larry R. Vandervert

The purpose of this paper is to provide a needed new way to understand epistemological and pedagogical questions related to the nature of the general education. There will be nothing said here of the traditional history and philosophy of general education. The great value of such accounts of general liberal education is surely recognized, but those discussions do not at all fall within the scope of this paper. It is not that traditional accounts are irrelevant to issues and processes addressed here, rather it is that traditional accounts address them at a different level.

During the last decade, computer systems have given rise to exceptionally rapid advances in both the availability and manipulation of knowledge in virtually every sector of what is becoming a global information society. Certainly, general education in our colleges and universities is no exception to this trend. Within general education, advances in knowledge availability is so rapid, that new, *fundamental* understandings of information growth are needed in order to develop pedagogical and curricular practices to manage them. To begin to chart broad notions of such fundamentals, I will (a) present basic socio-cultural mechanisms of information growth that are connected to newer conceptions of the evolution of the functional organization of the human brain, and (b) describe pedagogical and curricular implications of the relationship between the brain's functional organization and the growth in knowledge availability and manipulation for interdisciplinary studies in general education.

Evolutionary Perspective

The general evolutionary perspective to be followed throughout this paper combines converging principles of mathematical evolutionary biology, evolutionary psychology, cognitive psychology, developmental psychology, and information science. By combining principles from these disciplines an explanation can be constructed for the progressive selection of information growth that is related to the advance of the full historical range of human culture.

The evolutionary mechanisms to be described are fully compatible with those of the substantial and rapidly growing field of *evolutionary psychology*:

> Evolutionary psychology is psychology informed by the fact that the inherited architecture of the human mind is the product of the evo-lutionary process. It is a conceptually integrated approach in which theories of selection pressures are used to generate hypotheses about the design features of the human mind, and in which our knowledge of psychological and behavioral phenomena can be organized and aug-mented by placing them in their functional context. *Evolutionary psy-chologists expect to find a functional mesh between adaptive problems and the structure of the mechanisms that evolved to solve them* [italics added]. (Cosmides, Tooby, & Barkow, 1992, p. 7)

See also Tooby and Cosmides (1995). A similar theoretical statement concerning the foregoing evolution of the "inherited architecture of the human mind" appears in the extensive body of cognitive domain spe-cificity research (see, for example, Hirschfeld & Gelman, 1994).

It may at first be difficult to conceive how fundamental evolutionary principles guide the progressive unfoldment of general education. But such conceptions have a considerable history among evolutionists and information scientists. In what follows I devote only the absolutely essential space to the more "arcane" evolutionary fundamentals, moving rapidly to more familiar ideas related to information growth in general education.

Information Growth: A Directional Arrow
in Biological Evolution

Biological evolution may be uninformed as to outcome, but like the directional arrows that describe how time unfolds in the physical evolution of the universe, biological evolution follows an information-based "arrow" or direction of unfoldment.[1] Mathematical biologist, Alfred Lotka (1922, 1945) developed the fundamental energy-information principle of *progressive* evolutionary selection. Earlier, Boltzmann (1905) had brought evolutionary processes into the energy realm in his classic statement on selection that, "[the] Struggle for existence is a struggle for free energy available for work," (p. 23). Then, further elaborating Boltzmann's conception, Lotka (1922) formulated the *maximum-power principle* of evolution. The maximum-power principle describes the competitive "*maximization* arrow" of the energy-information flow through the system of organic nature: "Evolution ... proceeds in such *direction* [italics added] as to make the total energy [and information] flux through the system a maximum," (Lotka, 1922, p. 147).

Odum and Odum (1981) and Odum (1983, 1988, 1996) have applied Lotka's maximum-power principle to the description of ecosystems. In his award-winning work Odum (1988, 1996) delineated energy-information flow *pathways* within the maximum-power principle which allow a rigorous scientific approach to the evolutionary dynamics of not only ecosystems, but, as will be seen below, to all other living systems. For the purposes of this paper I will present Odum and Odum's (1981) generalized version of the maximum-power principle in the relevant informational terms:

> *Those systems that survive in the competition among alternative choices are those that develop more information inflow and use it to meet the needs of survival.* They do this by: (1) developing storages of high-quality information; (2) feeding forward and feeding back information from the storages to increase inflows; (3) recycling information as needed; (4) organizing informational control mechanisms that keep

the system adapted and stable; (5) setting up exchanges with other systems to supply special information needs; and (6) contributing useful information to the surrounding environmental system that helps maintain favorable conditions. (pp. 32-33)

The maximum-power information flow through the system is, by selective design, *autocatalytic*. That is, maximum-power information flows tend toward maximization in a self-organizing, self-referential (feeding forward and feeding back) manner and follow, precisely, thermodynamic principles. I will return to the idea of self-organization in table 1 to be presented below.

How the Maximum-Power Principle is Manifest in Consciousness

Consciousness, like everything else in nature, can be understood as an outcome of dynamic energy principles. When circuits in a brain play-out the maximum-power principle, a consciousness that parallels the dynamics of the ecosystem in which they are embedded becomes manifest in the experience of that brain. This parallelism selectively embeds the creature's nervous system in the ecosystem. Following this thesis I proposed that consciousness originates in a mostly hardwired autocatalytic, self-referential neuromatrix in the brain (Vandervert, 1995).

This neuromatrix was postulated by Melzack (1992) to explain the experience of phantom limbs in amputees and in those with *congenital limb deficiencies*. The experience of phantom limbs is a fully *conscious* experience (in the same manner that one might be conscious of their own bodies or their own thoughts) of the phantom presence of the missing limb. The person experiencing a phantom limb may, for example, try to stand on a phantom foot or pick up a cup with a phantom hand (see Melzack, 1992, p. 120; Melzack, Israel, Lacroix & Schultz, 1997, Tables 2A & 2B).

The conscious *attributes* of the three brain circuits of Melzack's neuromatrix illustrate how the phantom limb experience is nearly indistinguishable from the experience of our everyday active "stream of consciousness." Melzack (1992) described these circuits and their phenomenal attributes as follows:

In essence, I postulate that the brain contains a neuromatrix, or network of neurons, that, in addition to responding to sensory simulation, continuously generates a characteristic pattern of impulses indicating that the body is intact and unequivocally one's own. If such a matrix operated in the absence of sensory inputs from the periphery of the body, it would create the impression of having a limb even when that limb is removed.

To produce all of the qualities I have described for phantoms, the matrix would have to be quite extensive, including at least three major neural circuits in the brain. One of them, of course, is the classical sensory pathway passing through the thalamus to the somatosensory cortex [giving rise to phantom experiences of the limb being physically extended in space as an 'entity' that can be moved and mentally manipulated, and having sensory experiences—pressure, warmth, cold, wet, itches].

A second system must consist of the pathways leading through the reticular formation of the brain stem to the limbic system, which is critical for emotion and motivation. I include this circuit in part because I and others have noted that paraplegics who suffer a complete spinal break high in the upper body continue to experience themselves as still being in their old body, and they describe the feelings in the denervated areas with the same kinds of affective terms as they did before they were injured, such as 'painful,' 'pleasurable' or 'exhausting.'

A final system consists of cortical regions important to the recognition of the self and to the evaluation of sensory signals. A major part of this system is in the parietal lobe, which in studies of brain-damage patients has been shown to be essential to the sense of self.

Indeed, patients who have suffered a lesion of the parietal lobe in one hemisphere have been known to push one of their own legs out of a hospital bed because they were convinced it belonged to a stranger. Such behavior shows that the damaged area normally imparts a signal that says, 'This is my body; it is a part of myself.' (p. 123; see also Melzack et al., 1997, for a detailed account, based on 46 people, of the attributes of phantom experiences)

The phantoms generated through the brain circuits Melzack describes have all of the attributes including the "feel" of everyday consciousness and self-consciousness. The fact that the phantoms occur not only in child and adult amputees, but in people congenitally limb-deficient is, I believe, convincing evidence that this continuously generating neuromatrix circuitry is largely hardwired and is the body reference frame's foundational neurophysiological source from which a dynamical maximum-power principle consciousness arises. Thus the neuromatrix is the creature's way of autocatalytically and self-referentially embedding itself within its environmental reference frame.

In the next section we see how culture is most fundamentally a maximum-power reference frame for the further evolutionary embedding of human consciousness in its environment.

Lotka's Ground-Breaking Ideas on Maximal Information Growth in Culture

Quite ahead of his time, Lotka (1945) extrapolated the progressive maximal energy-information arrow of evolution to the accelerated adaptation rate of human culture:

> Man, one of the latest, and in his own judgment the highest product of evolution, has hitherto signally conformed with the principle of increasing energy flux [information flow, for our purposes]. By ingenious contrivances he has immensely refined and multiplied the operation of his receptor-effector apparatus. The excess of energy [information] captured, over the energy [information] barely sufficient for mere maintenance, has in his case grown to a wholly unparalleled magnitude. Normally this leaves him with a large balance available for 'play' activities and luxuries. And some of his play activities have turned out to be a most profitable reinvestment. For among them must be classed scientific research indulged in primarily out of curiosity, but resulting among other things in that complete recasting of methods of production which is known as the industrial and agricultural revolution. Aside from its direct benefits this has made it possible to spend relatively large amounts on sanitary improvements, on medical education and research, and, above all, on better living among the masses of the people. (p. 188)

Thus Lotka set the stage for an information-based evolutionary analysis of the development of culture. Were Lotka writing today, he no doubt would cite the profound acceleration of the flow of information occurring in the present *information revolution*. In today's allied information growth among computing systems, businesses and industries (coming together in, for example, parcel delivery systems) and education, the six information flow features of the maximum-power principle can clearly be seen to be necessary to efficient, competitive operations.

Information Growth in General Education

Odum and Odum's identification of the six real-world information flow features of maximum-power principle evolution described earlier has been profoundly useful in understanding how the principle applies to the evolution of educational systems. In an extension and refinement of Lotka's above description of the energetic evolution of culture, Odum (1988) applied the maximum-power energy-information arrow to the growth of energy-information quality over levels of educational attainment.

Figure 1 describes the energy-information quality of the educational attainment "arrow" from preschool to legacies, just as one would describe the progressive arrow of an ecosystem food chain (say, from 762 pounds of plant matter to 59 pounds of moose to a pound of wolf).[2] The progression of levels of education toward legacies can be viewed as the advancing development of levels of mental processing (thinking, learning, creating) with increasing energy-information quality, territory and influence—informational legacies of principles and processes comprising the greatest *embodied* energy-information (see note 2). In addition, in accordance with the maximum-power principle, each level of education and each legacy *feeds back* its high-quality energy-information in the downward control of larger flows of lower-quality energy-information. This feeding back is accomplished, for example, through teaching and the embodied energy-information of books, journals, and other information systems, and results in an increased inflow of energy-information to those systems. Through this feedback, "A few Calories of higher-quality energy [and information] have the ability to [downwardly] determine the time and place of work of a larger flow of low-quality energy [and information]" (Odum & Odum, 1981, p. 81). Thus, while not meaning to deglamorize education, it is solely the higher-quality information embodied in teachers' and professors' nervous systems that places them in a position to control the time and place of the larger, lower-quality flows which comprise those of the students.[3]

At the same time, in order to generate the maximum amount of work and problem solving possible, each type of energy-information depicted in figure 1 must interact with an energy-information flow of another quality. For example, high-quality energy-information is wasted if it is not amplified through interaction with a larger flow of low-quality energy-information. So as an energy-information system, the professor needs the student to maximize the quality of his or her energy-information flows.

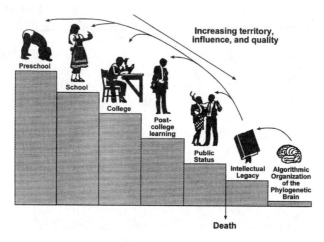

Fig. 1. Hierarchical levels of education attained in human development through the acquisition of cultural-level mental models, and the theoretical capacity of the algorithmic organization of the phylogenetic brain of Homo sapiens sapiens. The population of the United States in each category is graphed as a function of energy-information quality. More energy-information is embodied (concentrated) per unit of human mental development in school than preschool, and so on down the hierarchy. That is, as concentration takes place from left to right in the hierarchy, each unit has the capacity to do more work and solve more complex problems. The theoretical capacity of the energy concentration of the modern human brain is estimated at 22 intellectual/artistic legacies. The curved arrows indicate that the energy quality of the phylogenetic level algorithmic organization of the brain determines the time and place of energy-information flows associated with the cultural-level mental models, and so on back up the hierarchy.

In the next section I will describe how the maximum-power principle and the hierarchy of educational attainment depicted in figure 1 are translated into neural mechanisms by which the brain develops and learns as it moves through the hierarchy. In turn, the implications of these neural mechanisms for the general education curriculum will be described.

The Energy-Information Capacity of the Human Brain

Elsewhere (Vandervert, 1991), I proposed a further extrapolation of Odum's (1988) energy-information hierarchy of levels in human education. At the far right in figure 1 the hypothetical energy-information quality of the algorithmic organization of the phylogenetic human brain (the raw, non-enculturated brain of Homo sapiens) has been placed at the top of the energy-information hierarchy. In precise accordance with the maximum-power principle of evolution, the human brain represents the quintessential energy-information "equipment configuration" (embodiment), and it constantly feeds its Caloric order back down the hierarchy thus increasing the inflow of energy-information for its use.

The actual energy-information quality of a fully-developed, fully-enculturated human brain can only be estimated at the present time.[4] An estimate based on the fact that the oxygen consumption of the human brain is about 20% of that of the total body (Chien, 1981) places the embodied energy-information of the adult brain at 45 billion solar emjoules per joule (sej/J).[5] Since Odum (1988) has calculated that an informational legacy of principles and processes constitutes approximately 2 billion (sej/J) (see figure 1), each fully enculturated (or *maximally* educated) human brain would be equivalent to the energy-information embodiment of approximately 22 legacies! This estimated production potential of 22 legacies *for each brain* can be looked upon as an upper "limit" imposed by the calculations of the brain's energy-information embodiment as it might function in a maximal overall educational system. Below, I will describe brain functions, which will provide insight into how such maximal educational designs might be approached.

The Brain's Energy-Information Relationship to Cultural Evolution

Following the maximum-power principle's necessary leveraging relationship between lower and higher quality energy-information flows described earlier, the maximally high-quality phylogenetic brain (45 billion sej/J) is literally driven in accordance with the energy laws to construct lower quality flows than itself in order to maximize its own potential. That is, the brain's high-quality energy-information constructs in a *downward* fashion the ongoing evolution of the organization and activity of culture. This is precisely what is taking place in Lotka's (1945) quote describing the evolution of culture presented earlier, and in figure 1 where the immense, hardwired embodied information of the phylogenetic brain has constructed an informational legacy of lower quality energy-information (2 billion sej/J) than itself to increase inflow to itself. Such increased inflows of energy-information to the brain rep-. resent the way in which culture is seen to influence the further maximization of brain activity. Within the framework of increasing quality in education depicted in figure 1, the lower quality energy-information flows which the brain constructs are described as cultural-level mental *models* delivered via educational materials and practices, books, journals and so forth that are pertinent to each level of education (Vandervert, 1991, 1993, 1997a, 1997b).[6]

But what, precisely, is going on in the brain as it is driven toward the foregoing cultural maximization? It is to the brain as a maximizing modeling structure that we now turn.

The Brain as a Modeling System

It is obvious to anyone who has studied the functional organization of the brain that it is some sort of a *mapping* system. And, if the maps are put into a constant combinatorial motion in information processing, as they in fact are always operating, the algorithmic organization of the brain is best understood as a "mapping machine" (Jerison, 1991, p. 16). The brain mappings with which most people are familiar are the motor-sensory maps, which can be seen at the top of figure 2 (each person's own personal map looks *proportionately* like them). When we walk around, these maps "walk around." In fact, we'll see in a moment, that the experience of walking around "is" the activity of these maps.

Not so commonly known is that, in addition, there is a complete mapping of each person in the cerebellum in the lower back region of the brain (see figure 2). The information processing function of the cerebellar mappings, many contend, is related to faster-than-real-time simulative prediction of future states (see, Paulin, 1993, 1997; Pribram, 1971, 1991; Vandervert, 1997a). Added to these mappings there are visual, auditory, and olfactory mappings in the brain. When taken together, all of this mapping machinery erects representational perceptual-cognitive models inside the brain which parallel what's going on "out there" in the environment. (A model is defined here as a representation of some aspect of reality—see note 6.)

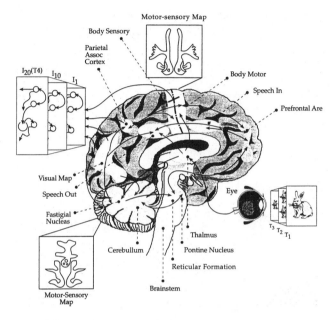

Fig. 2. A minimalist illustration of motor-sensory mappings in the central nervous system. The interconnections are meant to illustrate that the brain functions as a mapping/modeling system. At the same time the mapping/modeling activities of the brain are useful only in the service of anticipating future states of imagined or real moving systems.

In terms of higher cognitive processes occurring in the uniquely human brain (for example, through its highly elaborated neo-frontocerebellar functions associated with planning and prediction [MacLean, 1991]), it is more appropriate to refer to the brain as a *modeling* system as opposed to simply a "mapping" system. The term modeling system is more accurate I think, because it emphasizes the linguistic and creative functions of the brain as a representational system. That is, the cognitive informational modeling capacities of the human brain move far beyond the conventional point-to-point relational functions of conventional maps, into highly abstractive symbolic domains of modeling where completely *new* types of conceptions can be constructed. Such an informational structure permits a high degree of *nonlinearity*, where the form of new representations is not predictable within a closed-end analysis. That is, the outcome of the nonlinear sequence is not immediately derivable through a closed-end formula, but only becomes apparent by actually stepping though the iterations indicated by the formula.

Taking into account the entirety of mapping and modeling functions of the human brain, including those of the language centers depicted in figure 2 (which represents a minimalist version of those functions), it can be understood how it is a powerful modeling system that both students and professors bring to class each day. A classroom is indeed a room full of *extreme* high-quality energy-information modeling systems, each and collectively with an inherent tendency to operate and "develop-forward" in accordance with the hierarchical maximum-power outcomes and feedback loops as shown in figure 1. It will be proposed below that most conventional educational materials and practices not only fall regrettably short of enhancing maximization of the work of students' and professors' brain capacities, they actually thwart development toward maximizing information flows.

How the Maximum-Power Principle Operates Within the Mapping-Modeling Machinery of the Brain

Mandler (1988, 1992), a developmental psychologist, has proposed that meaning in the human brain arises in the form of perceptual-motor abstractive analogues she calls conceptual primitives that are *image-schemas*. Mandler further theorizes that such image-schemas provide the "conceptual basis for the acquisition of the of the relational aspects of language" (1992, p. 273)—thus connecting the two levels of image *mapping* and language neural *modeling*. I have proposed that information processing among the various mapping-modeling systems in the brain can be described as being carried out on the basis of Mandler's image-schemas (Vandervert, 1997a).

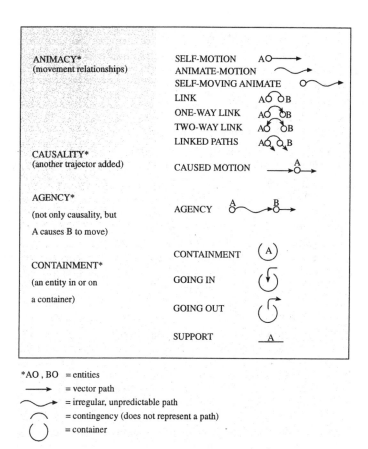

*AO , BO = entities
⟶ = vector path
⤳ = irregular, unpredictable path
⌒ = contingency (does not represent a path)
◯ = container

Fig. 3. Pictorial representation of Mandler's image-schemas which through evolutionary dynamics interconnect the mapping/modeling systems.

Figure 3 illustrates Mandler's (1992) depictions of image-schematic meanings as they are inferred from the behavior of infants. It is important to realize that these image-schemas are not meant to represent actual images experienced in the brain. Image-schemas are not like the everyday visual images we experience, but they perform all of the problem solving (informational) operations necessary to concept formation. As such, image-schemas are adaptive mechanisms which parallel the functions of vision, but which, because they are *abstractive* of everyday visual processing (Mandler, 1992; Vandervert, 1997a), constitute higher-quality algorithmic energy-information flows than visual processes. This higher energy-information quality of image-schemas is a powerful adaptive outcome that enables them to not only run parallel with visual experience, but also, and this is the important point, to at the same time operate energetically cheaper and faster than the real-time of visual experience. Compare T1,T2,T3 (real-time unfoldment) with I1 through I20 and T4 (faster than real-time *iterations* leading to a predicted future state) in figure 2.

Since the iterative flow of image-schematic information I1 through I20 downwardly determines the time and place of future (T4) perceptual-motor activity of the organism, image-schemas are *causal*.[7] In the absence of such an energetic organization of differing energy-information qualities in the causal chain of brain algorithms, it is difficult to imagine by what informational means organisms would be enabled to engage in cognitive-level, adaptive *anticipatory* behavior.

Although not relating image-schemas to energy-information quality, Mandler (1992) defined their organizational and processing character-istics in the following complementary manner:

> Image-schemas can be defined as dynamic analogue representations of spatial relations and movements in space. They are analog in that they are spatially structured representations. They are dynamic in that they can represent continuous change in location, such as an object moving along a path ... Because image-schemas are analog in nature, they have parts. One can focus on the path itself, its beginning, or its ending. In this sense, image-schemas embed. BEGINNING OF PATH can be embedded in PATH; each can be considered an image-schema in its own right. Similarly, perception of contingent motion is recoded into the contingent notion of coupled paths or LINK. I propose that image-schemas such as PATH (with focus on the BEGINNING OF PATH) and LINK constitute the meanings involved when a concept such as animacy is formed. (p. 591)

The foregoing features of image-schemas constitute the dynamics and contents of the iterative anticipatory sequences (I1 through I20) described above and depicted in figure 2. Algorithms inherent in the dynamics of these features extrapolate to anticipatory future states (T4), and drive perceptual-motor mapping and modeling processes (figure 2) toward perceptual-motor behavior in probabilistic manner. Thus through the dynamical characteristics of image-schemas, we have seen in some detail how maximum-power principle information processing *within* and *among* the various mapping-modeling systems in the brain (see figure 2) is achieved.

Educational Practices that Help Maximize the Brain's Potential

In the preceding sections it has been described how the brain maximizes energy-information quality through its mapping and modeling strategies. Educational practices can be designed that are direct extensions of those brain strategies. The purpose of this final section is to propose what these extensions are, and to relate them to other contemporary currents of general educational reform.

General Education as Modeling

The overall energy-information picture presented in figures 1, 2, and 3 shows how the maximum-power principle of evolution applies to information growth. This picture translates into an epistemological position and corollary educational practices. Epistemologically, the energy-information hierarchy extended to the brain shown in figure 1 means that all cultural-level mental models (collectively, knowledge) are based upon brain transformations and occur through the evolution of culture and in learning during ontogeny. Thus within this view, the origin, nature and limits of human knowledge are based upon phylo-genetic brain algorithms, as knowledge-related algorithms develop in a reciprocal relation toward maximization in the evolution of culture and in the individual.

Corollary general educational practices can be derived directly from features of brain algorithms, and the manner in which they develop in cultural-level mental models. As suggested earlier, cultural-level mental models are constructed in accordance with the six features of the maximum-power principle. Table 1 lists five corollary "brain features" derived from the maximum-power principle, along with comparisons between conventional general educational practices and "maximal information growth practices."

Table 1
Brain Functions and Corollary Maximal
Information Growth in General Education

Brain Feature	Conventional Practices	Maximal Information Growth Practices
1. Brain is a mapping-modeling system.	1. Topics emphasizing fragments of information become assessment focus.	1. All ideas and processes are interconnected; assessment is based upon modeling activity.
2. Brain is a simulator of future states.	2. "Closed-end" activities emphasize "current states" of systems.	2. Anticipatory modeling of future states of system guides teaching, curriculum and assessment.
3. Brain is a translational/transformational system.	3. Elements are emphasized (people, ideas, and things).	3. Mechanisms of change and forces are emphasized.
4. Brain is a natural feedforward/feedback system.	4. Overtly teach people how to think, analyze.	4. Thinking and analysis are by-products of the above processes.
5. Brain is a self-organizing system.	5. Most decisions are made for students (objectives, goals, and activities).	5. Students in groups feed forward and feed back most decisions among themselves.

Brain Feature #1. Since brain functions consist essentially of mapping/modeling activities, they can maximize information flows by following educational practices which emphasize the interconnections which exist among all ideas and processes—that is, how ideas and processes are embedded in maps and models. Assessments of such information growth can be based upon mapping and *modeling skill development* (see note 6).

Brain Feature #2. Fox (1988) has pointed out that, "The biological significance of the nervous system is that it can predict" (p. 144). The simulative manner in which the brain anticipates future states (predicts) is depicted in figure 2. Energy-information flows among mapping/ modelings in the brain can be maximized only through the *anticipatory* modeling of future states. Educational practices should emphasize how present information is useful only in relation to hypothetical future states. Assessment of anticipatory information growth can be based upon simple linear and nonlinear modeling (not necessarily involving advanced mathematics) which *extrapolates to future states* of the system(s) in question.

Brain Feature #3. Undergirding the progressive development of influence and territory depicted in figure 1 are energy-information translational and transformational processes. Therefore, educational processes should emphasize dynamics (how people, ideas, things change over time, and what mechanisms underlie change). The basis of dynamics should be emphasized. All assessments in education should reveal the mechanisms of change that are involved in the system(s) studied.

Brain Feature #4. Brain functions automatically feedforward energy-information flows in order to increase energy-information inflow to themselves. This source of "intrinsic motivity" drives the anticipatory simulation process described above and in figure 2. Educational practices should emphasize the development of *feedforward* skills. Feeding forward appears in human behavior as "suggesting," "proposing," "leading," and so on. In educational practice, groupings of students should be asked to formulate and execute most of their own curricular decisions. Assessment of the development of feedforward skills can be made by other "outside" groupings of students on the basis of a variety of *affective* behavior measurements, thereby further developing their own feedforward skills.

Brain Feature #5. The overarching dynamic of the maximum-power principle of brain development is self-organization. In order to improve assessment outcomes, conventional educational practices often attempt to teach people to "think," "analyze," and "synthesize." In actuality these cognitive operations are part and parcel of, or appearances of the four brain features described above. That is, critical thinking skill development will always be a natural constituent to and outcome of the first four maximal information growth practices. Assessment for self-organization is completely pragmatic; it is based upon the assessments of the above four brain function assessments— that is, in terms of brain functions, they define maximal critical thinking. Critical thinking is a natural by-product of mapping-modeling behavior in the brain.

Discussion

Most everyone is at least intuitively aware that conventional general educational practices can not maximize the absolute potential of the mind of each student. Part of the problem is that the idea of an "absolute potential" is difficult, if not impossible, to nail down. In this article, I have attempted to describe some of the essentials of an information-based approach to the notion of the brain's potential. While the evolutionary, energy-information approach may not be completely adequate; it seems that its mechanisms represent a critical part of the picture.

Certainly, there exists a great gulf between general educational practices that result in only an occasional legacy from millions of people on the one hand, and maximal information growth practices which, at least in theory, could result in several legacies from each person on the other. It may be wondered what the human race would do with so many legacies. One answer lies in the fact that information science and technology has been contriving computing system networks which, in the not too distant future, could easily place such vast amounts of knowledge into useful order(s) for *everyone*. In accordance with the maximum-power principle, legacies in the field of information science (informatics) have naturally gravitated toward this purpose.

The immense growth of knowledge can be followed through the unique patterns of energy-information growth in differing cultures as they have managed to amplify their available power to different levels. Tribus and McIrvine (1971) have calculated that, through technological contrivances, the worldwide per-person energy amplification ratio is about 25 to one (i.e., technology has amplified muscle-power 25 times). But in the U.S., higher and more widely-spread technology has led to an energy amplification of muscle-power of 250 to one. However, the potential amplification of *information* is much greater than that of energy. Tribus and McIrvine estimated that through information systems we could amplify the information processing capacity of a person 10^{24} times. This figure represents an enormous amplification over what presently exists anywhere in the world. If this level of information amplification were achieved, it would mean that a single person could have at their immediate disposal enough information processing capacity to solve all the problems presently being solved by everyone!

Such a single world-controller capacity is not likely to develop. But what is likely to occur is a profound expansion of the need for us to learn to use vast amounts of information—it has already been taking place for several decades. But what good would it be to have a million times as much information in the hands of people who are educated to manage with the comparative poverty of information we have today? Educational practices must change radically toward packing more information manipulation skills into learning.

With information processing systems developing as they are and information amplifying as it is, it seems that general educational delivery systems that approach the efficiency of brain functions will be needed (table 1). When the features of the maximum-power principle of information growth are applied to general education (right hand column, table 1), a theoretical model of pedagogy for *interdisciplinary* studies is the result. In my view, this is precisely what a maximal information growth future must hold for general education.

Requests for reprints should be sent to Larry R. Vandervert, Ph.D., American Nonlinear Systems, 1529 W. Courtland, Spokane, WA 99205-2608, USA. Phone: (509) 533-3583, e-mail: larryv@sfcc.spokane.cc.wa.us

Notes

[1]See the three arrows of the physical evolution of the universe (thermodynamic, psychological, and cosmological) described in lay terms by Hawking (1988, pp. 143-153).

[2]Different kinds of energy-information differ in quality in the sense of doing more with less, for example, solving more problems with less energy/information. As increasing amounts of energy-information are concentrated in food chains and substances (energy-information embodiment), the resulting energy increases its capacity to do work. A Calorie of sunlight cannot do the work or release the problem solving capacity of a Calorie of wood. The highest know quality of energy-information is that inherent in the problem solving (algorithmic) organization of the human brain, which stores and processes an enormous amount of information on a mere 10 watts (see, for example, Fischler & Firschein, 1987, p. 30).

[3]The same principle applies to eleemosynary activity. Large bequests to educational and other institutions make available high-quality energy-information embodied in money of the monetary system to form linkages with lower-quality manpower, which will help maximize the goals of the giver or charitable organization.

[4]Human brains at each stage of development (infancy through adulthood) and respective representative level of enculturation (see figure 1) would have attained a unique level of energy-information embodiment and quality.

[5]This estimate is based on calculations kindly provided by H.T. Odum in a personal letter to the author. Solar emjoules per joule is the measure of energy-information embodiment quality.

[6]A common breakdown of types of cultural-level mental models, in order of increasing abstraction and complexity, include the following: (1) *iconic* (for example, a toy car represents an automobile), (2) *analogic* (for example, the rotation of hands on a clock represents the rotation of the earth), and (3) *symbolic* (for example, the mathematics of the normal probability curve represent empirical distributions) (Ackoff, Gupta, & Minas, 1962, Chapter 4, "Models"). The superior, supervenient energy-information quality of the algorithmic organization of the phylogenetic brain over its constructed cultural-level models is attested to in many ways. First, Odum's (1988) hierarchy of educational attainment shown in figure 1 indicates that the various energy-information embodiments of the cultural level models are far less than that of the brain. Second, even the mental models of artificial intelligence (AI),

perhaps the most powerful symbolic mental models algorithms known, have not been able to approach the energy-information efficiency of the human brain. In fact, the entire legacy of AI has not provided mental models capable of guiding the development of the algorithmic efficiency of even the brain of a fly. Finally, the brain has the energy-information efficiency to refute and modify existing legacies, feats that only its higher-quality energy flows could accomplish.

[7]This idea bears importantly on the controversy as to whether mental images play an adaptive role (see, for example, Richardson, 1994). Fox (1988) and Vandervert (1997a) have proposed that the brain is essentially a *simulative* system, which operates in an iterative manner. For a downward-influencing, simulative system, prediction by imagery (or vicarious trial and error, which includes vicarious prediction [Vandervert 1997a]) is simply the most efficient energy-information method of anticipating future states. That is, imagery is an option among causative informational structures, one, which maximizes information amplification. This view is completely consistent with the large amplification potential of information over the amplification of energy. The reader who is further interested in the adaptive role of imagery is encouraged to consult Tribus and McIrvine's (1971, esp. pp. 183-184) very readable account on the differing relationships between energy and information amplification.

References

Ackoff, R., Gupta, S., and Minas, J. 1962. *Scientific method: Optimizing applied research and decisions*. New York: John Wiley and Sons.

Boltzmann, L. 1905. *The second law of thermodynamics*. Dordrecht: Reidel.

Chien, S. 1981. Cerebral circulation and metabolism. In *Principles of neural science*, edited by E. R. Kandel and J. H. Schwartz. New York: Elsevier/North Holland.

Cosmides, L., Tooby, J., and Barkow, J. 1992. Introduction: Evolutionary psychology and conceptual integration. In *The adapted mind: Evolutionary psychology and the generation of culture*, edited by J. H. Barkow, L. Cosmides, and J. Tooby. New York: Oxford University Press.

Fischler, M., and Firschein, O. 1987. *Intelligence: The eye, the brain, and the computer*. Reading, MA: Addison-Wesley.

Fox, R. 1988. *Energy and the evolution of life*. New York: W.H. Freeman and Company.

Hirschfeld, L., and Gelman, S. 1994. *Mapping the mind*. New York: Cambridge University Press.

Hawking, S. 1988. *A brief history of time*. New York: Bantam Books.

Jerison, H. 1991. *Brain size and the evolution of mind.* New York: American Museum of Natural History.

Lotka, A. J. 1922. A contribution to the energetics of evolution. *Proceedings of the National Academy of Science* 8:140-155.

———. 1945. The law of evolution as a maximal principle. *Human Biology* 17:167-194.

MacLean, P. 1991. Neofrontocerebellar evolution in regard to computation and prediction: Some fractal aspects of microgenesis. In *Cognitive microgenesis*, edited by R. Hanlon. New York: Springer-Verlag.

Mandler, J. 1988. How to build a baby: On the development of an accessible representational system. *Cognitive Development* 3:113-136.

———. 1992. How to build a baby: II. Conceptual primitives. *Psychological Review* 99:587-604.

Melzack, R. 1992. Phantom limbs. *Scientific American* 266 (April):120-126.

Melzack, R., Israel, R., Lacroix, R., and Schultz, G. 1997. Phantom limbs in people with congenital limb deficiency or amputation in early adulthood. *Brain* 120:1603-1620.

Odum, H. T. 1983 . *Systems ecology: An introduction.* New York: John Wiley and Sons.

———. 1988. Self-organization, transformity, and information. *Science* 242: 1132-1139.

———. 1996. *Environmental accounting: Emergy [with an "m"] and environmental decision making.* New York: John Wiley and Sons.

Odum, H. T., and Odum, E. C. 1981 . *Energy basis for man and nature.* New York: McGraw-Hill.

Paulin, M. 1993. The role of the cerebellum in motor control and perception. *Brain Behavior Evolution* 41:39-50.

———. 1997. Neural representations of moving systems. In *The cerebellum in cognition: International review of neurobiology.* Vol. 14, edited by Schmahmann. New York: Academic Press.

Pribram, K. 1971. *Languages of the brain.* Englewood Cliffs, NJ: Lawrence Erlbaum.

———. 1991. *Brain and perception: Holonomy and structure in figural processing.* Hillsdale, NJ: Lawrence Erlbaum.

Richardson, A. 1994. *Individual differences in imaging.* Amityville, NY: Baywood Publishing Company.

Tooby, J., and Cosmides, L. 1995. Mapping the evolved functional organization of mind and brain. In *The cognitive neurosciences*, edited by M. Gazzaniga. Cambridge, MA: The MIT Press.

Tribus, M., and McIrvine, E. 1971. Energy and information. *Scientific American* 225 (September):179-188.

Vandervert, L. 1991. A measurable and testable brain-based emergent interactionism: An alternative to Sperry's mentalist emergent interactionism. *The Journal of Mind and Behavior* 12:201-209.

————. 1993. Neurological positivism's evolution of mathematics. *Journal of Mind and Behavior* 14:277-288.

————. 1995. Chaos theory and the evolution of consciousness and mind: A thermodynamic-holographic resolution to the mind-body problem. *New Ideas in Psychology* 13(2):107-127.

————. 1997a. The evolution of Mandler's conceptual primitives (image-schemas) as neural mechanisms for space-time simulations structures. *New Ideas in Psychology* 15:105-123.

————. 1997b. Quanta within the Copenhagen interpretation as two-neuro-algorithm referents. In *Understanding Tomorrow's Mind: Advances in Chaos Theory, Quantum Theory, and Consciousness in Psychology*, edited by L. Vandervert. *The Journal of Mind and Behavior* 18:229-246.

Chapter 2

Modern Philosophical Culture, Education and the Fragmentation of Consciousness: Giambattista Vico and the Road Not Taken

E. Paul Colella

"There is poetry without prose,
but there can be no prose without poetry."

Benedetto Croce, *Estetica* (1902)

It has become something of a commonplace that both geographically as well as intellectually, Giambattista Vico stood outside of the mainstream of early modern philosophy. From his birth in 1668 to his death in 1744, Vico spent no significant length of time away from Naples. In spite of the relative insularity of his native city, Vico kept abreast of the philosophical developments in northern Europe. The intellectual reconfiguration of Nature carried out in the north had led to a rethinking of traditional philosophical problems in order to render them consistent with these revolutionary premises. As a maturing thinker, the new ideas of Descartes, Grotius, Bacon and Spinoza were not unknown to him.

Francesco DeSanctis likens Vico to Dante, and this comparison serves us well for orientation. Like the immortal poet, Vico was at odds with the general cultural tendency of his age. Finding themselves at the intersection of two centuries and two worlds, Vico as Dante could accept neither. Such resistance stood at the heart of their creativity. In the case of Vico, DeSanctis writes that while he believed himself to be an ancient, he was, in fact, a modern.[1]

Yet, his allegiance to what is ancient made him a unique species of modern, and this is especially true in his treatment of human consciousness. By drawing upon ancient sources, and by virtue of his divergence from the mainstream of modern thought on the issue of human nature and mind, Vico preserves an integrated model of human consciousness that avoids the traps which had ensnared so many of his better known contemporaries. He did this by urging a humanist model of mind and education which embraced the best of ancient culture and still incorporated the advances made by the moderns. This more humanistic view of consciousness stands as a persistent critique of the tendencies of modern philosophy which emphasized a fragment as if it were the totality of conscious mind.

Descartes, Humanism and Fragmented Consciousness

The characteristically modern view of consciousness is said to originate in the work of Rene Descartes. Humanistically educated by the Jesuits, Descartes turned his penetrating gaze inward in order to survey the terrain of the inner world of consciousness. What he discovered there proved to be every bit as revolutionary as what Galileo saw in the heavens. Framed as autobiography, Descartes announces the modern conception of consciousness.

> For myself, I have never presumed that my mind was in any respect more perfect than anyone else's. In fact, I have often longed to have as quick a wit or as precise and distinct an imagination or as full and responsive a memory as certain other people. And I know of no other qualities that aid in the perfection of the mind. For as to reason or good sense, given that it alone makes us men and distinguishes us from animals, I prefer to believe that it exists whole and entire in each one of us.[2]

The traditional powers of the mind are all here; wit, imagination, memory and reason. Within the context of his Humanistic studies, these powers and the conscious states that they represent formed a unified whole. However Descartes already reveals the nature of his intellectual revolution. He will define the mind solely in terms of rationality, that which "alone makes us men and distinguishes us from animals". These other non-rational powers must be de-emphasized.

In his *Discourse on Method* of 1637 Descartes surveys the humanistic curriculum and eliminates much of the traditional course of study. His own education left him "embarrassed by so many doubts and errors" and served only to convince him of his own ignorance. The elements of humanistic education are enumerated; the languages and fables of the classical world, histories, literature, eloquence, poetry, mathematics, philosophy, theology, law and medicine are all named, together with their supposed advantages. Nevertheless, Descartes dismisses all but the most rational as fruitless. Starting with classical language, the Humanists' key to ancient wisdom, Descartes writes:

> But I thought that I had already given enough time to languages and also even to the reading of ancient books—to their histories and to their fables. For it is about the same to converse with those of other centuries as it is to travel ... But when one takes too much time traveling, one becomes finally a stranger in one's own country; and when one is too curious about things that took place in past centuries, one ordinarily remains quite ignorant of what is taking place in one's own century. [3]

The study of myth and fable fares little better, leading us to "imagine many events to be possible which really are impossible."[4] Histories, even the most accurate ones, "if they neither alter nor augment the significance of things, in order to render them more worthy of being read, at least almost always omit the basest and least illustrious details, and thus the remainder does not appear as it really is."[5] People who look to these constructions as behavioral guides soon meet trouble by "falling into extravagances of the knights of our novels and to conceiving plans that are beyond their powers."[6]

Eloquence and poetry are dismissed entirely, being "gifts of the mind—not fruits of study" to which Descartes is quick to add that, at least on the matter of eloquence, the most effective speaker is the one who is in possession of "the most forceful power of reasoning" and who is able to "best order their thoughts so as to render them clear and intelligible". Such a person is the most effective speaker by far, even though they may only command a provincial dialect and be untutored in the principles of oratory.

On the other hand, mathematics has great potential. Its foundations seemed to be "solid and firm", even though up until now nothing "more noble" had been raised upon them".[7] Descartes intends to remedy that oversight with the articulation of the rules of a new universal method drawn from mathematics. Taking reason as the definitive activity of human consciousness, Descartes narrows the range further by demanding that the fruits of reason conform to the exacting standard of indubitable certainty. In the enactment of methodological doubt, he proposes to "reject as absolutely false everything in which I could imagine the least doubt, so as to see whether, after this process, anything in my set of beliefs remains that is entirely indubitable."[8] His mathematical method is a universal method. Descartes expects its application beyond algebra to the other sciences to be promising in the establishment of certainty.[9]

The elimination of the subject areas whose content fails the standard of indubitable certainty corresponds to a parallel narrowing of subjective elements of consciousness. Mental processes which do not correspond to the ideal processes carried on in mathematics are relegated to a subordinate place in the Cartesian model of the consciousness. In his rejection of language, history, poetry, fable and eloquence, Descartes is simultaneously devaluing the place of imagination, metaphor and memory in the life of the mind. Conscious mind is now defined as the locus of rational deductive activity, and from this the systematic fragmentation of the human being follows. Let us examine a sampling.

Defining body after the manner of emergent science of his day, Descartes sees it as a quantifiable entity only; that is, as extension. Mind on the other hand is not extended in space, it possesses a completely different set of properties, leaving him to posit as absolute the metaphysical dualism of *res cogitans* and *res extensa*. Yet the problem persists; how to explain their interaction? Is it not the case that minds direct bodily actions? Do not bodies influence mental states? Arguing that the rational soul is different from the body and hence must have been expressly created, Descartes leaves the issue of their unity in somewhat of an ambiguous condition. "It is not enough for it to be lodged in the human body, like a pilot in his ship, unless perhaps to move its members, but it must be joined and united more closely to the body so as to ... make up a true man."[10] The *Discourse* never succeeds in resolving this difficulty, leaving Descartes to posit the improbable solution of the pineal gland as their point of union. The difficulty in recombining mind and body to produce a true human individual in any coherent manner is indicative of the fragmentation in his thought.

This fragmentation likewise extends to the realm of practical action in human affairs. Descartes had established his paradigm of the solitary thinker early on in the *Discourse*. He is isolated in his room, by himself, surveying the contents of his own consciousness in the pursuit of atoms of certainty. The primacy of the solitary thinker is made clear in Descartes' choice of the metaphor of the engineer. Descartes asserts that,

> often there is less perfection in the works made of several pieces and in the works made by the hands of several masters than in those works on which but one master has worked. Thus one sees that buildings undertaken and completed by a single architect are commonly more beautiful and better ordered than those that several architects have tried to patch up.[11]

Hence, consciousness is fragmented from other human beings, it is constituted and acts solely within the boundaries of itself. There is no social construction of consciousness, nor is such necessary. All that is needed is a single, individual mind.

This individualistic position may well be expected to cause problems for social action and practical affairs. In matters of morality, Descartes is left with finding his way back from the solitary deductive reasoner to moral decision and action in a world which is populated by others and in which precision and certainty prove elusive. We have seen how Descartes had rejected classical fable, history and literature as a guide to conduct because of its uncertainty. They lead one to "conceive of plans that are beyond their powers".[12] Having doubted anything which is uncertain, it seems that ethics stands in need of a new, more solid, rational foundation. Yet by what means are such values to be discovered? And once found, what is there to inspire human beings to actively pursue them? Descartes' temporary response in the *Discourse* is a provisional morality, which is in essence a plea to observe local customs and follow the opinions of the most sensible and moderate persons. Descartes' reasons for such a code is so that he can still act as a moral agent while in his condition of methodological doubt. As was the case with the mind/body dualism, the issue of ethics is likewise unresolved in the *Discourse*, leaving the reader to wonder whether a scientific morality on the basis of his own premises—and from the point of view of the solitary deductive reasoner adhering to the standard of indubitable certainty—might be possible at all.

These examples sufficiently illustrate the inherent fragmentation of consciousness which resides in Descartes' thought. Conscious states are fragmented from one another as are the various powers of the mind, with the primacy going to the deductive and the rational, since only these can yield certainty. This rational mind is then fragmented off from the body in the human individual, leaving a physical - psychological dualism which would prove stubbornly resistant to Descartes' efforts to overcome it. Further, the individual reasoner is set off from others in the conviction that only the products of a solitary mind conducting its own rational processes can attain beauty and be well-ordered. Finally, this model of consciousness renders human ethical conduct problematic, since his model of consciousness is one in which consciousness dwells apart from others in its own deductive solitude. From this position, early modern philosophy takes its point of departure.

Cicero and the Tradition of Rhetoric

Vico's alternative road to consciousness begins in Rome. In the opening pages of *De Inventione*, Cicero orients his reader through the vehicle of myth. There was a time, he writes, before the emergence of civilized life, when human beings lived like feral beasts. They wandered through the wilderness, they lived on wild fare, "did nothing by the guidance of reason, had neither an ordered system of religion nor social duties."[13] Such basic institutions as law and family were lacking as well. In their blind and unreasoning passion, these human beasts acted and responded to their world on the basis of the only thing available to them, namely, physical strength.[14] Humanity would have remained in such a dismal condition had it not been for the intervention of "a great and wise" individual, who had become aware of the latent powers of the human and had developed them. The impact was profound. Human beings were scattered in the fields, writes Cicero,

And hidden in sylvan retreats when he assembled and gathered them according to a plan; he introduced them to every useful and honorable occupation, though they cried out against it at first because of its novelty, and then when through reason and eloquence they had listened with greater attention, he transformed them from wild savages into a kind and gentle folk.[15]

This is a remarkable story, for within it Cicero provides us with a paradigm for human consciousness and education. Human beings are transformed from beasts who can only understand the world in terms of power, into civilized beings who have become kind and gentle. They have taken on a truly human shape in a genuinely human community. This achievement is ostensibly the result of the intervention of a super-human figure who is as divine as the rest are bestial. More significantly, the transformation is brought about by a constellation of qualities possessed by this individual. We can isolate them as wisdom, eloquence, and the power to convert these into the service of the good, which Cicero defines as prudence. The humanity of this individual which places him far above his bestial companions resides in a *wholeness* which is made manifest by the interrelation of these three virtues. Wholeness and the integration of character is communicated to the savage ones, and from a scattered and fragmentary herd they form a human, communal whole.

There is nothing integrative in wisdom, eloquence and prudence taken by themselves. If they have the power to generate wholeness it is because they represent a gathering and an activation of the various powers of the human person in a combined and focused manner. Let us not forget that Cicero's reputation is based, to a large extent, upon his involvement with rhetoric as both a theoretician as well as a practitioner. His insistence upon the unity of philosophy (wisdom) and rhetoric (eloquence) reflects the deeper truth that human consciousness is composed of both rational and imaginative elements.

Rhetoric and eloquence had wider meanings in the Ciceronian tradition. While we tend to associate them with effective and persuasive speech alone, this view fails to capture the deeper epistemological characteristics which Cicero had attributed to rhetoric. Alongside of the rational powers of the mind that Greek philosophy had explored in such great detail, Cicero speaks of the non-inferential cognitive powers of discovery by means of which human beings first grasp their world. Invention and discovery precede inference, and it is through the power of *ingenium*, that is, through an original insight into similitude between previously unrelated things, that the starting points for rational argumentation begin to emerge. Drawing upon Aristotle's work in rhetoric and topics,[16] Cicero divides the art of eloquence into its constituent elements of invention, arrangement, expression, memory, and delivery. While invention concerns itself with the complex processes of discovery, it is through arrangement that this material is ordered into coherent arguments, and through expression and delivery that the proper language is affixed to the invented materials.[17]

The power of *ingenium*, which is vital to the epistemological side of eloquence, operates through the construction of images and metaphor.[18] The human being invents images, discovers connections, and then can fashion these materials into logically coherent inferences and arguments. The point is that through this recovered, wider notion of eloquence, the unity of imagination and thought, discovery and critical articulation, is placed in the forefront of importance. Wisdom emerges as a complex structure drawing together a wide range of human powers and capacities. It sets the whole person in motion. The fruits of invention, cast in argument, are communicated, taking pains to affect the emotions as well as appeal to reason, to move the souls of others to act. And such action, as we have seen in the myth that Cicero tells, promotes the shared ends of civilized communal living which is the sphere of morality and politics.[19]

Vico's Alternative: Towards an Integrated Consciousness

Giambattista Vico spent his career as Professor of Eloquence at the University of Naples. His specialty in rhetoric and in law required him to study Roman authors in great detail. As the son of a bookseller, and as an intimate of learned yet non-academic men, Vico had also become familiar with the most influential philosophies emanating from the North. For some time, he had been an enthusiastic Cartesian himself, but in the first decade of the eighteenth century, he gradually distanced himself from this school of thought. The pivot of his disagreement lies in the issue of consciousness.

One can measure the distance between Vico and Descartes by simply considering their respective goals. The difference in goal will color the different accounts of consciousness that each will put forward. Descartes establishes unshakable certainty as the desideratum and rejects anything which can be doubted. Difficulties are to be divided into as many parts as possible, and our thoughts must proceed from "the simplest and easiest to know objects" and rise in degrees, "to the knowledge of the most composite things".[20] Complexes of knowledge are, according to Descartes' rules of method, resolvable into their simplest atomic components of certainty. Armed with this method and proceeding with care, one can expect to achieve certainty in any area of human inquiry.

As was true of Cicero, Vico's concern is wisdom. This concerns the continuity between knowing, speaking and acting, wisdom demands a more integrated view of consciousness and its powers. For this reason, wisdom cannot be concerned with the analysis of wholes into their ultimate parts, nor with the reduction of complexes into the simples out of which they are constituted. Wisdom is totalizing—Vico employs Cicero's definition of wisdom as knowledge of the full range of human and divine things. Nothing is left out of such comprehensive knowledge. Clearly the totalizing object of consciousness is a reflection of the fusion of subjective powers. Wisdom sets into motion the full breadth of powers residing in consciousness: intellect, reason, imagination, language, memory, and passion; the outcome is right action. Certainty on the other hand sets into motion the rational powers of mind only in accordance with a strictly construed protocol of mathematical judgment. The remainder of these conscious powers are deemed irrelevant.

The human being experiences a Scriptural fallen-ness in the fragmentation of consciousness; in its being unable to know things human and divine (wisdom), the inability to render these ideas in true and proper speech (eloquence), and the complete inability to act in accordance with the good in any deliberate manner. Cartesianism is but a modern expression, in philosophical-scientific terms, of these ancient diagnoses of fragmented consciousness. For the Cartesians, the solution is to prune off everything that fails to attain the level of mathematical certainty. For Vico, the only solution is to start with a new model of consciousness as integrated totality.

In the Inaugural Oration for 1699 on humanistic education, knowledge of the self is put forward as the most necessary project for the young scholar. Humanistic studies become the pathway to this self-knowledge, which in turn, contributes to the flowering of wisdom. In the Oration, Vico exhorts his audience to study and mastery of the "full universe" of learning, including the study of language, mathematics, physics, oratory, metaphysics, and theology. The point to keep in mind is that these studies are not merely meant to reveal the structural character of the external world, nor is their purpose that of providing human beings with mastery over that world. Rather, they reveal the subjective structure of human consciousness as a complex yet unified reality.

It is in the Oration for 1708 where Vico develops his most cogent critique of Cartesianism as well as his alternative model of human consciousness. Published as *De Nostri Temporis Studiorum Ratione*, the work stands as his most impressive philosophical statement prior to the appearance of *Scienza Nuova* in 1725. Couched in terms of a comparison of ancient and modern study methods, the *De Nostri* is an aggressive argument in favor of the restoration of imagination and memory to a status equal to that enjoyed by mathematical reason in the Cartesian view of mind. This, of course, becomes the powerful core idea of Vico's masterwork of 1725.

While the Cartesians argue that the art of rational demonstration and criticism, that is, the ability to move from premise to conclusion, and to evaluate long chains of deductive reasoning is what is most essential, Vico pleads the case for the ancient Art of Topics as just as necessary to intellectual culture. Introduced by Aristotle and developed by the Roman rhetoricians, the Art of Topics emphasizes invention and discovery over deduction and criticism. Before rational demonstrations can be evaluated, they must be constructed. Arguments must be invented, initial fundamental relationships established, and starting points must be found. Only then can deduction proceed. This invention, maintains Vico, has been overlooked by the Cartesians. It is an act not of the rational powers but rather of the imaginative, poetic powers of the mind. Metaphor is the fundamental product of conscious invention; it forges new connections between previously unrelated things.

Consciousness is a continuum embracing imagination and reasoning, invention and logical inference, the eloquence of poetry and the precision of prose. This view requires a fuller model of consciousness than the Cartesians are able to supply. The inclination of the latter to neglect imaginative invention is fatal to their theory of mind. The Greeks were the first to introduce the distinction between invention and judgment "because they did not pay attention to the proper faculty of knowing. This faculty is mother wit, the creative power through which man is capable of recognizing likenesses and making them himself".[21] Only after this power is developed can one profitably engage in rational criticism. Later in his *On the Most Ancient Wisdom of the Italians* of 1710, Vico advises Paolo Doria on the impact that this model of consciousness must have on education.

> in the education of your prince, do not send him straight to the critical art, but have him imbued with examples for a long time before he is initiated into the art of making judgments about them. Why else is this but first to bring his mother wit into full bloom and then to let it be cultivated by the art of judgment?[22]

Building upon this view of education, Vico generates a comprehensive theory of history in his great work, *Scienza Nuova.*

Giambattista Vico: Towards a New Science of Human Consciousness

Vico's masterwork begins with a myth of its own, one that echoes Cicero in many ways. After the Flood, the gentiles were separated from the Hebrews who had retained their relationship with God, and were dispersed in the wilderness. The gentiles had forgotten divine wisdom, they lost their powers of articulate speech, and they obeyed the proddings of passion and lust. Gradually, they lost human form, growing to gigantic proportions and sinking into a feral wandering. One day, a chance flash of lightning and roar of thunder frightened these grotesque beasts. The more ingenious among them imagined these fearsome events to be the expression of anger on the part of some supremely powerful being, and Jove was invented. In creating the new connection between disturbing natural phenomena and what they had experienced in themselves when agitated in anger, they laid the foundations for both a nascent wisdom and for civilization itself. Through a creative act of the imagination, that is, through the power of *ingenium*, these beasts took the first step towards becoming a civilized human community. A profound metaphorical connection is made between the inanimate world of nature and the more familiar world of the human, which these beasts knew firsthand. Inanimate nature now takes on a whole new meaning, as do the behavioral responses of the humans living in that world.

The imagination's construction of Jove creates a poetic wisdom which refashions the world into a place where there are both divine and human realms. It is a world in which the characteristics of humanity and divinity are fleshed out in a language dominated by imagery, metaphor, and fable. From this poetic wisdom and poetic language engendered by this crude metaphysics, there arises a poetic morality which provides the context for secure group life. Thus for Vico, imagination and poetic expression initiate the move to civilization. A poetic and metaphorical language is developed in order to give adequate expression to this poetic wisdom, and its communication becomes the basis of what Vico calls a poetic morality.[23] As Andrea Battistini writes, for Vico, rhetoric is essential "not only to create a persuasive discourse but also to be able to create thought."[24]

Vico sets out from this powerful myth and provides a theory of historical development in which the primary motive force lies in the modifications of consciousness itself. Human consciousness is a whole which embraces the powers of *ingenium*, imagination, reasoning, emotion, memory and desire. Rational modes of thought develop out of, and form a continuous whole with imaginative forms. They form a single whole and this wholeness expresses itself in the three virtues of wisdom, eloquence and prudence. What is lost in the Fall is recovered through the historical process in the life of humanity and in the individual through the educational process itself.

The result is most evident in ethical matters. Indeed, Vico reserves his most aggressive criticism of modern consciousness for the discussion of ethics. The great failure of Cartesianism—and for the culture of modernity itself—is "that we pay an excessive amount of attention to the natural sciences and not enough to ethics."[25] The inquiry into the human character is neglected, and with it, the relationship between the human passions and public life. Crippled by this overweening rationalism, the young generation is "unable to engage in the life of the community, to conduct themselves with sufficient wisdom and prudence".[26] Vico admonishes his contemporaries that,

> it is well for us to keep in mind that human events are dominated by Chance and Choice, which are extremely subject to change and which are strongly influenced by simulation and dissimulation (both pre-eminently deceptive things). As a consequence, those whose only con-

cern is abstract truth experience great difficulty in achieving their means, and greater difficulty in attaining their ends. Frustrated in their own plans, deceived by the plans of others, they often throw up the game. Since, then, the course of action in life must consider the importance of the single events and their circumstances, it may happen that many of these circumstances are extraneous and trivial, some of them bad, some even contrary to one's goal. It is therefore impossible to access human affairs by the inflexible standard of abstract right.[27]

Vico realizes well that the soul is not moved by dry abstractions. The world of public affairs—that is, politics and morality—cannot be reconstructed along strictly logical-rationalistic lines. Perhaps this is why Descartes leaves us with the provisional morality and nothing more. In the closing pages of *Scienza Nuova*, Vico emphasizes the link that he had forged his entire career; the need to integrate the rational and the non-rational aspects of consciousness in practical affairs. Invoking one of the most eminent scientific names of his day as the representative of modernity, as well as an intellectual forerunner of modernity from the Greek world Vico writes:

Let Bayle consider then whether in fact there can be nations in the world without any knowledge of God! And let Polybius weigh the truth of his statement that if there were philosophers in the world there would be no need in the world of religions! For religions alone can bring the peoples to do virtuous works by appeal to their feelings, which alone move men to perform them; and the reasoned maxims of the philosophers concerning virtue are of use only when employed by a good eloquence for kindling the feelings to do the duties of virtue.[28]

Here one finds the true purpose behind Vico's alternative view of consciousness. Taking the religious to include the full spectrum of the non-rational aspects of human consciousness, we find that without these, there can be no meaningful moral or political action. A nation of philosophers can discuss virtue in its most minute detail, but philosophical wisdom without eloquent voice remains, as Cicero had argued, mute and ineffective. Imagination must be kindled to burning life in the service of the maxims of virtue if, indeed, human beings shall ever have a hope of constructing a more human and humane world. To Vico, the Cartesians, those quintessential moderns, have reduced human consciousness into a rational fragment, thereby distorting the human person and human experience beyond recognition. The most troubling consequence, yet far from the only consequence, is for Vico the moral failure of modernity.

Vico's contribution to the history of philosophy is his New Science of the history of Nations. In it, consciousness develops socially and historically, manifesting itself in its external products, namely, in the institutions and the cultural artifacts of civilization. In the process of this development from bestial to civilized humanity, consciousness passes through determinate ages. The earlier ages are dominated by the supremacy of imagination, image, metaphor and poetic fable. The later by abstract rational philosophy. In an age dominated by reason, philosophy reflects upon consciousness in an attempt to comprehend it. Fashioning its object on the model that it itself provides, rational inquiry discovers a consciousness which is, as Descartes had believed, made in its own image. The non-rational powers of consciousness; especially the imagination with its Herculean power of creating fundamental metaphors without which thought is impossible, remain concealed. This error, which Vico describes as the "conceit of scholars", "who have it that what they known is as old as the world", is as pernicious as Bacon's Idols of the Mind. It can only distort what it seeks to understand. Before metaphysics received rational formulation, it was expressed poetically in fable. Prior to this mythical expression, this poetic metaphysics dwelt in the unarticulated connections forged in the imagination. The creation of Jove is the first and greatest poetic construction of human consciousness. Vico's all-embracing New Science is a history of the civilized institutions which result from this first great creative act, and through them, it is a history of the human mind itself. Vico writes that such a science is a history of the divine:

> from *divinari*, to divine, which is to understand what is hidden *from* men—the future—or what is hidden *in* them—their consciousness. [29]

Notes

[1]DeSanctis, The history of Italian Literature, Volume II, (Barnes & Noble: New York, 1959), pp. 796-798.

[2]Descartes, *Discourse on Method*, translated by Donald Cress, (Hackett: Indianapolis, 1980) pp. 1-2.

[3]Ibid, pp. 3-4.

[4]Ibid., p. 4.

[5]Ibid.

[6]Ibid.

[7]Ibid.

[8]Ibid., p. 17.

[9]Ibid., p. 12.

[10]Ibid., p. 31.

[11]Ibid., p.6.

[12]Ibid., p. 4.

[13]Cicero, *De Inventione*, I. ii.

[14]Ibid.

[15]Ibid.

[16]See Aristotle, *Posterior Analytics*, 72a27.

[17]Cicero, *De Inventione*, I.vii.9. See also Ernesto Grassi, *Rhetoric as Philosophy: The Humanist Tradition,* (University Park: The Pennsylvania State University, 1980).

[18]Cicero, *Topica*, I.5.

[19]Cicero, *De Inventione*, I.iv.6. Cicero remarks that in cities, human beings keep faith, observe justice, and work for the common good because of eloquence.

[20]Ibid., p. 16.

[21]Giambattista Vico, *De Antiquissima Italorum Sapientia* (1710). See also Giambattista Vico, *On the Most Ancient Wisdom of the Italians*, translated by L.M. Palmer, (Ithaca: Cornell University), Press, 1988), pp. 101-102.

[22]Ibid.

[23]Vico, *Principi di scienza nuova*, (Milano: Mondadori, 1992), paragraphs 361-519. See also Bergin & Fisch, *The New Science of Giambattista Vico*, (Ithaca: Cornell University Press, 1988).

[24]Andrea Battistini, "Three Essays on Vico: Vico and Rhetoric", *New Vico Studies*, Volume 12, 1994, p. 5.

[25]Giambattista Vico, *De Nostri Temporis Studiorum Ratione* (1708). See also Giambattista Vico, *On the Study Methods of Our Times*, (Ithaca: Cornell University Press, 1990). p.33.

[26]Ibid.

[27]Ibid., p. 34.

[28]Vico, *Scienza Nuova*, paragraph 1110.

[29]Ibid., paragraph 342.

Chapter 3

The Strange Attraction of Sciousness: William James on Consciousness

Andrew Bailey

William James' account of consciousness has been quite influential in the back-rooms of the recent philosophical and scientific study of consciousness. Gerald Edelman, for example, credits James for pointing out that consciousness is a process and not a substance or thing.[1] Daniel Dennett has cited James approvingly as suggesting a "purely functional" model of introspective consciousness,[2] while Owen Flanagan parades James' robust notion of a phenomenological stream of consciousness.[3] Several of the papers in the proceedings of the first major interdisciplinary conference on consciousness ("Toward a Science of Consciousness," at Tucson in 1994) take James' doctrines as a central starting point.[4] As work in the burgeoning field of 'consciousness studies' reaches fever pitch, James' thoughts in this area have increased in importance and influence correspondingly.

Yet *it is not at all clear* just what James thought consciousness was—or even whether he thought it *existed*. He had a lot of things to say about consciousness, and it's not so simple to pile those mental nuggets all together so that they fall into any consistent pattern. Consider the tension between the following two quotations:

> The first and foremost concrete fact which everyone will affirm to belong to his inner experience is the fact that *consciousness of some sort goes on.*[5]

> I believe that consciousness (as it is commonly represented, either as an entity, or as pure activity, but in any case as being fluid, unextended, diaphanous, devoid of content of its own, but directly self-knowing—spiritual, in short), I believe, I say, that this sort of consciousness is pure fancy.[6]

In fact, the situation is even worse than it appears here. At least James' careful wording of these two aphorisms preserves the distinction between consciousness of *some* sort (which does exist) and consciousness as *commonly understood* (which does not). But exactly how James can consistently draw the distinction between these two kinds of consciousness is not at all clear. The conceptual tangle is made more difficult by James' habitual differentiation between his writings—and thus his conclusions—to do with *natural science* and those concerning *metaphysics.*

This difficulty has struck several commentators in the current consciousness debate, even those who consider themselves strongly influenced by his work. Thus, for example, Bernard Baars, a well-known cognitive scientist, notes in his book on consciousness that many have "found James to be a great source of confusion, for all his undoubted greatness, and James himself felt confused."[7] This view is also shared by a number of James scholars, such as Gerald E. Myers:

> James wanted to hold that in one way consciousness does not exist, but that in another way it does; yet he was never able, even to his own satisfaction, to define the two ways clearly enough to show that they are consistent rather than contradictory.[8]

So I try to do two things in this paper:

a) briefly bring together and explain all the main things that James has to say about experiential consciousness, and

b) show that all his positions can be seen as mutually consistent *without*, for example, relying on the assumption that some of his 'naturally scientific' methodological assumptions in fact turn out to be false within the final system as a whole.

It turns out, I suggest, that looked at carefully James' theory of consciousness is even more unique and suggestive than has previously been realised. It encompasses gritty realism about the phenomenal data of consciousness, a sort of dualism between the mental and the physical, his radical metaphysics of pure experience and, perhaps most interesting of all, a view of consciousness as a kind of control capacity without agency—a position that I think can fruitfully be compared with the role of attractors in chaotic systems.

In what follows I shall try to explicate James' ideas in four parts:

I. First, his writings about the *stream of thought*, drawing a contrast between these and standard notions about conscious-ness, but noting his assertions to the effect that this phenomenon certainly does exist.

II. Then those parts of his writings which suggest that one of the things which is true about consciousness is that it is *non-physical*. That is 'consciousness exists' in the traditional sense that something inhabits the universe 'in addition to' the physical, and these extras correspond to what we normally label 'the mental.'

III. Third, those segments of James' thought which treat of con-sciousness as a *causal agent*, and which suggest consciousness exists not just as a melody or a shadow exist, but in a more substantial way.

IV. And finally I will briefly discuss James' metaphysical doctrine of '*radical empiricism*,' which views consciousness as existing as an arrangement of pure experience.

By the time I am finished, I hope to have shown that all James' manifold pronouncements in this area can be made consistent and coherent in an extremely interesting way.

The Stream of Thought

James has two fundamental points to make in this area, I think. First, to put it at its simplest, James holds that *states of consciousness* exist, in the form of the 'stream of thought,' but calls into question the status of *consciousness itself*. Second, James asserts that psychology, as a natural science, must hold certain data to be fundamental; like every science it must rely upon certain assumptions which it cannot call into question on peril of ascending/descending into metaphysics. Among these basic postulates are the data of consciousness.[9] Thus when we introspect and look into our own minds, "*everyone agrees that we there discover states of consciousness.*"[10] In accordance with this: "the definition of Psychology may be best given ... as the description and explanation of states of consciousness as such."[11]

So James can be seen as having a strong positive thesis about the existence of consciousness: such things as sensations, desires, emotions, cognitions and the rest of the list—the standard furniture of our mental lives—positively do exist, and indeed are the very subject matter of the science of psychology. However, this view is coupled with his, perhaps more famous and controversial, negative account of consciousness: all that James is willing to admit at the outset, by way of (so to speak) fleshing out the stream of consciousness, is that "thought goes on."[12] He goes on to describe more of its characteristics, and in particular these five:

- every thought is part of a personal consciousness;

- thought is in constant change;

- within each personal consciousness thought is sensibly continuous;

- thought appears to deal with objects independent of itself; and

- thought is selectively attentive.[13]

James claims that *all* that is evident about consciousness, as we actually experience it, amounts to nothing more than the sequence of thoughts with roughly the five kinds of property listed above.[14] "When we turn to consciousness, to examine it in its own specific being, we find not an 'entity' distinct from its objects but just this cognitive *function* of having objects."[15]

This empirical description of the stream of thought is, for James, not only compatible with a very attenuated metaphysical account of consciousness, but seems to *demand* it because of the absence of evidence for any other hypotheses.

> I believe that 'consciousness,' when once it has evaporated to this estate of pure diaphaneity, ... is on the point of disappearing altogether. It is the name of a nonentity.[16]

Thus, for example, we do not experience consciousness as being a sort of container through which unchanging, simple ideas pass: it, itself, *is* the continuous stream of thought, and it is natively selective.[17] Nor do we experience a *soul* or *ego* behind or within our consciousness. Nor do we have any direct evidence, James asserts, that the medium of the stream of thought is a different kind of *substance* than the 'rest' of the world.[18]

So James is opposed even to the neo-Kantians, who, though they reduce consciousness to merely a logical correlative of 'content'—the consequence of the irreducible subject-plus-object character of experience—however also suppose that we "have an immediate consciousness of consciousness itself. ... [T]he consciousness is believed to ... be felt as a kind of impalpable inner flowing."[19]

Perhaps the most central part of all of this is that James claims we have no evidence for the duality of *content* and *consciousness*. The contemporary prevailing view, James says, was that experience is essentially dualistic, made up of both 'content' and 'consciousness, or reference to a self,' and it is possible to mentally subtract one, so that the other remains 'in the mind's eye.'[20] (Indeed, such a view is not unheard of today!) But

> *experience, I believe, has no such inner duplicity; and the separation of it into consciousness and content comes, not by way of subtraction, but by way of addition*—the addition, to a given concrete piece of it, of other sets of experiences ... [A] given undivided portion of experience, taken in one context of associates, play[s] the part of a knower, of a state of mind, of 'consciousness'; while in a different context the same

undivided bit of experience plays the part of a thing known, of an objective 'content.'[21]

This preserves a sort of dualism—"since [experience] can figure in both groups simultaneously we have every right to speak of it as subjective and objective both at once"[22]—but it is not any longer a mysterious dualism, James suggests:

> [I]t becomes verifiable and concrete. It is an affair of relations, it falls outside, not inside, the single experience considered, and can always be particularized and defined.[23]

Consciousness, according to James, is thus not another entity juxtaposed to the entities it knows, with an internal structure of its own, but is rather the 'function' of the objectification; its forms and structure come from its objects.[24] And so:

> It seems as if consciousness as an inner activity were rather a *postulate* than a sensibly given fact, the postulate, namely, of a *knower* as correlative to all this known; and as if '*scious*ness' might be a better word by which to describe it. But 'sciousness postulated as an hypothesis' is practically a very different thing from 'states of consciousness apprehended with infallible certainty by an inner sense.'[25]

Non-Physical Consciousness

One might be tempted at this point to think that James is in some way bent on collapsing the mental into the physical; this, within the modern terms of this debate, perhaps seems to us a natural way of showing that 'consciousness does not exist.' However, though consciousness is clearly not for James a separate *substance* from the physical, nor is it to be *identified* with the physical.

> Although we affirm that the *coming to pass* of thought is a consequence of mechanical laws ... we do not in the least explain the *nature* of thought by affirming this dependence, and in that latter sense our proposition is not materialism.[26]

In *Human Immortality* James describes what he calls "the great psycho-physiological formula: *Thought is a function of the brain.*"[27] However, nowhere (as far as I know) does he seriously propose the prospect that thought is *the same thing* as the brain (in the commonsensical sense we would understand that phrase today—I am ignoring for the present his doctrine of pure experience but adopting his 'methodological dualism').[28] "The admitted fact of functional dependence,"[29] for James, is here a relation between separate terms. Indeed, when James lists the possible varieties of functional dependence—productive, permissive or transmissive—none of them constitute self-identity.[30]

Further, James lists many attributes of consciousness which he considers not to be predicable of the physical. For example, he dwells at some length on the fact that consciousness is unique in that it can have 'ends' or 'interests.'[31] Considered merely physically, the reactions of our brain

> cannot be properly talked of as 'useful' or 'hurtful' at all … All that can be said of them is that *if* they occur in a certain way survival will as a matter of fact be their incidental consequence. The organs themselves, and the rest of the physical world, will, however, all the time be quite indifferent to this consequence, and would quite as cheerfully, if the circumstances changed, compass the animal's destruction. (p. 141)

This has the additional consequence that the *fundamental character of consciousness*, for James, is as a 'fighter for ends.' It is not purely cognitive—rather, cognition is subservient to ends (p. 141).

Other central examples of non-physical predicates, for James, are the property of 'knowing' or 'reporting' and of being 'personal.' In addition, all sorts of things are true of 'mental objects' (that fire may play over them and not affect them, that they only came into existence moments ago) that are false of their corresponding 'physical' counterparts, and *vice versa*.[32] All of this goes to show that James was firmly opposed to any claims to the effect that consciousness or mentality are identifiable with, and thus reducible to, anything physical.

Causal Consciousness

Another way of downplaying the 'reality' of consciousness is to strip it of its causal agency, a view which "banishes [consciousness] to a limbo of causal inertness" (p. 135), where it exists more like a 'melody,' or a 'shadow' than like a 'real thing' (p. 133).[33] James remarks, however, that he finds this prospect unconvincing. "It is to my mind quite inconceivable that consciousness should have *nothing to do* with a business which it so faithfully attends" (p. 136).

Psychology as a natural science, James opines, has a duty to be *naïve* about the status of causes—if something *seems* like a cause, then they had better treat it as if it is (pp. 137–8). Further, "the *particulars of the distribution of consciousness*, so far as we know them, *point to its being efficacious*" (p. 138).

i)   "Consciousness grows the more complex and intense the higher we rise in the animal kingdom" (p. 138).

ii) Consciousness might help "maintain the animal in the struggle for existence" (p. 138).

iii) The defects of the 'other' human organs "are such as to make them need just the kind of help that consciousness would bring provided it *were* efficacious" (p. 138).

iv) Therefore "the plausible inference [is] that it came just *because* of its efficacy" (pp. 138–9).

It is in defending the second and third premises of this informal argument that James moves into exciting and speculative new territory. The higher nervous system—the cerebral hemispheres—is highly unstable, James asserts; its operations are "indeterminate and unforeseeable" compared to those of the brain stem (p. 139). James, had he had the terminology, seems on the verge of calling the brain a *chaotic system*:

> what discharge a given small impression will produce may be called *accidental*, in the sense in which we say it is a matter of accident

whether a rain-drop falling on a mountain ridge descend the eastern or
western slope. (p. 139)

This provides for an extremely high capacity for adaptation to
minute changes in circumstances (p. 139). However, it also leads to the
problem that "I do not see how one could reasonably expect from it any
certain pursuance of useful lines of reaction" (p. 140). It may be hugely
adaptable, but "we can never be sure that its equilibrium will be upset in
the appropriate direction" (p. 140). *Consciousness*, James claims, is
"primarily a selecting agency" (p. 139). Its role, always, is to attend to
one thing in particular out of the range of things presented to its notice,
and it does so in line with some particular interest. Consciousness, then,
acts something like an attractor in a chaotic system "by bringing a more
or less constant pressure to bear in favour of *those* of its performances
which make for the most permanent interests of the brain's owner."[34]
Consciousness is not a causal agent that mysteriously impinges upon the
physical world like a kind of ectoplasmic billiard ball; rather it is a non-
physical causal force which stabilizes the brain.[35]

At first sight there seems to be something deeply implausible about
James' Darwinian claims in this argument. He claims that "the brain is
an instrument of possibilities, but of no certainties," and that the organ
is just as apt to move in the direction of ends "which are not the proper
ones of the animal, but often quite opposed," as the reverse (p. 141).
But if the brain is a purely mechanical, deterministic system, then, for
any given set of circumstances, it will have a given behavioural output.
If that output is inappropriate, then it will lessen the organism's chances
of surviving and reproducing—natural selection should take care of the
rest. So, if this story is complete, nothing in addition to the unconscious
brain is needed to explain the totality of human behaviour.

However, James' claims look more plausible once we understand
him as claiming that the brain is a *chaotic* system;[36] that is, in a nutshell,
that the brain's activities have a very great dependence on initial
conditions, such that a minuscule change in conditions might lead to
radically different outcomes. Think, for example, of a pencil balancing
on its point, or the 'butterfly effect' on weather systems.[37] This *general*
chaotic character would, as James says, vastly increase the brain's
responsiveness to its environment (by definition, in fact). However it
would, as James notes, lead to the danger of the brain responding in
widely different ways to two very similar situations, because of small
differences in 'irrelevant' conditions: for example, faced with a sheer

cliff, a chaotic organism might either jump or back away depending on, say, the prevailing wind-speed.

The solution is to introduce the notion of an attractor: a set of points to which the system is especially 'attracted' within the space of possible outputs. Thus chaotic systems are, in fact, to some degree predictable: they always end up at some point on the attractor. *This* is the role that consciousness plays, and James' conclusion stands: consciousness need not be an external causal agent acting upon the brain—it is more like a *principle of organisation* of the brain; a higher level pattern which describes the complex activities of the brain.

Radical Empiricism

> My thesis is that if we start with the supposition that there is only one primal stuff or material in the world, a stuff of which everything is composed, and if we call that stuff 'pure experience,' then knowing can easily be explained as a particular sort of relation towards one another into which portions of pure experience may enter. The relation itself is a part of pure experience; one of its 'terms' becomes the subject or bearer of the knowledge, the knower, the other becomes the object known.[38]

Thus James introduces his notion of 'radical empiricism'—the doctrine that the most fundamental 'substance' is not matter, nor mind, but pure experience. Hence consciousness *qua* substance-like entity, or *qua* something radically distinct from the physical, does *not* exist.

James' evidence for this hypothesis seems to consist largely of an examination of consciousness as it is seen pre-theoretically.[39] Here is his puzzle: We see a room, which commonsensically is a physical object in space, and which commonsensically we have 'in our mind.' How can the room be in two places at once: the world and the mind? It might be that what is in the mind is only a *representation* of the room; but 'the reader's sense of life' knows no intervening image but seems to see the room immediately.[40] His solution: "Reality is apperception itself. ... Our sensations are not small inner duplications of things, they are the things themselves in so far as the things are presented to us."[41] The commonsensical solution to the problem, James thus urges, is to hold that the room exists in two places at once just as a single point can be on two lines at once: if it is at their intersection.[42]

The two 'lines' or processes or sets of relations in question are these:

a) the reader's personal biography, a set of mental, 'inner,' operations;

b) the history of the house of which the room is part, a train of physical operations.

That these two groups of operations are "curiously incompatible" (as we saw in section II above) is a matter of their differing contexts only, "just as the same material thing may be both low and high, or small and great, or bad and good, because of its relations to opposite parts of an environing world."[43]

So, for James, what kind of 'stuff' is pure experience—that is, what is consciousness fundamentally 'made of,' on this view?

> There are as many stuffs as there are 'natures' in the things experienced. If you ask what any one bit of pure experience is made of, the answer is always the same: 'It is made of *that*, of just what appears, of space, of intensity, of flatness, brownness, heaviness, or what not.'[44]

At least three major questions about all this arise at once. First, why do the natures of things differ so much depending on whether they are taken as consciousness or content? Indeed, these two kinds of nature seem to *contradict* each other—one is heavy, the other not; one spatial, the other not—and yet they are supposed to be attributes of the self-same thing. How can this be? Second, how can one bit of pure experience *know* another? How can a bit of pure experience 'know' anything? Yet there certainly seems to be knowing going on. And third, how can my *point of view* be accounted for? If 'mind' and 'matter' are fundamentally the same, and all the universe is pure experience, then what is it that traces 'my' passage through 'the external world'? What *is* 'the given'?

James does have responses to these problems, but I do not have the space to do more than gesture at them here. In brief: James' response to the first is basically to claim that the 'mental' and 'physical' do *not* differ in their natures, but only in the *relations* of these characteristics.

The general group of experiences that *act* ... comes inevitably to be contrasted with the group whose members, having *identically the same natures*, fail to manifest them in the 'energetic' way.[45]

Thus, for James, the thought of a fire *is* hot; the mental image of a foot-rule *does* have extension; it is just that the fire fails to warm my body, and the imagined foot-rule need not be in a stable 'spatial' relationship with other mental objects. "The two worlds differ, not by the presence or absence of extension, but by the relations of the extensions which in both worlds exist."[46]

On the second question, James has this to say:

What does exist and constitutes the portion of truth covered over by the word 'Consciousness' is the susceptibility possessed by the parts of experience to be reported or known ... This susceptibility is explained by the fact that certain experiences can lead some to others by means of distinctly characterized intermediary experiences, in such a fashion that some play the role of known things, others that of knowing subjects ... These two roles can be defined perfectly without departing from the web of experience itself, and without invoking anything transcendent ... The attributes 'subject' and 'object,' 'represented' and 'representative,' 'thing' and 'thought' mean, then, but a distinction which is of a *functional* order only, and not at all ontological as understood by classical dualism.[47]

Either, then, something is an object present to perception, in which case it is simply the self-same piece of experience in its 'known' aspect, or our mental image of it is related in certain ways to other parts of pure experience, such as our being able to direct someone to the thing, knowing something about its background and present uses.[48]

On the third point above, regarding our point of view, part of James' response is to say that

the world experienced (otherwise called the 'field of consciousness') comes at all times with our body as its centre, centre of vision, centre of action, centre of interest. Where the body is is 'here'; when the body acts is 'now'; what the body touches is 'this'; all other things are 'there' and 'then' and 'that.'[49]

Bringing It All Together

As I noted at the outset, there is much general dissatisfaction with the coherence of James' various pronouncements about consciousness.[50] With one breath, James is a dualist; with the next he is asserting a 'radical empiricist' form of monism. On one page he calls consciousness the fundamental datum of psychology, and an unshakeable reality of our everyday experience; overleaf he is busy trying to persuade us that consciousness does not exist. With one hand he gives us the causal efficacy of consciousness; with the other he takes it away as an agent or activity or entity.

At least one commentator, Wesley Cooper, takes the line that all apparent conflicts can be resolved by keeping clear James' distinction between the level of 'natural science' and that of metaphysics.[51] In general, he says, James can adopt the position that certain metaphysical positions are possibly true, and can argue about them in certain works, while still holding that the phenomena of a particular science can account for all relevant *empirical* aspects. For example, he says at one point, "our reasonings have not established the non-existence of the Soul; they have only proved its superfluity for scientific purposes."[52]

The relationship between these two levels, for James, is not exhaustively characterised by Cooper.[53] However, there seem to be two ways of construing the relation. It could be that:

a) the assumptions of the science of psychology are *false* but instrumentally useful, or

b) the assumptions of the science of psychology are actually *true*, but only partial, restricted only to 'unmetaphysical' matters which are not controversial.

On the former reading, James can be inconsistent in what he says about consciousness: for some of the things he asserts, for example in the *Principles*, may be strictly speaking *false*. Cooper, at times, seems to tend towards this view. For example, he claims that James is an instrumentalist in science,[54] which might be taken as symptomatic of a cavalier attitude towards truth. And it is true that James, for example, cheerfully admits that psychology's assumption of determinism is likely to be false.[55]

However, I do not think that we need to treat James this uncharitably; the second reading b) is also possible.[56] John Danisi, for instance, suggests that James' real intention in insisting on psychology's status as a 'natural science' was to strip psychology of its dubious underpinnings and concentrate solely on the *facts* of experience.[57] And I think we do have now before us an interpretation of James' account of consciousness in which—though very far from unproblematic—each of the parts are mutually consistent, at least when broadly construed: his dualism is consistent with his monism; his anti-epiphenomenalism with his attacks on consciousness as a causal agent; his crypto-functionalism with his phenomenal realism. Here, then, is how all of what James says about consciousness can be true together:

1. All that our experienced mental life shows us is that thoughts follow each other in a stream with the five characteristics identified by James in *The Principles of Psychology*. This data is the subject of psychology; and, as far as it goes, it reveals truth—the stream of consciousness actually exists.

2. The dualism between the mental and the physical also *exists*; however, it is not a dualism of substance, it does not classify our 'real' ontology. It is a dualism of *higher level patternings* of the relations entered into by bits of pure experience. The mental and the physical are two quite different kinds of 'process.'

3. Consciousness can be spoken of, if only rather metaphorically, as 'causal.' However, it is a mistake to think of it as an *agency*. Rather the fact of consciousness in an organism should be thought of as the appearance of a kind of *patterning* within its behaviour, along the lines of the way an attractor 'causes' chaotic behaviour to follow a certain complex trajectory; and this patterning is, of course, highly causally relevant.

4. The fundamental metaphysical reality is pure experience: both the mental and the physical consist in 'pieces' of pure experience 'seen' in the context of different sets of relations.

Reprinted with permission from *Transactions of the Charles Peirce Society* 34 (spring 1998): 414-434.

Notes

[1] Gerald Edelman, *Bright Air, Brilliant Fire* (New York: Basic Books 1992) 37.

[2] Daniel Dennett, "Toward A Cognitive Theory of Consciousness," *Brainstorms: Philosophical Essays on Mind and Psychology* (Cambridge, MA: MIT Press 1978) 160.

[3] Owen Flanagan, *Consciousness Reconsidered* (Cambridge, MA: MIT Press 1992) 153ff.

[4] See, for example, David Galin's "The Structure of Subjective Experience," Güven Güzeldere's "Consciousness and the Introspective Link Principle," John Taylor's "Modelling What It Is Like To Be," and José-Luis Díaz's "The Stream Revisited: A Process Model of Phenomenological Consciousness," all in S. Hameroff, A. Kaszniak and A. Scott (eds), *Toward A Science of Consciousness: The First Tucson Discussions and Debates* (Cambridge, MA: MIT Press 1996).

[5] William James, *Psychology: Briefer Course* (Cambridge, MA: Harvard University Press 1984 [1892]) 140.

[6] William James, "The Notion of Consciousness" in *Essays in Radical Empiricism* (Cambridge, MA: Harvard University Press 1976 [1905], Appendix III) 7.

[7] Bernard Baars, *A Cognitive Theory of Consciousness* (Cambridge: Cambridge University Press 1988) 6.

[8] Gerald E. Myers, *William James: His Life and Thought* (New Haven: Yale University Press 1986) 64.

[9] Just as "all the natural sciences, for example, in spite of the fact that farther reflection leads to Idealism, assume that a world of matter exists altogether independently of the perceiving mind." *Psychology* 9.

[10]William James, *The Principles of Psychology, Vol. 1* (New York: Dover 1918 [1890]) 185. James continues: "So far as I know the existence of such states has never been doubted by any critic, however sceptical in other respects he may have been. ... *I regard this belief as the most fundamental of all the postulates in Psychology*, and shall discard all curious enquiries about its certainty as too metaphysical for the scope of this book." *Principles* 185.

[11]"By states of consciousness are meant such things as sensations, desires, emotions, cognitions, reasonings, decisions, volitions, and the like." *Psychology* 9.

[12]*Principles* 225. Henceforth page references to this book will be included in the text.

[13]See *Principles* Ch. IX.

[14]*Psychology* gives a similar list of five properties.

[15]James M. Edie, "William James and Phenomenology," *Review of Metaphysics* **23** (1970) 481–526. 512.

[16]William James, "Does 'Consciousness' Exist," in *Essays in Radical Empiricism* (Cambridge, MA: Harvard University Press 1976 [1904], 3–19) 3.

[17]As Schuetz puts it, James rejects "Locke's simile of a 'white paper' soul." (Alfred Schuetz, "William James' Concept of the Stream of Consciousness, Phenomenologically Interpreted," *Philosophy and Phenomenological Research* **1** (1941) 442–452. 444.) See also John J. McDermott (ed), "Introduction," *The Writings of William James* (Chicago: Chicago University Press 1977 xix–1) xxxv.

[18]For example: we think we perceive our mental life "as a sort of interior current—active, light, fluid, delicate, diaphanous, so to speak—and absolutely different from what is material. ... I believe ... that this sort of consciousness is pure fancy, and that the sum of concrete realities which the word consciousness should cover deserves quite a different description." "The Notion of Consciousness" 2–7.

[19]"Does 'Consciousness' Exist" 5.

[20]"Does 'Consciousness' Exist" 6. "...[I]t is always considered as possessing an essence absolutely distinct from the essence of material objects which, by a mysterious gift, it can represent and know. Taken in their

materiality, material things are not *felt*, they are not objects of *experience* as such, nor are they *related* as such. In order that they may assume the form of the system in which we feel ourselves to be living, it is necessary that material things *appear*; and this fact of appearance, superadded to their raw existence, is called the consciousness we have of them...." "The Notion of Consciousness" 1.

[21]"Does 'Consciousness' Exist" 6–7.

[22]"Does 'Consciousness' Exist" 7.

[23]"Does 'Consciousness' Exist" 7.

[24]Edie 518.

[25]*Psychology* 400.

[26]*Psychology* 13.

[27]William James, *Human Immortality: Two Supposed Objections to the Doctrine* (New York: Dover Publications, 1956 [1897]) 10.

[28]When he does, at one point, note the possibility, he (a little dismissively) calls it 'the *monistic* theory,' where mind and brain are 'inner and outer aspects' of 'One and the Same Reality.' After mentioning the theory, he then proceeds to discuss its two alternatives ('the *spiritualistic* theory' and 'the *atomistic* theory') in more detail, suggesting that these are the two really live options. *Psychology* 396.

[29]*Human Immortality* 12.

[30]*Human Immortality* 12–14.

[31]"Nothing can more strikingly show, it seems to me, the essential difference between the point of view of consciousness and that of outward existence. We can describe the latter only in teleological terms, hypothetically, or else by the addition of a supposed contemplating mind which measures what it sees going on by its private teleological standard, and judges it intelligent. But consciousness itself is not merely intelligent in this sense. It is *intelligent intelligence*. It seems both to supply the means and the standard by which they are measured. It not only *serves* a final purpose, but *brings* a final purpose—posits, declares it." "Remarks on Spencer's Definition of Mind as

Correspondence" in *Essays in Philosophy* (Cambridge, MA: Harvard University Press 1978 [1878]) 27–28.

[32]"Does 'Consciousness' Exist" 8–9.

[33]The contrast with a 'real thing' here is mine rather than James'.

[34]*Principles* 140. For example, pleasures are generally associated with beneficial acts, and pains with harmful ones. A good reason for this would be if mental states were causally efficacious: then, if harmful acts were pleasurable, organisms would be made to pursue them and thus come to harm. "An animal that should take pleasure in a feeling of suffocation would, if that pleasure were efficacious enough to make him immerse his head in water, enjoy a longevity of four or five minutes." *Principles* 143–4.

[35]"In claiming this efficacy for consciousness James is not simply noting that there is a functional commerce between an organism and its environment, but rather he is explaining this functional relationship by referring to a nonphysical cause." W.E. Cooper, "William James' Theory of Mind," *Journal of the History of Philosophy* **28** (1990) 571–93. 578.

[36]On all of this see, for example, James Gleick, *Chaos* (New York: Viking 1987), or Stephen Kellert, *In the Wake of Chaos* (Chicago: University of Chicago Press 1993).

[37]Note too, if you like, that Jeff Goldblum's chaos mathematician character in the film *Jurassic Park* illustrates the phenomenon of chaos by showing that a drop of water, landing in the same place, will run in a different direction off someone's hand each time because of tiny variances in initial conditions. Compare James' rainfall on a mountain ridge example!

[38]"Does 'Consciousness' Exist" 4–5.

[39]"Let the case be what it may in others, I am as confident as I am of anything that, in myself, the stream of thinking (which I recognize emphatically as a phenomenon) is only a careless name for what, when scrutinized, reveals itself to consist chiefly in the stream of my breathing. ... *The entity is fictitious, while thoughts in the concrete are fully real. But thoughts in the concrete are made of the same stuff as things are.*" "Does 'Consciousness' Exist" 19.

[40]"Does 'Consciousness' Exist" 8.

[41]"The Notion of Consciousness" 3. "This present actuality with which things confront us, from which all our theoretical constructions are derived and

to which they must return ... is homogenous—nay, more than homogenous, but numerically one—with a certain part of our inner life." "The Notion of Consciousness" 3.

[42]"If the 'pure experience' of the room were a place of intersection of two processes, which connected it with different groups of associates respectively, it would be counted twice over, as belonging to either group. ... In one of these contexts it is your 'field of consciousness'; in another it is 'the room in which you sit,' and it enters both contexts in its wholeness, giving no pretext for being said to attach itself to consciousness by one of its parts or aspects, and to outer reality by another." "Does 'Consciousness' Exist" 8. The same rule applies for concepts or imaginings (as opposed to percepts). Imaginings or memories for example, can be seen to have a dual objective-subjective nature. There is the context of the inner history of a person, and there is the context of all the impersonal associations and relations—spatial, temporal, logical etc.—between the experiences. That is, in one context these experiences form part of the 'field of objects,' and in another they are 'states of mind.' (See "Does 'Consciousness' Exist" 9–10.) Our concepts and imaginings are 'objective phenomena:' a dream of a golden mountain appears to the dreamer *as* physical; remembrance of one's childhood in a far-off land is presented *as* about a part of the world, truly distant in time and space. ("The Notion of Consciousness" 3–4.)

[43]"Does 'Consciousness' Exist" 13. The difference between things perceived and things imagined is not a difference in kind: "It is simply that a present object has a vivacity and a clearness superior to those of the representation. ... But this present object, what is it in itself? Of what stuff is it made? Of the same stuff as the representation. It is made of *sensations*; it is something perceived." "The Notion of Consciousness" 4.

[44]"Does 'Consciousness' Exist" 14–15.

[45]"Does 'Consciousness' Exist" 17, my italics.

[46]"Does 'Consciousness' Exist," pp. 16–17.

[47]"The Notion of Consciousness," p. 11.

[48]But, James goes on to explain, *everything* in our mental life contains reference to some 'other.' "Sensational experiences *are* their 'own others,' then, both internally and externally. Inwardly they are one with their parts, and outwardly they pass continuously into their neighbors, so that events separated by years of time in a man's life hang together unbrokenly by the intermediary

events." "The Continuity of Experience," in McDermott, p. 295. Yet is every kind of connectedness to constitute intentionality? Part of a table-top forms a continuum with the rest; it can lead one to another point on the table. This does not mean it 'knows' it: here is a serious problem that James does not adequately address.

[49]"Does 'Consciousness' Exist" 16–17.

[50]Consider, for example, Myers' final verdict: "Whether the phenomenon is called experience or consciousness, James' testimonial words to it lead us irresistibly to view it not merely as a function but as something with an inherent nature, by which it is a causal agent that produces effects. ... James wanted to hold that in one way consciousness does not exist, but that in another way it does; yet he was never able, even to his own satisfaction, to define the two ways clearly enough to show that they are consistent rather than contradictory." Myers, 64.

[51]"Generally, one should resolve apparent contradictions in James' system by apportioning the conflicting propositions to different levels." W.E. Cooper, "William James' Theory of the Self." *Monist* **75** (1992) 504–20. 505.

[52]*Principles* 350, quoted in Cooper 1992. "At the scientific level of James' system a proposition is expected to pay its way in the coin of prediction, verification and control, and, judged by this standard, references to the soul lack explanatory value. At the metaphysical level a proposition's function is to make as much sense as possible of one's experience and the human condition generally." Cooper 1992, 508.

[53]He suggests that "the natural sciences do the indispensable spadework for metaphysics, and they may point suggestively away from or towards a metaphysical conclusion; but typically they leave options open with respect to ultimate questions." Cooper 1990, 574.

[54]"The kind of psychology which could cure a case of melancholy, or charm a chronic insane delusion away, ought certainly to be preferred to the most seraphic insight into the nature of the soul." *Essays in Psychology* 277, quoted in Cooper 1990, 584.

[55]*Psychology* 395.

[56]Cooper, too, sometimes seems to sway in this direction. "The pure experiences of the *Essays* are what the sensations of the *Principles* become when sensations are no longer being classified as mental or physical. This

classification is still legitimate; it is salient for ordinary life and fundamental for scientific psychology. But for metaphysical purposes it is superficial." Cooper 1990, 584.

[57]"Instead of starting with some *a priori* scheme of entities, psychology must turn, as he says, to what can be immediately verified by everyone's consciousness so that a central mass of experience can be described, which all may accept as certain, however different their ulterior philosophic interpretations of it may be." John Danisi, "The Vanishing Consciousness of William James," *International Philosophical Quarterly* **29:1** (1989) 3–16. 8.

Chapter 4

Recasting Dewey's Critique of the Reflex-arc Concept via a Theory of Anticipatory Consciousness: Implications for Theories of Perception

J. Scott Jordan

Almost 100 years ago to the date, John Dewey (1896) published his seminal review, *The Reflex-arc Concept in Psychology*. In that paper, Dewey made clear the peculiar way one must describe human action when constrained to the stimulus-response distinction. The problem, he felt, was that the words stimulus and response represented nothing more than conceptual abstractions from what was an otherwise continuous, coordinated sequence of events. Descriptions of action based upon these abstractions, claimed Dewey, stripped the coordination of its very essence; namely, the process of maintaining a particular state of organization. Thus, he proposed that action be modeled, not as a linear chain of stimulus-response contingencies, but rather, as a circuit (i.e., an organized coordination) whose outputs are fedback into the system as inputs. According to Dewey then, instead of using *stimulus* to refer to an external event, it should be used to refer to that part of the coordination which specifies the state of affairs (i.e., state of organization) the coordination is maintaining, while *response* should refer to that aspect of the coordination which serves as the means by which the specified state of affairs is maintained:

> The stimulus is that phase of the forming coordination *which represents the conditions which have to be met in bringing it to a successful issue* [italics added]; the response is that phase of one and the same forming coordination which gives the key to meeting these conditions, which serves as instrument in effecting the successful coordination. (as quoted in Sahakian, 1968, p. 225)

The purpose of the present paper is to present a recasting of Dewey's critique by bringing together data which shed light on the nature of Dewey's coordination-specifying "stimulus." This will be accomplished via a synthesis (Jordan, 1996) of Vandervert's (1995) neuroalgorithmic theory of anticipatory consciousness and a series of studies on a recently reported perceptual phenomenon known as the Phantom Array (Hershberger, 1987). This synthesis will reveal that the primal stimulus within any organism-environment coordination resides within a continuously-generated anticipatory "feel" of the body in space-time that is not derived from afference (i.e., it is not a "caused-effect" of "environmental stimulation"), yet is essential to controlled action.

Having made this point, the paper will then address the implications of this anticipatory phenomenal context for *theories* of perception. It should be stressed that the present paper does not challenge traditional stimulus-response *methodology*. The practice of manipulating and controlling independent variables in order to assess their relationship to dependent variables has proven invaluable in its ability to reveal dynamic contingencies between the observations of physicists and that which we find in common phenomenology; an endeavor traditionally referred to as psychophysics. What the present paper does challenge is the literal translation of these *methodological* concepts into *theoretical* concepts. That is, once perception is *theorized* to be a response to environmental stimuli, as is often done in what are perhaps best known as *representationalist* theories of perception (Costall, 1984), it appears theoretically appropriate to assume that (1) perception "lags" behind the environment, and (2) perception is inherently inaccurate because the perceptual response (i.e., representation) cannot be equal to the total environmental stimulus available. The recasting of Dewey's critique counters these arguments, and further makes it clear, in a new way, that this sort of representationalist theorizing results from the non-parsimonious assumption that perception is the process of constructing "appearances" of the real, physical world. The paper will conclude by making the argument that it was just this sort of non-parsimonious theorizing that J. J. Gibson was attempting to overcome in his theory of direct perception.

Phantom Limbs and the Phantom Array: Evidence of the Anticipatory Nature of Consciousness

As one looks from one target to another within the visual environment via saccadic eye movements, the spatial location of a stationary object appears to remain stable despite the fact that the retinal locus of the object's image changes with each change in eye position. Researchers claim that the nervous system achieves this perceived constancy across saccades, what is perhaps best known as visual direction constancy (VDC, Shebilske, 1976) by producing a corresponding shift in the spatial coordinates of the retina (i.e., retinal local signs) via a neural signal representing eye position (Bridgeman, 1986; Grüsser, 1986; Hallet & Lightstone, 1976a, 1976b; Hansen & Skavenski, 1985; Hershberger & Jordan, 1992, 1996, in press; Hershberger, Jordan, & Lucas, in press; Jordan & Hershberger, 1994; Matin, 1972, 1982; Shebilske, 1976; Skavenski, 1990; Steinbach, 1987). Given that the true nature of this neural signal is unknown, it is often referred to as the *extraretinal* signal.

Interestingly, researchers are now claiming there to be a similar sort of signal for the entire body; an *extrabody* signal that codes the coordinates of the body in space-time (Melzack, 1992; Stapp, 1993; Vandervert, 1995). Melzack (1992) models this *extrabody* signal as a hard-wired neuromatrix spread-out over three major brain circuits that continuously generates a pattern of impulses letting one know, "the body is intact and unequivocally one's own" (p. 123). Vandervert (1995), referring to the work of Melzack, refers to this *extrabody* signal as a "continuously-generated feedforward template of the active body universe" (p. 113). He then claims that the activity of this continuously-generated template of the body in space-time constitutes one's basic level of awareness of one's self as something different from the environment; that is, it is *consciousness*:

> I propose that conscious experience is the continuously-generated entirety of the activity of the pure space-time template of the body in the brain—it feeds forward the integrity and 'whereabouts' of the genetically-derived template of the body universe. (p. 113)

Theoretical Underpinnings of Vandervert's Theory

Vandervert refers to the activity of this proposed space-time template as a *neuroalgorithm*, and points out that the phylogenetic emergence and genetic embedding of such a neuroalgorithm is the result of millions upon millions of selective iterations, over the course of evolution, of what Lotka (1945) referred to as the prey-predator scenario.

Survival within this scenario demands that both the prey and the predator be able to discriminate changes in perception brought about by self-motion versus environmental motion, what von Holst and Mittelstaedt (1950) referred to as reafference and exafference, respectively (cf. Hershberger, in press). It further demands that the neuroalgorithms regarding the body in space-time that are used in making this reafference-exafference distinction, be feedforward (anticipatory) in nature. The predator must control the motion of its body as a whole towards positions it anticipates the prey will occupy, while the prey must accomplish the same feat, but toward positions it anticipates the predator will *not* occupy. Vandervert believes it was the need for this organism-environment, reafference-exafference sort of figure-ground distinction that brought about the emergence of such anticipatory (i.e., feedforward) body-in-space-time neuroalgorithms:

> It is my view that consciousness constructs this model of space time in the brain as a comparator system by which the brain can movement-by-movement, moment-by-moment differentiate itself from, and make sense of, the constant barrage of incoming sensory information (1995, p. 113)

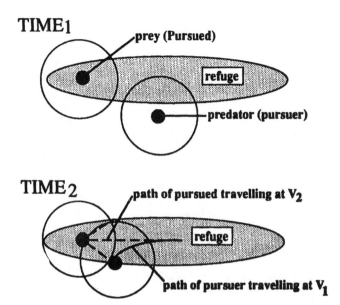

Fig. 1. "Countless millennia of iterations of selective processes in this generalized prey-predator scenario resulted in the encapsulation of space-time algorithms in the brain. Algorithms are patterns of energy pathways (methods of work) that solve problems." (Figure and quoted caption from "Chaos Theory and the Evolution of Consciousness and Mind: A Thermodynamic-Holographic Resolution to the Mind-Body Problem" by L. Vandervert, 1995, in *New Ideas in Psychology* 13(2):107-127. Copyright 1995 Elsevier Sciences Ltd, The Boulevard, Langford Lane, Kidlington 0X5 1GB, UK. Reprinted by permission of the publisher and the author.)

Phantom Limbs: Empirical Support of Vandervert's Theory

As evidence of this continuously-generated neurotemplate of the body in space-time, Vandervert (1995) cites Melzack's (1992) work on phantom limbs. Melzack points out the following: (1) A person missing a limb continues to experience the limb as if it were still intact, (2) the phantom limbs are experienced in spatial locations that are consistent with the person's ongoing behavior, and (3) loss of a limb is not necessary: Phantom limbs are also experienced by those who are born without a limb. From these findings, Melzack concluded, the existence of phantoms in people born without a limb or who have lost a limb at an early age suggests that the neural networks for perceiving the body and its parts are built into the brain. The absence of inputs does not stop the networks from generating messages about missing body parts; they continue to produce such messages throughout life. (p. 126)

Investigations of a recently discovered perceptual phenomenon known as the Phantom Array (Hershberger, 1987) further support this notion of a continuously-generated neuroalgorithmic template of the body in space-time. The Phantom Array also provides empirical evidence which supports the notion that the template is a template, not of *actual, proximal limb position*, but rather, of the *intended, distal action* in which the limb is to be engaged. The "feel" of the body in space-time, then, is the moment-to-moment discrepancy between the anticipated and the actual location of the body in space-time.

Further Empirical Support of Vandervert's Theory: The Phantom Array

One experiences the Phantom Array while producing saccadic eye-movements across a rapidly blinking (200 Hz) light-emitting diode (LED) in an otherwise darkened room. While saccading from left-to-right, one sees something akin to that depicted in figure 2 (Hershberger & Jordan, in press). Specifically, one sees a horizontal row of flashes in which the flashes materialize sequentially in the direction opposite the saccade. This, of course, is brought about by the sweeping motion of the retina across the blinking LED. However, the fact that one sees an array indicates that the shift in eye-position and the shift in the extra-retinal signal (i.e., space-time template of retinal spatial coordinates) are asynchronous, for if they were synchronous, the retinal local signs would be shifted in the direction of the saccade at the same rate as the eye, and every flash would appear at the same spatial location. The nature of this asynchrony can be deduced to some extent from the spatial location of the Phantom Array. Specifically, the entire array appears on the side of the LED associated with the intended direction of gaze (Hershberger & Jordan, 1992; in press), with the first flash appearing abruptly displaced from the pre-saccadic location of the LED to its position at the right-end of the array. Given that the first flash is presented at or before the moment the eyes begin the saccade, (this is assumed from its appearance as part of the array which, of course, is brought about by the actual movement of the eyes), its abrupt displacement in the direction of the impending saccade indicates that by the onset of the saccade, the local signs of the retina have shifted in the direction of the impending saccade. Jordan and Hershberger (1994) conducted an experiment to determine when this anticipatory shifting of the template occurs.

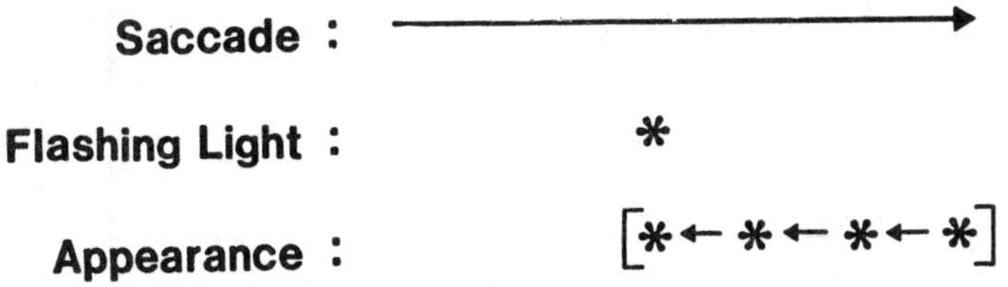

Saccade : ————————————————▶

Flashing Light :   ✱

Appearance :   [✱ ← ✱ ← ✱ ← ✱]

Fig. 2. "If you shift your gaze saccadically from the left to the right of a point light source in a darkened room, blinking on and off at 120 Hz, you will see phi movement to the left within a phantom array that is *displaced* to the right." (Figure and quoted caption from "Saccadic Eye Movements and the Perception of Visual Direction" by W. [A]. Hershberger, 1987, in *Perception & Psychophysics* 41(1):35-44. Copyright 1987 Psychonomic Society, Inc.. Reprinted by permission of the publisher and the author.)

Timing the Template. Four trained subjects produced 1600 left-to-right saccades in the dark from a fixation point (F) to a saccadic target (T). The spatial layout and the onsets and offsets of all stimulus LEDs are depicted in figures 3 and 4, respectively (for a thorough examination of the methodology, see Jordan & Hershberger, 1994). At the start of every trial, F glowed red for a randomly varied interval ranging from 1-2 sec (the unpredictable duration of F reduced the frequency of anticipatory saccades). As can be seen in figure 4, exactly 50 msec following the offset of F, T glowed red for 100 msec. Subjects, having been told to "follow the red light" saccaded (S, figure 4) from F to T. A 150-250-msec latency normally exists between target onset and the actual initiation of a saccade (Robinson, 1975); consequently, both F and T were extinguished before the eyes began to move.

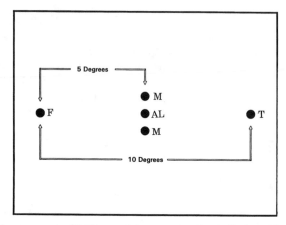

Fig. 3. "Arrangement of LEDs used to generate visual displays. F = fixation light, T = target light, AL = array light, M = Marker." (Figure and quoted caption from "Timing the Shift in Retinal Local Signs that Accompanies a Saccadic Eye Movement" by J. S. Jordan, & W. A. Hershberger, 1994, in *Perception & Psychophysics* 55(6):657-666. Copyright 1994 Psychonomic Society, Inc. Reprinted by permission of the Publisher.)

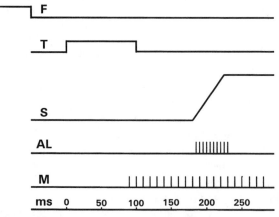

Fig. 4. "The chronology of events comprising a single trial. F = fixation, T = target light, S = saccade from F to T, AL = array light, M = marker flash; the bottom trace indicates milliseconds in relation to T onset." (Figure and quoted caption from "Timing the Shift in Retinal Local Signs that Accompanies a Saccadic Eye Movement" by J. S. Jordan, & W. A. Hershberger, 1994, in *Perception & Psychophysics* 55(6):657-666. Copyright 1994 Psychonomic Society, Inc. Reprinted by permission of the Publisher.)

The LED labeled AL (Array Light) began flashing green at 200 Hz, 5 msec after the subject began the saccade from F to T, and stopped flashing 1 msec after the subject completed the saccade (see figure 4). This green flashing LED produced a green phantom array. The two LEDs labeled M (Marker) flashed simultaneously for 1 msec at a pre-determined moment during the trial. As can be seen in figure 4, there were 20 possible moments for each subject, each being separated by a 10 msec interval. This "window" of potential marker moments was temporally situated around the subject's average saccadic latency, which had been determined prior to the onset of experimental trials (Figure 4 depicts a hypothetical subject having an average saccadic latency of 180 msec). The actual marker moment utilized on any given trial was unknown to the subject. The pair of yellow marker flashes produced by the Ms generated a vertical yellow hash-mark that intersected the green phantom-array. Given that these yellow flashes would be displaced just as the green flashes had been, and further given that one could, in a post-hoc manner, determine the moment of the M flash in relation to the onset of the saccade, the location of the yellow hash mark within the green phantom array provided a reliable measure of when the first flash (or any flash for that matter) in the Phantom Array appeared, relative to the onset of the saccade.

To obtain this measure, subjects indicated where the yellow vertical line had appeared relative to the Phantom Array. They did so on a 5-point scale on which a 1 meant "the left-end of the array," a 5 meant "the right-end of the array," and a 3 meant "the middle of the array" (2 and 4, of course, meant positions between 1 and 3, and 3 and 5, respectively). Figure 5 illustrates the change in the average Marker-Position Judgment (MPJ) as a function of the temporal relativity of M and the saccadic onset (Marker-Saccade Asynchrony; MSA).

Illustrating the Shift in the Template. The first thing to point-out about figure 5 is the pattern of MPJs during the saccade (i.e., MSAs ranging from 0-40 msec). Clearly, markers flashed at the beginning of the saccade were seen at the right end of the array, while markers flashed during the saccade (i.e., MSAs between 0 and 40) were seen at array locations nearer and nearer to the left-end of the array. The extreme overlap of the 4 subjects during this range of MSAs rather robustly indicates that subjects were very capable of judging the location of M within the Phantom Array, and further serves to validate the MPJs obtained at different MSAs. For example, during the 80-msec interval preceding the onset of the saccade (i.e., MSAs of -80 to 0), the MPJs are very close to 5. This indicates that Ms flashed as soon as 80 msec prior to the onset of the saccade were seen at the right-end of the array, which further indicates that the first flash in the Phantom Array appears in its displaced location roughly 80 msec prior to the onset of the saccade. Given that the subjects were still fixating F during this interval, the appearance of the first flash in this new displaced location indicates that the space-time template of the retina had shifted in the direction of the *impending* eye-position, despite the fact that the eyes had yet not begun the saccade that would bring them to that impending position.

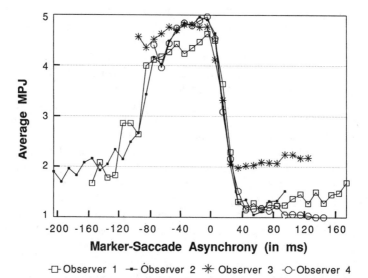

-□- Observer 1   -•- Observer 2   -✳- Observer 3   -○- Observer 4

Fig. 5. "The observer's average marker-position judgments (MPJs) plotted as a function of the marker-saccade asynchrony." (Figure and quoted caption from "Timing the Shift in Retinal Local Signs that Accompanies a Saccadic Eye Movement" by J. S. Jordan, & W. A. Hershberger, 1994, in *Perception & Psychophysics* 55(6):657-666. Copyright 1994 Psychonomic Society, Inc. Reprinted by permission of the Publisher.)

Clearly, the shift in retinal local signs accompanying a saccade is anticipatory. Further support for this claim can be found in the work of Becker and Jürgens (1975), for they found that the amplitude of a saccade may be altered by retinal information that is presented as late as 80 msec prior to a saccade, indicating that the shift in retinal local signs is finalized just in time to generate the pre-saccadic portion of the Phantom Array. Further, Duhamel, Colby, and Goldberg (1992) reported finding neurons in the monkey inferior-parietal lobe that shift their retinal receptive fields to the same degree and in the same direction as an impending saccade well before the onset of the saccade (e.g., 80 msec or more). Collectively, these data support the claim that the shift in the template is anticipatory, and led Jordan and Hershberger (1994) to conclude the following:

> The traditional interpretation of the perisaccadic illusion of visual direction is that the brain shifts the retinal local signs in order to compensate for an eye movement, and generally dismisses the alternative possibility that the brain moves the eyes saccadically in order to compensate for an abrupt shift in retinal local signs. (p. 665)

The Anticipatory Nature of Consciousness

Both phantom limbs and the Phantom Array indicate that "felt" egocentric space (i.e., phenomenal body-in-space-time experience) is "of," or "about," the discrepancy between intended and actual body-in-space-time location, with shifts in the former preceding shifts in the latter. This supports Vandervert's (1995) claim, derived from the "flight" and "pursuit" curves of the Lotka scenario, that the continuously-generated template of the body in space-time is feedforward (anticipatory) in nature, and further indicates that our immediate awareness of ourselves in space-time, which Vandervert (1995) claims is consciousness, resides within the discrepancy between the actual, proximal position of the body in space-time, and the distal, intended action in which the body is to be engaged.

This notion that experience is influenced by both intended and actual effector-position is not completely new. Helmholtz claimed as early as 1867 that perceived visual direction depends more upon the "effort of will" necessary to produce eye movements than upon proprioceptive feedback. This hypothesis has often been cited as being synonymous with von Holst and Mittelstaedt's (1950) efference copy hypothesis, which claims, essentially, that the extraretinal signal (neuroalgorithmic template) mediating visual direction constancy is a copy of the neural commands sent to the oculomotor nuclei (Dassonville, Schlag & Schlag-Rey, 1992; Hallet & Lightstone, 1976a, 1976b; Hansen & Skavenski, 1985; Honda, 1989; Matin, 1972, 1982; Shebilske, 1976).

The existence of phantom limbs and the Phantom Array, however, challenge the idea that it is a copy of *efference* that is fedforward. Specifically, the fact that subjects experience phantom limbs in positions consistent with on-going behavior, despite the lack of the limb, indicates that the template of the body-in-space-time is a template of "feels" that *are not derived from afference*. This is consistent with Melzack's interpretation of Phantom Limbs:

> In short, phantom limbs are a mystery only if we assume the body sends sensory messages to a passively receiving brain. Phantoms become comprehensible once we recognize that the brain generates the experience of the body. Sensory inputs merely modulate that experience; they do not directly cause it. (1992, p. 126)

Since these "feels" are not the result of afference, one might be tempted to refer to the neuroalgorithms mediating such "feels" as efference. And since both Lotka's prey-predator scenario and the Phantom Array indicate these "feels" are anticipatory, one might further contend that the involved neuroalgorithms constitute an anticipatory *efference copy*. But this is also problematic, since *efferent* signals are traditionally associated with effector movement, not effector "feels." It seems as though the neuroalgorithms mediating these anticipatory "feels" are neither afferent nor efferent, at least not in terms of the *inflow* and *outflow* they traditionally denote.

Hershberger (1976, in press) was aware of this problem with efference-copy explanations of spatial constancy. Thus, he coined the phrase *afference copy* in order to capture the idea that the neuroalgorithm mediating constancy was an anticipatory "feel" versus an anticipatory motor command (efference-copy). This notion of an anticipatory "feel" of an effector in space time is precisely what was eluded to by William James in his classic description of voluntary behavior;

> I trust that I have now made clear what that 'idea of a movement' is which must precede it in order that it be voluntary. It is not the thought

of the innervation [efference copy] which the movement requires. It is the anticipation of the movement's sensible effects [afference copy], resident or remote, and sometimes very remote indeed. (1890, Vol. 2, p. 521)

The nature of these anticipatory "feels" and their relationship to what is traditionally denoted by *afference* is made clear by research on perceived visual direction during oculomotor paralysis (Stevens et al., 1976; von Graefe, 1854). Specifically, those experiencing anatomical or neurochemical oculomotor paralysis report that the visual scene seems to "jump" in the direction of an attempted saccade, yet do not report that the visual world remains in this position for long. Apparently, feedback from the un-moved orbs keeps the generation of the afference-copy in "check", and thus prevents long-term experience of phantom-like phenomena. This notion is supported by the existence of phantom limbs. Specifically, the feedforward neuroalgorithms of the body in space-time are present, while feedback is not. Given this de-coupling of the neuroalgorithms regarding intended and actual effector location, the generation of anticipatory "feels" continues "unchecked" as it were, and the missing limb is experienced in positions consistent with on-going behavior (i.e., the intended orientation of the rest of the body). Thus, while the Phantom Array is brought about by the relatively brief de-coupling of intended and actual eye-position that exists both before and during saccadic eye-movements, phantom limbs are the result of the same sort of de-coupling playing itself out at a temporally-larger, more permanent scale. And this de-coupling is not between an efference-copy and feedback. It is between an anticipatory afference-copy and feedback.

Implications of the Anticipatory Nature of Consciousness for Theories of Perception

This notion of an anticipatory feedforward "feel" of the body in space-time provides new insight into Dewey's (1896) claim that the word *stimulus* should refer to the part of the organism-environment coordination specifying the state of organization the coordination is striving to maintain. *If the word stimulus is to be used, it should refer to the anticipatory "feel" of the body in space-time the organism is specifying and striving to attain.*

This recasting of Dewey's critique has profound implications for theories of perception, for it reveals conceptual shortcomings that arise within representationalist *theories* which claim that perception is the act of generating mental/neural representations in response to environmental stimuli. Such representationalist theories are perhaps well-represented by the following quotation:

> perception consists of a sequence, stretching from events in the physical world external to the perceiver through the translation of those events into patterns of activity within the perceiver's nervous system, culminating in the perceiver's *experiential and behavioral reactions* [italics added] to the events. (Sekular & Blake, 1994, p. 1)

These authors later state the following:

> The perceiver's view of the world is necessarily inaccurate, because the perceiver's sensory system both *limits* the information that is available and *augments* the information that is available ... To sum up: In order to understand perception as fully as possible, one must study not only the properties of the physical world but also those of the perceiver. (p. 11)

Even though the word representation is not utilized in the preceding quotation, there is an obvious commitment to the representationalist notion that perception is a response to an environmental stimulus. The anticipatory, feed-forward "feel" of the body-in-space-time, revealed via phantom limbs and the Phantom Array, makes clear three conceptual shortcomings inherent within such a theory of perception. The first is its sequencing of environmental awareness. The second is its claim that the perceiver's view of the world is necessarily inaccurate. And the third is its implicit assumption that there exits a real "physical" world of which we experience but appearances.

The Sequence of Perception

Implicit in the sequence outlined in representationalist theories of perception is the notion that awareness of the world necessarily lags "behind" the world due to the transfer delays of the nervous system.

Though the notion of transfer delays seems appropriate, the notion that perception is thus a post-hoc phenomenon, does not. The locations of the flashes in the Phantom Array clearly indicate that those flashes occurred within an anticipatory (feedforward) phenomenological context; 80 msec prior to the onset of the saccade, phenomenal space had already shifted in the direction of the intended direction of gaze.

This notion that perception is constrained and contextualized by control of the body in space-time was touched upon by Dennett (1991) in his critique of Libet's (1981) arguments regarding the temporal relationship between environmental events and perception. Specifically, Dennett claims that the temporal order, or sequence, in which the nervous system distributes information is not dictated by the order in which the information is transduced by the sense organs. Rather, it is dictated by the temporal constraints imposed by the on-going control of the body in space-time. Dennett refers to these constraints as "temporal control windows" and contends that the nature of these windows is a function of the relevant sensory-motor coordination.

> When we are engaged in some act of manual dexterity, 'fingertip time' should be the standard; when we are conducting an orchestra, 'ear time' might capture the registration. (p. 162)

Phantom limbs and the Phantom Array enhance Dennett's contention by pointing out that whatever we "experience" about these temporal control windows is contextualized by the changing intended orientation of the body in space-time. For example, as regards "saccade time" the temporal-control window "opens" with the observer's decision to look to a new position, and closes roughly 80 msec prior to the onset of the saccade, from which point the afference-copy "jumps" and becomes "locked-in" at the intended direction of gaze. Visual experiences unfold as if the eyes have moved in the direction of the intended saccade, and subsequent retinal information (i.e., the Phantom Array), that reaches the appropriate thresholds, is experienced within the context of this locked-in, intended "feel." Further, even though the *visual* location of a perisaccadic flash follows the pattern made clear by the Phantom Array (i.e., it is illusory), one can nonetheless accurately point (Miller, 1993) and guide hammer blows (Hansen & Skavenski, 1985) toward the location of such flashes. These data indicate that "saccade-time," "manual-pointing time," and "hammer-blow time" function according to control windows involving different levels of temporal scale, and the sequence of perception within such windows is determined more by the temporal scale of that window than temporal constraints imposed by transfer delays.

Interestingly enough, there are data to indicate that even though these control windows operate at different temporal scales, they are, nonetheless, coordinated and can influence one another. Specifically, Lucas (1994) found that a brief (1 msec) peri-saccadic flash presented at the onset of a saccade to a target located 8 degrees from the fixation point, can result in hypermetric adaptive saccades even though the peri-saccadic flash originates from a hypometric location (e.g., 6 degrees from the fixation point). The perisaccadic flash must be presented during the de-coupling of intended and actual eye position (i.e., from roughly 80 msec prior to the saccade to the end of the saccade), because hypometric flashes presented at the end of the saccade produce hypometric adaptive saccades. Further, the peri-saccadic flash must be brief, for if it is presented at saccadic onset and lasts an entire second, the result is hypometric adaptive saccades. Thus, in order for the flashes comprising the Phantom Array to impact eye-movements, they must be presented in isolation during the de-coupling of intended and actual eye position.

How does one use the words *stimulus* and *response*, or *cause* and *effect* to describe the sequence of perception that is playing itself out among these temporally-nested control windows? Once can rightfully make the methodologically-oriented statement that the flashes comprising the Phantom Array constitute an effect of the blinking LEDs. However, one can also rightfully state that the spatial extension of the flashes comprising the array constitutes an effect of the interaction between the subjects' intended and actual action. In the former description, the environment constitutes stimulus, while in the latter, the organism does so. Some might be satisfied by declaring a draw and making the claim that perception is influenced by both environmental stimuli and top-down influences residing within the subject. But such thinking makes it appears as if both environment and organism are imbued with equal causal efficacy. The question is, are they?

Prinz (1997) addressed this issued directly. His claim is that in any experimental setting, the first and primary stimulus is to be found in the instructions given to the subject. Thus, in the Phantom Array experiment, the instructions given to the subjects to follow the red lights and to assess the location of the hash mark relative to the marker flashes, provided subjects with a sensory-motor coordination to maintain throughout the experimental session. *This is how the LEDs obtained their status as stimuli.* If the subjects had been placed in the experimental laboratory without having been asked to maintain the afore-described sensory-motor coordination, the LEDs would have had minimal, if any, causal efficacy in regards to the subjects' perceptions.

Costall (1984) too, was aware of the primacy of the subject's perceptual expectations and the fact that such expectations are manipulated within experimental settings;

> the psychological laboratory is the very microcosm of the Cartesian scheme [environment as stimulus]. After all, our major experimental paradigms are designed explicitly to prevent the organism from transforming the experimental situation, as would be possible to some degree in real life ... The subjects are free only in the sense that they can *react to*, [italics added] rather than change, the conditions which are imposed upon them. (p. 114)

This point may appear contrived and trivial, but it brings to a head, rather robustly, the fact that in experimental settings, environmental events derive their conceptual power as stimuli via experimental instructions. Of course, this is the very purpose of experimental control— to minimize the subject's contribution to his/her own experiences. By doing so, one assumes one's experiment to be revealing phenomenally-independent "physical-world" parameters which serve as the causes of perception. This methodology may sound atheoretical, as if one is simply sticking close to the "facts." But the statement, in fact, implicitly makes the theoretical claim that perception is an effect of environmental causes. This philosophical maneuver makes it appear equally "factual" to claim that perception lags behind the world due to transfer delays. The only place this statement approaches being appropriate is in a laboratory setting in which the subject's contribution is supposedly minimized.

Environmental events are ultimately granted causal efficacy because such events are relevant to an organism's controlled sensory-motor coordination. The maintained sensory-motor coordination (i.e., intention, afference-copy, etc.) is the final cause. It is the primary stimulus. An organism controlling its relationship to the environment predetermines, via its intentions (i.e., afference copies), which environmental events have the potential to influence that control. We can *refer* to those environmental events as stimuli, but we cannot theorize such environmental events to be the *causes* of perception, for newly-detected environmental information always resides within a world of phenomenal body-in-space-time anticipation. Transfer delays do exist, but the "pursuit" and "flight" curves of the prey-predator scenario clearly indicate that natural selection favors those systems whose phenomenology plays itself out on the forward, anticipatory edge of the present. Phantom phenomena indicate that this anticipatory edge is provided by the anticipatory feels associated within temporally nested control windows. And as pointed out by Hershberger (1976) and James (1890), such "anticipatory images" are a necessary prerequisite of controlled action.

This notion, then, that perception begins with an organism's need to control, leads to the second conceptual inadequacy that the present recasting of Dewey's critique reveals about the representationalist tendency to utilize *methodological* stimulus-response distinctions within *theories* of perception. That it, it challenges the notion that an organism's perceptions are necessarily inaccurate because the organism's sensory systems augment and limit the information transduced.

Perception as Limited and Inaccurate

The claim that perception is necessarily limited and inaccurate is based upon the fact that organisms cannot transduce all of the information available within the environment, thus, any "representation" they construct of that world must be inherently incomplete (i.e., inaccurate). This definition of perceptual accuracy, however, results from labeling the environment as stimulus and perception as response— perception is theorized to be an act of representation construction. If the intentions of the organism are labeled as stimulus, however, perceptual accuracy becomes something different. For if environmental information is transduced according to its relevance to the control of body-in-space-time relationships, perceptual accuracy comes to be measured in terms of sensory-motor success. Over the course of evolution, success on this scale has been dictated by the dynamics of the prey-predator scenario, with successful sensory-motor coordinations being those that lead to escape for the prey, and capture, for the predator. Vandervert (1996) discusses how these successful neuroalgorithms (sensory-motor coordinations) come to be:

a given algorithm is independent of its source system and can be moved from system to system by purely algorithmic processes. For example, algorithms which obtain among systems of physical sources of nature do not in any way 'belong' to those systems, and they may be transported from those dynamical nonliving substrates into substrates of living systems such as nervous systems by another algorithm, for example, the 'natural selection algorithm.' (p. 5)

Thus, countless selective iterations of the prey-predator scenario (the algorithm of "natural selection") have resulted in sensory-motor coordinations (neuromuscular algorithms) whose dynamics are a mirror image of the forces, or dynamics, they must counteract in the environment (environmental algorithms). "Accurate" perceptions within these successful sensory-motor coordinations would be those perceptual events that facilitate "escape" and "capture" for the prey and predator, respectively.

As regards perception of the body, phantom phenomena indicate that the "accurate" way to perceive the body is in terms of the discrepancy between its "intended" and "actual" location, thus allowing the control of anticipatory "flight" and "pursuit" paths. Given these paths must be directed toward locations the prey and predator are expected to occupy or not occupy, respectively, it follows that what organism's specify to be "attained" is not just body-position, but rather, body-in-environment position. This means that both body and environment locations must exist within an anticipatory phenomenal context.

Recent studies in cognitive psychology support this notion. Specifically, it has been demonstrated (Finke, Freyd, & Shyi, 1986; Freyd & Finke, 1984; Hubbard, 1995) that the remembered final position of a moving target is displaced in the direction the target was traveling just prior to its offset. Further, the magnitude and direction of the displacement is consistent with the laws of physics. For example, the remembered final position of an upward-traveling target is displaced in the direction of the target's motion, but to a lesser extent than a downward-traveling target. This, of course, is consistent with the law of gravity. Likewise, the remembered final position of a horizontally-moving target is displaced to a decreasing extent as one increases the number of surfaces the target "slides" across. This is consistent with the dynamics of friction.

In addition to following the laws of physics, it has been found that such displacements cannot be eliminated by error feedback (Freyd,

1987). Apparently, the dynamics of the environment (i.e., environmental algorithms) have been transferred, via the algorithm of natural selection, into the algorithms of sensory-motor control in such a way that the location of a moving target, just as the "location" of the body in space-time, is contextualized by the target's "anticipated" location. Further data indicate that these anticipated locations are body-in-space-time relative. Specifically, Reed and Vinson (1996) found that displacements were larger when subjects were told that a vertical, descending line was a "rocket" versus a "church steeple." However, the finding that displacement occurs, even if what actually happens to the target is inconsistent with the observer's expectations (i.e., the target "crashes through" a barrier, versus "bouncing off" the barrier; Hubbard, 1994) indicates that while these anticipated locations are body-in-space-time relative, they nonetheless play themselves out according to the rules dictated by the environmental algorithms from which they emerged.

Thus, it appears that the algorithm of natural selection has endowed us with sensory-motor control systems whose dynamics are algorithmically isomorphic with environmental dynamics as well as body-in-space-time dynamics. This algorithmic isomorphy allows organisms to control "anticipatory" flight and pursuit curves toward "anticipated" locations. Vandervert touches upon this isomorphy of algorithms and, in doing so, makes a telling comment about the nature of algorithms:

> Of course, the neuro-algorithms that link the fish's visual perception with the neuroalgorithms that control the fins equally reflect algorithms inherent in the hydrodynamic properties of the water. In sum, algorithms are neither their source system's nor matter-energy; algorithms are *patterns* of information. (1996, p. 5)

Vandervert's equating of environmental and neural algorithms with "patterns of information" seems to get to the heart of what J. J. Gibson (1979) meant by his use of the word "information":

> Locomotion and manipulation are neither triggered nor commanded but *controlled*. They are constrained, guided, or steered, and only in this sense are they ruled or governed. And they are controlled not by the brain but by information [algorithms], that is, by seeing oneself in the world. Control lies in the animal-environment system. Control is by the animal *in* its world. (p. 225)

Gibson's equating of information with 'seeing oneself in the world' casts a different spin on what it is that organisms actually control. For though our language habits lead us to claim that what organisms control is "behavior," Gibson seems to be claiming that what they control is relationships between what we *call* body and what we *call* environment. In other words, what organisms control is "oneself in the word," and this is neither body nor environment, but rather, anticipatory body-environment relationships (Jordan, 1997).

This notion that what organisms control is body-environment relationships, and that such control demands anticipatory feels of both the body and the environment, sheds new light on the question of perceptual accuracy. For according to such a notion, there is no need to construct representations of the environment in the nervous system. The sensory-motor control systems of any organism, of which its nervous system is a part, are already mirror images, or "re-presentations" (the hyphen is intended) of the dynamics of the organism-relative environment. The isomorphic coherence between organisms and environments was settled long-ago via the prey-predator scenario and has been passed on, phylogenetically, ever since. Organisms need not "represent." Rather, what they need do is place themselves in positions that allow their anticipatory phenomenal world to be modulated by environmental information. These variations in the nervous system brought about via such positioning and transduction can be *modeled* as representations, but *theorizing* perception to be the process of constructing such *environmentally-caused representations*, and then claiming perception to be inherently inaccurate or incomplete because these environmentally-caused representations cannot be exact replicas of the entire environment, is to put the cause, or stimulus, of perception in the environment, and simply translate the methodology of psychophysics into a theory of perception. Yes, there does exist a plethora of psychophysical data indicating organisms can transduce only a small portion of information available within the environment. But to describe perception as inaccurate or incomplete because only certain levels of thermodynamic structure (i.e., levels of information) are relevant to an organism's control, is to ignore the fact that these non-immediate levels of information are not open to us until we bring them, via technology, into the realm, or scale, of immediate experience. Once revealed, *these non-immediate levels of information can also be said to be inaccurate because they too represent a particular scale of observation.* In order to describe a given level of information, *one must necessarily ignore other levels of information during the act of measurement, thus all measurements are inherently inaccurate and incomplete.*

These arguments indicate that the notion of perception being inherently inaccurate or incomplete has got it backwards. Perception is not inherently incomplete, it is inherently scale-dependent, as are all measurements. Psychophysical data do not reveal that perception is wrong. They reveal that the informational dynamics which qualify as "environment" for a particular organism are determined by that organism's need to control its relationship to certain aspects of that which lies beyond itself. The algorithms encapsulated in the organizational dynamics of an organism's sensory-motor control systems are exactly the algorithms necessary for that organism to control its propulsion through space-time on anticipatory paths toward anticipated locations. It is this isomorphic relationship among algorithms and their coordination in successful sensory-motor coordinations that truly serves as the yardstick of perceptual accuracy, not the degree of correspondence between the levels of information revealed via physics and immediate experience. Perception is not about "representing," it is about successful control. And it is not inherently incomplete, it is inherently scale-dependent.

Again, the purpose here is not to question the value of psychophysical research. To the contrary, the research on the Phantom Array, which ultimately led to the theory of perception presented in the present paper, was conducted in accordance with the principles of psychophysics. What is being questioned is the translation of this methodology into a theory of perception. The confusion of scale-dependence and accuracy inherent in representationalist theories is the direct result of putting the cause, or stimulus, for perception *in the environment.* Having done so, it seems appropriate to claim that perception is inherently inaccurate. But the arguments of the present paper support Dewey's claim that if we are to use the words cause or stimulus in reference to organism-environment coordinations at all, they are best used to describe the state of coordination the organism is striving to attain. With stimulus and cause defined in this manner, perception suddenly becomes inherently scale-dependent and *extremely* accurate.

This notion that an organism's need to control it propulsion determines, in a phylogenetically a priori manner, which levels of information (i.e., thermodynamic structures) can be transduced and thus qualify as objects for that organism, leads to the third point by which

phantom phenomena challenge representationalist models of perception—that there exists a real "physical" world of which we
experience but appearances.

The World of Perception

In his book, *Our Knowledge of the External World*, Bertrand
Russell (1914) gives an eloquent description of what it means to see a
table. It is worth repeating:

> A table viewed from one place presents a different appearance from
> that which it presents from another place. This is the language of
> common sense, but this language already assumes that there is a real
> table of which we see the appearances. Let us try to state what is know
> in terms of sensible objects alone, without any element of hypothesis.
> We find that as we walk round the table, we perceive a series of
> gradually changing visible objects. But in speaking of 'walking round
> the table,' we have still retained the hypothesis that there is a single
> table connected with all the appearances. What we ought to say is that,
> while we have those muscular and other sensations which make us say
> we are walking, our visual sensations change in a continuous way, so
> that, for example, a striking patch of colour is not suddenly replaced by
> something wholly different, but is replaced by an insensible gradation
> of slightly different colours with slightly different shapes. This is what
> we really know by experience, when we have freed our minds from the
> assumption of permanent 'things' with changing appearances. What is
> really known is a correlation of muscular and other bodily sensations
> with changes in visual sensations. (p. 84)

While Russell may appear to be taking the long-way-home approach
to describing a table experience, what his observation makes clear is
that the short-cut provided by common sense (i.e., the belief in the
existence of "physical" objects of which we experience "appearances")
is not parsimonious, for it demands the "inferred" existence of such
objects. The more parsimonious account is that what we know is "a
correlation of muscular and other bodily sensations with changes in
visual sensation." What phantom phenomena add to this idea is the notion that what we know are scale-dependent exafference (environmental
information dynamics) and reafference (body-in-space-time information
dynamics) as they are contextualized by the organism's need to control

its propulsion along anticipatory trajectories towards anticipated locations.

Within this account then, it is more parsimonious to refer to perception as an act of "information detection" versus one of "representation construction." The former does not demand the existence of a material world in need of representation, as does the latter. All that is ontologically demanded by the former is the existence some degree of thermodynamic invariance, what one might refer to as "information structures." The theoretical advantage of the concept "information structure" over "object" is its lack of epistemological connotation. The word "object" connotes a certain degree of a priori givenness—the objects we find in our phenomenal world are material "givens" which exist outside phenomenology and, therefore, must be "represented" before they can reside within phenomenology. The concept "information structure" however, recognizes that the "objects" we find in our phenomenal world are those invariant aspects of the thermodynamic storm beyond the organism that are relevant to that organism's control. Aspects of that storm become corpuscularized (i.e., becomes "objects") within an organism's field of control (Jordan, in press). They therefore do not exist as neural representations in the organism's brain or as material objects in the environment—they exist as invariant thermodynamic information structures that are realized within an organism's field of control.

This notion, that invariant thermodynamic structures (i.e., information structures) are realized (i.e., are given their objectivity) within an organism's field of control, is consistent with Niels Bohr's (1934) description of the "objects" of physics, "In our description of nature the purpose is not to disclose the real essence of phenomena but only to track down as far as possible relations between the multifold aspects of our experience" (p. 18). Within this context, the claim to be able to measure the "physical world" really translates into the ability to manipulate (i.e., control) thermodynamic invariants (i.e., information structures) in such a way as to make certain experiences possible. This notion is also consistent with Henry Stapp's (1997) quantum-theoretical description the mind-matter relationship:

> This description shows how our experiencings become woven into the fabric of the quantum mechanical description of nature: they are the identifiers of events that are the comings into being of these experiencings, and that also act efficaciously upon the mathematical

structure that represents the physical aspect of nature. In this new picture of nature the physical aspect constitutes the more subtle aspect of reality: it acts merely as a substrate of *propensities* for experiential events to occur. These experiential events are the more robust basic realities. (p. 177)

What Stapp refers to as "a substrate of propensities," I have referred to as "information structures," and it is within an organism's field of control that such propensities obtain their "objectivity." Once this is realized, words like "mind" and "matter" come to be seen for what they truly are; crude symbols we utilize in the attempt to communicate to one another the algorithmic order of, or form within, our experiences. In the words of Bertrand Russell,

'Mind' and 'mental' are merely approximate concepts, giving a convenient shorthand for certain approximate causal laws [algorithms]. In a completed science, the word 'mind' and the word 'matter' would both disappear, and would be replaced by causal laws [algorithms] concerning events. (1927)

Conclusions

Perhaps the best trick that evolution ever played on us was the materialization of the world. This perceptual trick, which Vandervert (1990) refers to as the "primordial constancy," reflects an evolutionary achievement on the part of organisms that have succeeded in controlling their progress through the information structures beyond themselves; it is a manifestation (i.e., a materialization) of their ability to recognize exafference—as opposed to mere afference. Accordingly, the notion that perceptions are re-presentations of material objects, inferred on the basis of sensory information, has it backwards. Material bodies are the inferences, not the origins, of consciousness. Perceived bodies are not delayed representations of real bodies. The perception of one's own body, its perceived position in space-time, clearly does not lag behind the body's own sensory transducers. Phantom limbs and the Phantom Array are experienced within the anticipatory phenomenological context provided by the control of body-environment relationships. These anticipatory feedforward "feels" allow organisms to propel themselves on anticipatory paths, and it is the control of this propulsion that determines "when" environmental information will be utilized, more so than transfer delays. Further, the spatial memory displacements reported by Hubbard (1995), and the finding that such displacements are consistent with the laws of physics, indicate that the algorithms of environmental dynamics have been rather "accurately" transferred, via natural selection, into the neuromuscular algorithms of sensory-motor control. Thus, while the exafference-reafference distinction resulting from control of body-environment relationships does give rise to the experience of there being something "out there," *it is the naming of exafference as physical, not the exafference (perception) itself, which qualifies as inference.*

This is the conclusion one comes to when one recasts John Dewey's "stimulus" (i.e., state of affairs to be maintained) in terms of an anticipatory "feel" of body-environment relationships. Interestingly enough, it seems to be the case that this recasting of the issue is exactly what J. J. Gibson (1979) was attempting to develop in his theory of direct perception. By recognizing that the cause of perception resides, not within the "environment," but rather, within an organism's need to locomote through the environment, Gibson was able to develop a theory in which perception was theorized to be an act of information detection (the control of the transduction of environmental algorithms into neuroalgorithms) that reveals affordances (future possibilities of sensory-motor control experienced within the phenomenological context provided by the current intended body-environment relationship). Viewed in this light, current arguments about whether a critical experiment can be designed to test the relative merits of informational and representational models of perception (Hecht, 1996) are misplaced; rather, the question is which model involves a more parsimonious account of the world. The ultimate criterion is Occam's razor.

Reprinted with permission from *New Ideas in Psychology* 16 (1998) 165-187.

I gratefully acknowledge the many helpful comments and encouragements given over the years by Wayne A. Hershberger. I am further grateful for the insightful comments given by Larry R. Vandervert during the various stages of manuscript preparation. Portions of this article were presented as a poster at *Tucson II: Toward of Science of Consciousness*, which took place on April 9, 1996 in Tucson, AZ.

References

Becker, W., and Jürgens, R. 1975. Saccadic reactions to double-step stimuli: Evidence for model feedback and continuous information uptake. In *Basic mechanisms of ocular motility and their clinical implications,* edited by G. Lennerstrand, P. Back-y-Rita, C. C. Collins, A. Jampolsky, & A. B. Scott. New York: Pergamon.

Bohr, N. 1934. *Atomic theory and the description of nature.* New York: MacMillan.

Bridgeman, B. 1986. Multiple sources of outflow in processing spatial information. *Acta Psychologia* 63:35-48.

Costall, A. P. 1984. Are theories of perception necessary? A review of Gibson's The Ecological Approach to Visual Perception. *Journal of the Experimental Analysis of Behavior* 41:109-115.

Dassonville, P., Schlag, J., and Schlag-Rey, M. 1992. Oculomotor localization relies on a damped representation of saccadic eye displacement in human and nonhuman primates. *Visual Neuroscience* 9:261-269.

Dennett, D. 1991. *Consciousness explained.* Toronto: Little, Brown and Company.

Dewey, J. 1896. The reflex arc concept in psychology. *Psychological Review* 3:359-370.

Duhamel, J. -R., Colby, C. L., and Goldberg, M. E. 1992. The updating of the representation of visual space in parietal cortex by intended eye movements. *Science* 225:90-92.

Finke, R. A., Freyd, J. J., and Shyi, G. C. W. 1986. Implied velocity and acceleration induce transformations of visual memory. *Journal of Experimental Psychology: General* 115:175-188.

Freyd, J. J. 1987. Dynamic mental representations. *Psychological Review* 94: 427-438.

Freyd, J. J., and Finke, R. A. 1984. Representational momentum. *Journal of Experimental Psychology: Learning, Memory, & Cognition* 10:126-132.

Gibson, J. J. 1979. *The ecological approach to visual perception.* Boston: Houghton Mifflin.

Grüsser, O. -J. 1986. Interruption of efferent and afferent signals in visual perception: A history of ideas and experimental paradigms. *Acta Psychologia* 63:2-21.

Hallet, P. E., and Lightstone, A. D. 1976a. Saccadic eye movements to flashed targets. *Vision Research* 26:101-107.

———. 1976b. Saccadic eye movements towards stimuli triggered by prior saccades. *Vision Research* 16:99-106.

Hansen, R., and Skavenski, A. A. 1985. Accuracy of spatial localizations near the time of saccadic eye movements. *Vision Research* 25:1077-1082.

Hecht. H. 1996. Heuristics and invariants in dynamic event perception: Immunized concepts or nonstatements? *Psychonomic Bulletin & Review* 3:61-70.

Helmholtz, H. von. [1867] 1962. *Treatise on physiological optics*. Edited and translated by J. P. C. Reprint, Southall. New York: Dover.

Hershberger, W. 1976. Afference copy, the closed-lop analogue of von Holst's efference copy. *Cybernetics Forum* 8:97-102.

————. 1987. Sacccadic eye movements and the perception of visual direction. *Perception & Psychophysics* 41:35-44.

————. in press. Control systems with a priori intentions register environmental disturbances a posteriori. In *Systems theories and a priori aspects of perception*, edited by J. S. Jordan. Amsterdam: Elsevier.

Hershberger, W. A., and Jordan, J. S. 1992. Visual direction constancy: Perceiving the visual direction of perisaccadic flashes. In *The role of eye movements in perceptual processes*, edited by E. Chekaluk. Amsterdam: Elsevier.

————. 1996. The Phantom Array. *Behavioral and Brain Sciences* 19(3):552-553.

————. in press. The Phantom Array: A peri-saccadic illusion of visual direction. *The Psychological Record*.

Hershberger, W. A., Jordan, J. S., and Lucas, D. in press. Visualizing the peri-saccadic shift of spatio-topic coordinates. *Perception & Psychophysics*.

Honda, H. 1989. Perceptual localization of stimuli flashed during saccades. *Perception & Psychophysics* 45:162-174.

Hubbard, T. L. 1994. Judged displacement: A modular process? *American Journal of Psychology* 107:359-373.

————. 1995. Environmental invariants in the representation of motion: Implied dynamics and representational momentum, gravity, friction, and centripetal force. *Psychonomic Bulletin & Review* 2(3):322-338.

James, W. 1890. *The principles of psychology (Vol. 2)*. New York: Henry Holt.

Jordan, J. S. 1996. Phantom limbs and the Phantom Array: Evidence for the volitional nature of Vandervert's continuously-generated feedforward template of the consciousness of the body universe. (From *Toward a Science of Consciousness 1996 "Tucson II"*, Tucson, AZ, Abstract No. 210).

————. 1997. Individual and group action as the control of image-schemas across fractal time-scales: A response to Vandervert. *New Ideas in Psychology* 15(2):127-131.

————. in press. Intentionality, perception, and autocatalytic closure: A potential means of repaying psychology's conceptual debt. In *Systems theories and a priori aspects of perception*, edited by J. S. Jordan. Amsterdam: Elsevier.

Jordan, J. S., and Hershberger, W. A. 1994. Timing the shift in retinal local signs that accompanies a saccadic eye movement. *Perception & Psychophysics* 55(6):657-666.

Libet, B. 1981. The experimental evidence for subjective referral of a sensory experience backwards in time: Reply to P. S. Churchland. *Philosophy of Science* 48:182-197.

Lotka, A. J. 1945. The law of evolution as a maximal principle. *Human Biology* 17:167-194.

Lucas, D. 1994. The effect of perceived visual direction on parametric adjustments of saccadic eye movements. *Unpublished Dissertation.*

Matin, L. 1972. Eye movements and perceived visual direction. In *Handbook of sensory physiology, Vol. 7,* edited by D. Jameson and L. Hurvich. Heidelberg: Springer.

―――. 1982. Visual localization and eye movements. In *Eye movements and psychological process,* edited by W. A. Wagenaar, A. H. Wertheim, and H. W. Leibowitz. New York: Erlbaum.

Melzack, R. 1992. Phantom limbs. *Scientific American* 266 (April):120-126.

Miller, J. M. 1993. Egocentric localization of a brief perisaccadic flash. *Investigative Ophthalmology & Visual Sciences* 34:1138. (From Proceedings of the Annual Meeting of the Association for Research and Ophthalmology, Sarasota, FL, Abstract No. 2142).

Prinz, W. 1997. Why Donders has led us astray. In *Theoretical issues in stimulus-response compatibility,* edited by B. Hommel and W. Prinz. Amsterdam: North-Holland.

Reed, C. L., and Vinson, N. G. 1996. Conceptual effects on representational momentum. *Journal of Experimental Psychology: Human Perception & Performance* 22:839-850.

Robinson, D. A. 1975. Oculomotor control signals. In *Basic mechanisms of ocular motility and their clinical implications,* edited by G. Lennerstrand and P. Bach-y-Rita . New York: Pergamon.

Russell, B. [1914] 1961. *Our knowledge of the external world.* Reprint, London: George Allen & Unwin.

―――. [1927] 1970. *An outline of philosophy.* Reprint, London: George Allen & Unwin.

Sahakian, W. S. 1968. *History of psychology: A sourcebook in systematic psychology.* Itasca, Illinois: Fe Peacock Publishers.

Sekuler, R., and Blake, R. 1994. *Perception (Third Edition).* New York: McGraw-Hill.

Shebilske, W. L. 1976. Extraretinal information in corrective saccades and inflow vs. outflow theories of visual direction constancy. *Vision Research* 16:621-628.

Skavenski, A. A. 1990. Eye movement and visual localization of objects in space. In *Eye movements and their role in visual and cognitive processes,* edited by E. Kowler. Amsterdam: Elsevier.

Stapp, H. 1993. *Mind, matter, and quantum physics.* New York: Springer-Verlag
———. 1997. Science of consciousness and the hard problem. *The Journal of Mind and Behavior* 18:171-193.
Stevens, S. S., Emerson, R. C., Gerstein, G. L., Kallos, T., Neufled, G. R., Nichols, C. W., and Rosenquist, A. C. 1976. Paralysis of the awake human: Visual perception. *Vision Research* 15:93-98.
Steinbach, M. J. 1987. Proprioceptive knowledge of eye position. *Vision Research* 10:1737-1744.
Vandervert, L. 1990. Systems thinking and neurological positivism: Further elucidations and implications. *Systems Research* 7:1-17.
———. 1995. Chaos theory and the evolution of consciousness and mind: A thermodynamic-holographic resolution to the mind-body problem. *New Ideas in Psychology* 13(2):107-127.
———. 1996. From idiots savants to Albert Einstein: A brain-algorithmic explanation of savant and everyday performance, *New Ideas in Psychology* 14:81-92.
von Graefe, A. 1854. Beiträge zür Physiologie und Pathologie der schiefen Augenmuskeln. *Von Graefe's Archiv für Opthalmologie* 1: 1-18.
von Holst, E., and Mittelstaedt, H. 1950. Das Reafferenzprinzip. *Naturwissenshafen* 37:464-476.

Chapter 5

Perceiving and Measuring of Spatiotemporal Events

Jochen Müsseler

Consciously Perceived Events and Measured Events

In one way or another, our consciously perceived world results from transformations in the retina and the brain. The present paper is concerned with the question of how these transformations establish the experienced metric of spatiotemporal events, and whether and how these transformations are related to the metric measurements which a physicist uses to survey the physical world.

Perceptual psychologists and physicists agree that the viewpoint contributes to what is perceived or measured when considering events. In perception, for example, the full moon low in the sky appears consciously up to one-third larger than the same moon overhead. The reason is that the moon on the horizon is judged against the landscape while, when it is overhead, no cues for size and distance are available. In physics, spatial length is also seen as constituting only a relative measure. This became obvious with the theory of relativity (more precisely with the so-called *Lorentz transformation*, cf. Einstein, 1905), which shows that length measurements depend on the movement relative to an observer.

When in the 1920s and 1930s the ideas of physical relativity theory flashed over to other scientific disciplines, psychologists were among the first to adopt the pragmatic principle of relativity of space and time. This view was supported by phenomena, which demonstrate considerable spatiotemporal interactions in perceptual judgments. For example, when observers judge the intervals of successively flashed lights, temporal judgments turns out to be dependent on the spatial distance between them—as well, spatial judgments prove to be dependent on the temporal interval (*kappa-tau effect*, e.g., Cohen, 1969; Helson & King, 1931; cf. also Piaget, 1955, 1965). These phenomena were sometimes taken as evidence for the existence of a relativity principle that overlaps scientific disciplines.

The present paper tries to evaluate a more formal attempt to apply physical spatiotemporal measurements to psychological phenomena. This is based on an analogy between the perception of moving stimuli and the spatiotemporal relationships between two physical frames of references that are in motion relative to each other. As has been argued, there is a formal similarity between these two situations which makes it possible to apply the Lorentz transformation to perceptual *contraction phenomena* (e.g., Caelli, 1981; Caelli, Hoffman, & Lindman, 1978; Drösler, 1979; Müsseler, 1987; Müsseler & Neumann, 1992). In other words, the analogy is of interest because the Lorentz transformation predicts a length contraction if one system moves at constant velocity relative to the other.[1]

In perceptual psychology contraction phenomena have been known for more than a century. The first author to report one variant was Zöllner (1862; cf. also Vierordt, 1868; Helmholtz, 1910, pp. 210). He presented figures moving behind a vertical slit a few millimeters in width and observed what he called 'anorthoskopische Zerrbilder' (anorthoscopic distorted pictures): Although only a small vertical section of the figure is uncovered at any time as the figure is in motion behind the slit, the observer sees a complete figure, with all its parts being *simultaneously* visible. This simultaneity impression is independent of whether the figure moves behind the slit, or the slit moves over the figure (Haber & Nathanson, 1968). However, only when the figure moves behind the slit does the figure appear to be *contracted;* that is, there is a reduction of the figure's phenomenal length in the direction of its movement. This phenomenon was rediscovered by Parks (1965) with an illustration of a camel as seen through the eye of a needle (figure 1).

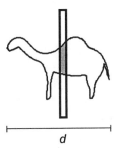 

Fig. 1. Stimulus presentation (left) and stimulus perception (right) of a moving camel as seen through the eye of a needle (see text). Note, the length contraction *d'* of the perceived camel as compared to its actual length *d*.

On the other hand, length contraction does not only occur with the slit paradigm. We used an arrangement in which the slit was enlarged to a window up to 80 mm and a pair of vertical rods traveled through it. In a figurative sense the leading rod replaced the head, the following rod the tail of the camel. If the rod distance was larger than the width of the window (e.g., 96 mm), then the first rod had physically left the window before the second rod entered. Nevertheless, the observer sees two rods travelling simultaneously through the window (*tandem effect*, cf. Müsseler, 1987; Müsseler & Neumann, 1992). Here, simultaneity is the qualitative indicator of the contraction phenomenon. A closer inspection of the data revealed that perceived distance depends considerably on rod distance, window width, and movement velocity (figure 2, upper panels).

The presence of a window does not constitute a necessary condition of length contractions. Ansbacher (1938, 1944) presented only a rotating arc, nevertheless the arc shrunk subjectively with optimal velocities. It has been speculated that Ansbachers' experiment was suggested by none other than Max Wertheimer who had an extensive exchange with Albert Einstein about relativity theory at the end of his life (cf. Drösler, 1979).

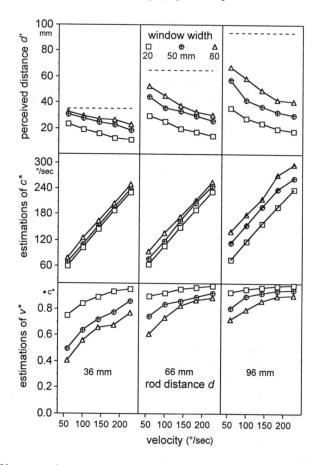

Fig. 2. Upper panels demonstrate perceived distance d' as a function of rod distance (vertical panels), window width (curve parameter), and movement velocity (abscissa) in the tandem-effect situation (dashed lines indicate physical distance d; data from Müsseler & Neumann, 1992, Experiment 2). The maximal propagation rate of signals in the human visual system c^* as estimated from d' is shown in the middle panels. Estimations of perceived velocity v^* as portions of a constant c^* are figured in the lower panels.

The question is, of course, whether at all these consciously perceived length contractions have something to do with physically postulated contractions. To answer this question a closer look at the relativistic assumptions and their psychological correspondents is needed.

A First Look at the Relativistic Approach

In physics the contraction is one of the consequences that followed from the so-called Lorentz transformation. These equations *(1)* transform the spatiotemporal coordinates of two reference systems which are in motion toward each other:[2]

$$x' = \frac{x - vt}{\sqrt{1 - v^2/c^2}}, \; y' = y, \; z' = z, \; t' = \frac{t - vx/c^2}{\sqrt{1 - v^2/c^2}} \qquad (1)$$

From equations *(1)* the reduction immediately follows: If d is some distance in system S, and if there is some system S' that moves at a uniform speed v relative to S, then d will be reduced to d' if observed from S' (see, e.g., Caelli et al., 1978, for a derivation of *(2)*).

$$d' = d \cdot \sqrt{1 - v^2/c^2} \qquad (2)$$

The reduction in equation *(2)* is only due to the limit velocity c between the systems, which is a consequence of the thesis that there are no instantaneous spatiotemporal propagations between systems. Since then v is always lower than c, the square root is always smaller than or equal to 1, hence d' is smaller than or equals to d.

Another way to phrase the situation described in equation *(1)* is that an observer measures spatiotemporal features of objects, which are in relative motion to him. Contraction occurs only because of this motion and because of the limited propagation rate of signals with which the observer is able to register spatiotemporal events. In this respect, the relativistic approach reflects a theory of measurement.

Caelli et al. (1978) and Drösler (1979) have attempted to apply the Lorentz transformation to perceptual phenomena. The only necessary modification they introduced was substituting c with c^*, the corresponding limit velocity of transmission in the visual system. c^* was assumed to be *"a measure of the finite propagation rate of signals in the human visual system"* (Caelli, 1981, p. 150). It was defined as the maximum of perceived velocity and empirically determined by the velocity at which observers were unable to report the direction of the movement. Then, in equation *(2)*, *d'* is perceived distance and *d* is physical distance. Caelli et al. (1978) as well as Drösler (1979) report quantitative evidence supporting this view.

However, one of the underlying assumptions of the relativistic approach is that *c* or *c** is a constant. We checked this assumption by solving equation *(2)* for *c**.

$$c^* = \frac{v}{\sqrt{1 - d'^2 / d^2}} \qquad (3)$$

Equation *(3)* can be used to estimate *c** from our perceived distances in the tandem-effect situation. We found that *c** varied from 61.0 to 294.9°/sec, and depended considerably on window width, rod distance, and movement speed (cf. figure 2, middle panels). These dependencies are damaging for a direct application of the Lorentz transformation to perceptual contraction data. Dzhafarov (1992) came to a similar conclusion based on another data set.

If a formal account—like the relativistic approach—is not consistent with the data, one or more of its underlying assumptions must be questioned. One deficiency of equation *(2)* is that it does not contain the variable 'window width.' Yet this variable strongly exerts an influence on perceived distance (figure 2). Therefore, one solution for the relativistic approach could be that in equation *(2)* physical velocity *v* has to be replaced by perceived velocity *v**, which is known to be affected by window width (e.g., Brown, 1931a, 1931c). Indeed, Dzhafarov (1992) found evidence that it could be perceived velocity and not physical velocity that contributes to the experienced metric.

When we transformed equation *(3)* to equation *(4)*,

$$v^* = c^* \sqrt{1 - d'^2 / d^2} \qquad (4)$$

and estimated *v** as portions of a constant *c**, we got *v** functions which obeyed psychophysical demands (cf. figure 2, lower panel). Similar psychophysical power functions of perceived velocity have been found by Mashour (1964) and Algom and Cohen-Raz (1984). The latter authors further reported that their power functions intersect at a common point due to a relationship of slope (exponents of the power functions) and intercept. This relationship and the common intersection is also present in the power functions depicted in figure 2 (for details, see Müsseler, 1987, p. 74).

To conclude, when physical velocity v is replaced by subjective velocity v^*, the application of the Lorentz transformation to our data became plausible. However, a critical evaluation of this account requires an additional explication of what c^* really stands for and what it means to speak of 'motions between systems' in a psychological context. Before doing so however, it is worthwhile to consider an attentional explanation of the contraction phenomena, which may, in turn, offer an explication of the relativistic assumptions.

An Attentional Approach

Phenomenal distance-reduction effects have been explained by accounts other than the relativistic framework (for a review of alternative accounts see Müsseler & Neumann, 1992). Another approach takes advantage of attentional considerations. It is based on the idea that the empirical properties of visual attention that have been revealed by studies with stationary stimuli should be equally applicable to situations in which stimuli are in motion. If we analyze the situation in which the tandem effect occurs in terms of attention shifts, then it can be shown that this reduction phenomenon falls off as a natural consequence of three well-known properties of visual attention.

1. *Localizing and pointing to a stimulus requires focal attention being directed to it* (for overviews see Neumann, 1996; Van der Heijden, 1992). Therefore, a phenomenal representation of a stimulus is assumed to be established at the end of an attention shift. To judge the distance between two moving rods, both have to be located. Since the rods travel through the window in succession, attention has to be focused on them successively. This implies that observers in a tandem-effect experiment have to shift their attention from the first to the second rod in order to estimate their distance.

2. *A shift of attention can be elicited by the appearance of a stimulus in the retinal periphery* (e.g., Jonides, 1981; Müller & Rabbitt,

1989). This implies that the attention shift from the first to the second rod can be initiated by the second rod when it enters the window.

3. *An attention shift takes time* (e.g., Sperling & Reeves, 1980; Tsal, 1983). Since the stimuli in the tandem-effect display are in motion, this implies that, after eliciting the attention shift, the second rod will have moved a certain distance before the focus of attention reaches it.

If we assume that the second rod is perceived at the position that it has attained when the focus shift reaches it, then the tandem effect will necessarily follow: The perceived position of the first rod is determined by its position at the beginning of the focus shift. The perceived position of the second rod is determined by its position at the end of the focus shift. Hence the perceived distance between them will be smaller than their physical distance by the distance that the second rod has covered during the focus shift.

The underlying cognitive mechanisms of this attentional explanation can be formulated as variants of a two-process account. Basically such accounts assume that there is pre-attended and attended state of processing and that the perceived environment results from the systems' state when attention is directed. In the present context, two formulations of the two-process account are considered in more detail.

The first account assumes that the presentation of a visual stimulus triggers two kinds of processes that take place simultaneously: *coding processes* and *attentional processes* (cf. Neumann, 1990). Coding processes encompass all operations that serve to create an internal code of the stimulus, for example, computing its contour, its color, size, location, etc. An attentional process is initiated by the transient response to the appearance of the stimulus and consists of a shift of the attentional focus to the stimulus, that is, towards its approximate location. Only after this focus shift has been completed will the result of the coding processes be phenomenally represented (i.e., be available for the observer's explicit report). It is assumed that as a result of the coding processes, the updating of an internal spatial map of the visual environment takes place, and that this updating has a short latency as compared to the time required for attentional processes. Hence, it is possible that the spatial map changes while the focus shift is still under way. Because only the state of the spatial map at the end of the focus shift is phenomenally available, changes of the stimulus that occur during the focus shift will go unnoticed (see also Neumann & Müsseler, 1990a, 1990b; Müsseler & Aschersleben, 1996, 1998; cf. the comparable account by Bachmann, 1984, 1994).

The second, not necessarily alternative account emphasizes the functional relationship between attentional processes and directed eye movements for space perception. There is growing evidence that eye movements and attentional mechanisms are closely linked, that is, covert attentional orienting normally interacts with overt orienting. However, covert and overt orienting can be independently observed by inhibiting the overt-action part (cf. the "premotor theory of attention," Rizzolatti & Craighero, 1998; Rizzolatti, Riggio, Dascola, & Umiltá, 1987; Umiltá, Riggio, Dascola, & Rizzolatti, 1991).

Given these two approaches we recently introduced an account which claims that in the visual perception of spatial position, that is, in the construction of the visual field, two densely connected maps with different codes or representations are involved: A visual *sensory map* (*V*), which is only conceived as an ordinal map and which thus contains mainly neighborhood relationships of objects, and a *motor map* (*M*), which codes (eye) positions on (map) positions and which thus introduces the metrics needed to execute goal-directed eye-movements (Van der Heijden, Müsseler, & Bridgeman, 1999). Both maps determine what is seen. This can be taken to mean that perceived positions result from map *V* being 'enriched' by map *M* (or vice versa) regarding spatial positions in the visual field in terms of realized and required eye positions. The only assumption to add in the present context is that the determination of saccadic amplitude and direction needs time, therefore temporarily delaying the enrichment (or update) of map *V* (or *M*, respectively). The enrichment is performed when the motor program for the eyes is prepared, that is, when attention is directed.

These attentional explanations of the tandem effect are attractive for several reasons. One is their parsimony. In contrast to other explanations of reduction phenomena they do not require any new principles or constructs. It simply extends, to the case of moving stimuli, what is known about visual attention in stationary displays. Moreover, it relates the contraction phenomenon to a broader class of phenomena (e.g., to metacontrast masking, cf. Neumann, 1979, 1982; to a mislocalization at the beginning of a movement, the so called the Fröhlich effect, cf.

Müsseler & Aschersleben, 1996, 1998; or to localization errors with stationary stimuli, Müsseler, Van der Heijden, Mahmud, Deubel, & Erstey, in press, Van der Heijden et al., 1999).

However, to explain the other variants of the reduction phenomenon mentioned above (i.e., the Parks' slit paradigm or the Ansbacher paradigm), additional assumptions are needed. For example, in the slit paradigm it has to be assumed that the attentional shift operates on an internal spatial representation, which extrapolates head and tail trajectories after they had been presented in the slit. The distance between head and tail would then be estimated by attentional shifts between these represented positions. The observation that the complete figure with all its parts appears simultaneously visible can be taken as an indication that such a representation exists.

The Ansbacher variant of the rotating arc is more problematic for an attentional account. An explanation of the contraction in terms of an attentional shift works only when the observer focuses the leading edge first. In this case the shift to the trailing edge and the direction of the movement are in opposite directions, 'meeting' at some point (as in the tandem-effect paradigm). If the observer were to first focus the trailing edge and then shift his/her attention to the leading edge, both directions would be identical, and the attention shift would have to 'catch up' with the leading edge's movement. A reversal of the contraction effect, that is, an expansion should be the consequence. This is indeed consistent with findings obtained in a modified tandem-effect situation (Müsseler & Neumann, 1992, Experiments 4 and 5).

This change from contraction to expansion describes a *Doppler effect*. This effect occurs, for example, when a fast moving train approaches a stationary observer standing on a platform. When the train reaches the observer, the sound appears to drop drastically. This is due to the fact that the sound and movement directions are identical before the platform and are opposite after the platform.

Nevertheless, the Ansbacher variant of the contraction phenomenon reveals the limits of the attentional explanation. In the slit or in the tandem-effect paradigm a shift from the leading to the trailing edge might provide a plausible account of the contraction. In fact, there are some hints that attentional mechanisms work in these situations (cf. Müsseler & Neumann, 1992). But it is too arbitrary in the Ansbacher variant whether contraction or expansion should occur.

A Second Look at the Relativistic Approach

The attentional explanation was not initially developed in terms of a relativity theory. However, the Doppler formulations above demonstrate a point of contact between psychological and physical procedures of measurement. The Doppler situation is different from the relativistic perspective in that the observer captures only a specific point of view within a stationary system. Obviously, the spatiotemporal distortions described in the Lorentz transformation *(1)* abstract from this specific view. However, it remains to be explicated what 'systems' and 'c^*' cognitively represent.

Are There Comparable Systems in Human Information Processing?

The attentional formulations above differentiate between an unattended state of the system, in which phenomenally inaccessible spatiotemporal information is coded, and an attended state, which represents the consciously perceived spatiotemporal relationships. Attentional mechanisms are assumed to determine the information that is transferred between these states. Thus, this formulation suggests two states, which might functionally represent two different representations. Are these representations comparable to physical systems?

Another cognitive implementation is also conceivable. Consider a stage model with an early stage representing peripheral processing and a later stage representing central processing. These stages can be assigned to different areas in the brain between which spatiotemporal information is transferred and which also can be assumed to represent comparable systems.

The problem with all these assumed cognitive 'systems' is that they are not equally available for empirical testing. To be more concrete, one presupposition of the Lorentz transformation *(1)* is that the spatiotemporal laws of one system are identical to the spatiotemporal laws of the other system, and these laws are independent from motions between the two systems *(relativity principle)*. In physics, a test of this principle raises no empirical difficulties, but in cognition it is in no way testable. This is because there is no means by which to compare isolated spatiotemporal observations of the peripheral stage with isolated spatiotemporal observations of the central stage.

An indication, however, that a perceptual relativity principle might work results from observations demonstrating the *symmetry principle*. This principle states that motion can be observed only relatively and that therefore an individual should not be able to identify motion in respect to an absolute coordinate system. In fact, this seems to be the case as demonstrated by driving and flight simulators. Instead, an observer uses the Gibsonian flow of the optical arrays to 'perceive' motion (Gibson, 1979); this is even true when the observer is stationary and others move a scene, as is realized in a movie.

Is There a Limited Propagation Rate c^* Between Perceptual Systems?

This second presupposition of the Lorentz transformation *(1)* seems to be less problematic than the relativity principle. It claims that there are no instantaneous propagations between systems, an assumption easy to accept in biological organisms. Consequently that c^* exists in human information processing is inferred from the spatial components of the retinal stimulation and the temporal propagation rate of the neural system (Drösler, 1979).

However, it is less plausible to determine c^* empirically by the velocity with which observers were unable to report the direction of a motion (Caelli et al., 1978; Drösler, 1979). First, this threshold varies too much with factors such as stimulus size and movement distance (cf. (Brown, 1931b) to represent a constant propagation rate of an internal neural system. And second, an inspection of equation *(2)* reveals that a moving stimulus which comes close to c^* should not be perceivable at all. On the other hand, if one would use this upper absolute threshold of motion for c^*, it would clearly be too high to account for the quantitative amount of observed contraction (cf. Müsseler, 1987). We therefore conclude that c^* cannot be accessed directly by perceptual observations. Instead, we speculate that c^* might reflect the spatiotemporal shifts of attention within the visual field. These shifts are never directly perceivable, only the state after completing the shift constitutes what is perceived.

Conclusion

The present paper aimed to compare physical spatiotemporal measurements with the cognitive mechanisms that establish perceived space and time. Our starting point was spatial contraction phenomena. In physics, contractions are a consequence of the Lorentz transformation and are observable when moving objects come close to c, the maximum signal propagation rate between systems. In cognition perceptual contractions are observed with velocities much lower than the physical c, nevertheless, the underlying mechanisms could be identical when c is replaced by c^*, the maximum propagation rate between cognitive levels of processing.[3]

As shown, this replacement of c by c^* is not sufficient to fit the observed contraction data to the relativity idea. Additionally, it is at least necessary to also replace the physical velocity v by v^*, the assumed perceived velocity. Although the scaled velocity obtained from our contraction data show a similar shape as compared to other psychophysical velocity functions, additional explications are needed in regards to what c^* stands for and what 'systems' means in a psychological sense. However, this analysis revealed that in a cognitive context there is in principle no means of testing the relativistic presuppositions. Maybe these presuppositions, on which the Lorentz transformation based, are fulfilled in human information processing, but they cannot be examined unambiguously.

From that it follows that a critical evaluation of the relativistic ideas requires further support. In this paper we are only concerned with spatial contraction phenomena, but the Lorentz transformation also predicts a subjective time dilatation, when stimuli are in motion relative to an observer. Further consequences would be that the addition law of velocities holds and that judgments of spatiotemporal coincidences depend on stimuli's motion. First steps in these directions have already been taken (cf. Caelli et al., 1978; Drösler, 1979).

A last point is worth to note. In this paper, one product of the information-processing stream is to the fore, namely, what observers report what they have seen in a specific experimental situation. From that the "consciously" perceived metric is inferred. This does not necessarily imply that the same metric is used, for example, to guide goal-directed actions or that this metric is an indisputable entity.

Instead, it is very likely that further, here unmentioned factors contribute to what and how something is perceived spatially.

Acknowledgments: I am very grateful to Scott Jordan for helpful comments and suggestions to a previous draft of the paper.

Notes

[1]It is worth noting that the present paper is only concerned with spatial distortions that are observable when stimuli are in motion. In the following sections it will become clear why spatial distortions with stationary stimuli are not under consideration. For example, to apply relativistic ideas to the kappa-tau situation, described above, a further assumption is needed, namely, stimulus presentations should evoke subjective *induced motions*. But even with this additional assumption, data of the original kappa-tau experiments do not fit to the relativistic ideas. For example, data indicate that higher induced motions reveal smaller temporal and spatial distortions; the opposite has to be assumed from a relativistic view.

[2]For the following it is sufficient to consider only the case of uniform motions between the systems. In fact, this restriction is a prerequisite of the special relativity theory.

[3]Note that even if relativity theory turns out to be invalid in the physical world—as modern quantum physics seems to claim (cf. Atmanspacher & Kronz, 1999)—perceptual relativity effects may still exist in the psychological world. For example, even if evidence is produced for instantaneous propagations in the physical world, thus damaging the physical relativity account, instantaneous propagations are not to be claimed for the human information processing.

References

Algom, D., and Cohen-Raz, L. 1984. Visual velocity input-output functions: The integration of distance and duration onto subjective velocity. *Journal of Experimental Psychology: Human Perception and Performance* 10:486-501.

Ansbacher, H. L. 1938. Further investigations of the Harold C. Brown shrinkage phenomenon: A new approach to the study of the perception of movement. *Psychological Bulletin* 35:701.

———. 1944. Distortion in the perception of real movement. *Journal of Experimental Psychology* 34:1-23.

Atmanspacher, H., and Kronz, F. 1999. Many realisms. In *Modeling consciousness across the disciplines*, edited by J. S. Jordan. Maryland: University Press of America, Inc.

Bachmann, T. 1984. The process of perceptual retouch: Nonspecific afferent activation dynamics in explaining visual masking. *Perception and Psychophysics* 35:69-84.

———. 1994. *Psychophysiology of visual masking: The fine structure of conscious experience*. Commack, NY: Nova Science Publishers.

Brown, J. F. 1931a. On time perception in visual movement fields. *Psychologische Forschung* 14:233-248.

———. 1931b. The thresholds for visual movement. *Psychologische Forschung* 14:249-268.

———. 1931c. The visual perception of velocity. *Psychologische Forschung* 14:199-232.

Caelli, T. 1981. *Visual perception: Theory and practice*. Oxford: Pergamon Press.

Caelli, T., Hoffman, W., and Lindman, H. 1978. Subjective Lorentz transformations and the perception of motion. *Journal of the Optical Society of America* 68:402-411.

Cohen, J. M. A. 1969. Relativity of psychological time. In *Psychological time in health and disease*, edited by J. M. A. Cohen. Springfield.

Drösler, J. 1979. Relativistic effects in visual perception of real and apparent motion. *Archiv für Psychologie* 131: 249-266.

Dzhafarov, E. N. 1992. Visual kinematics: III. Transformation of spatiotemporal coordinates in motion. *Journal of Mathematical Psychology* 36(4):524-546.

Einstein, A. 1905. Zur Elektrodynamik bewegter Körper [Electrodynamics of moving objects]. *Annalen der Physik* 17:891-921.

Gibson, J. J. 1979. *The ecological approach to visual perception*. Boston: Houghton Mifflin.

Haber, R. N., and Nathanson, L. S. 1968. Post-retinal storage? Some further observations on Park's camel as seen through the eye of a needle. *Perception and Psychophysics* 3:349-355.

Helmholtz, H. v. 1910. *Handbuch der physiologischen Optik [Handbook of physiological optics]*. (Vol. 3). Hamburg: Voss.

Helson, H., and King, S. M. 1931. The Tau effect: An example of psychological relativity. *Journal of Experimental Psychology* 14:202-217.

Jonides, J. 1981. Voluntary versus automatic control over the mind's eye's movement. In *Attention and performance*, edited by J. B. Long and A. D. Baddeley. Hillsdale, NJ: Erlbaum.

Mashour, M. 1964. *Psychophysical relations in the perception of velocity*. Stockholm: Almquist and Wiksell.

Müller, H. J., and Rabbitt, P. M. 1989. Reflexive and voluntary orienting of visual attention: Time course of activation and resistance to interruption. *Journal of Experimental Psychology: Human Perception and Performance* 15:315-330.

Müsseler, J. 1987. *Aufmerksamkeitsverlagerungen und Relativität. Ein experimenteller Beitrag zur Raum-Zeit-Wahrnehmung anhand eines Kontraktionsphänmomens (Tandem-Effekt). [Attention shifts and relativity. An experimental study to the perception of space and time with a contraction phenomenon (tandem effect)]*. München: Minerva.

Müsseler, J., and Aschersleben, G. 1996. Zur Rolle visueller Aufmerksamkeitsverlagerungen bei der Etablierung einer (subjektiv berichtbaren) Raumrepräsentation [The role of attentional shifts in establishing a (subjectively reportable) spatial representation]. In M. B (Ed.), *Aktives Sehen in technischen und biologischen Systemen [Active vision in technical and biological systems]*. Sankt Augustin (Germany): Infix.

————. 1998. Localizing the first position of a moving stimulus: The Fröhlich effect and an attention-shifting explanation. *Perception & Psychophysics* 60(4):683-695.

Müsseler, J., and Neumann, O. 1992. Apparent distance reduction with moving stimuli (Tandem Effect): Evidence for an attention-shifting model. *Psychological Research* 54(4):246-266.

Müsseler, J., Van der Heijden, A. H. C., Mahmud, S. H., Deubel, H., and Ertsey, S. in press. Relative mislocalizations of briefly presented stimuli in the retinal periphery. *Perception & Psychophysics*.

Neumann, O. 1979. Visuelle Aufmerksamkeit und der Mechanismus des Metakontrasts [Visual attention and the mechanism of metacontrast]. In *Bericht über den 31. Kongress der Deutschen Gesellschaft für Psychologie*, edited by L. Eckensberger. Göttingen: Hogrefe.

————. 1982. *Experimente zum Fehrer-Raab-Effekt und das 'Wetterwart'-Modell der visuellen Maskierung* [Experiments on the Fehrer-Raab effect and the 'weather station' model of visual masking]. Bochum: Department of Psychology, Ruhr University, Report No. 24.

————. 1990. Visual attention and action. In *Relationships between perception and action. Current approaches*, edited by O. Neumann and W. Prinz. Berlin, Heidelberg: Springer.

————. 1996. Theories of attention. In *Handbook of perception and action*, edited by O. Neumann and A. F. Sanders. London: Academic Press.

Neumann, O., and Müsseler, J. 1990a. "Judgment" vs. "response": A general problem and some experimental illustrations. In *Psychophysical explorations of mental structures*, edited by H. G. Geissler. Göttingen: Hogrefe.

————. 1990b. Visuelles Fokussieren: Das Wetterwart-Modell und einige seiner Anwendungen [Visual focusing: The Weather-Station Model and some of its applications]. In *Bielefelder Beiträge zur Kognitionspsychologie [Bielefeld contributions to cognitive psychology]*, edited by C. Meinecke and L. Kehrer. Göttingen: Hogrefe.

Parks, T. E. 1965. Post-retinal visual storage. *American Journal of Psychology* 78:145-147.

Piaget, J. 1955. The development of time concepts in the child. In *Psychopathology of childhood*, edited by P. H. Hoch and J. Zubin. New York: Grune & Stratton.

————. 1965. Psychology and philosophy. In *Scientific psychology: Principles and approaches*, edited by B. B. Wolman, and E. Nagel. New York: Basic Books Inc. Publishers.

Rizzolatti, G., and Craighero, L. 1998. Spatial attention: Mechanisms and theories. In *Advances in psychological science* (Vol. 2: Biological and cognitive aspects), edited by M. Sabourin, F. Craik, and M. Robert. Hove, UK: Psychology Press.

Rizzolatti, G., Riggio, L., Dascola, I., and Umiltá, C. 1987. Reorienting attention across the horizontal and vertical meridians: Evidence in favor of a premotor theory of attention. Special Issue: Selective visual attention. *Neuropsychologia* 25: 31-40.

Sperling, G., and Reeves, A. 1980. Measuring the reaction time of a shift of visual attention. In *Attention and performance*, edited by R. S. Nickerson. Hillsdale, NJ: Erlbaum.

Tsal, Y. 1983. Movement of attention across the visual field. *Journal of Experimental Psychology: Human Perception and Performance* 9:523-530.

Umiltá, C., Riggio, L., Dascola, I., and Rizzolatti, G. 1991. Differential effects of central and peripheral cues on the reorienting of spatial attention. *European Journal of Cognitive Psychology* 3:247-267.

Van der Heijden, A. H. C. 1992. *Selective attention in vision*. London: Routledge.

Van der Heijden, A. H. C., Müsseler, J., and Bridgeman, B. 1999. On the perception of position. In *Cognitive contributions to the perception of spatial and temporal events*, edited by G. Aschersleben, T. Bachmann, and J. Müsseler. Amsterdam: Elsevier.

Van der Heijden, A. H. C., Van der Geest, J. N., De Leeuw, F., Krikke, K., and Müsseler, J. 1999. The perception of position of a single small bar. *Psychological Research* 62: 20-35.

Vierordt, K. 1868. *Der Zeitsinn nach Versuchen [The sense of time in experiments]*. Tübingen (Germany): Laupp.

Zöllner, F. 1862. Ueber eine neue Art anorthoskopischer Zerrbilder [About a new kind of anorthoscopic distorted figures]. *Annalen der Physik. Poggendorfs Annalen* 117:477-484.

Chapter 6

A Physiologically Based System Theory of Consciousness

L. Andrew Coward

Introduction

A scientific theory of consciousness must have a number of characteristics. It must propose a one to one correspondence between psychological and physiological states. For example any psychological state X must have a corresponding physiological state x. Causal connections between physiological states at the physiological level of description must exist whenever there are causal connections between psychological states at the psychological level of description. For example, if physiological states x and y correspond with psychological states X and Y and state X causes state Y at the psychological level of description, then state x must cause state y at the physiological level of description. The same physiological state x cannot correspond with multiple psychological states X1, X2, X3, etc., although multiple physiological states could correspond with the same psychological state. For example, experiences of the colors red and blue cannot correspond with the same physiological states. Differences between experiences at the psychological level between, for example, different individuals, must correspond with differences at the physiological level in a consistent fashion (i.e., when there is a difference between the experience of the color red described at the psychological level and these differences are observed in a number of instances, the corresponding physiological states must differ in a consistent fashion). If the difference in the feel of the color red between two individuals can be described by an outside observer then it must be reflected in a difference at the physiological level. An individually unique feel must therefore correlate consistently with an individually unique physiological state.

Electronic systems have been designed and built which can perform extremely complex combinations of functions using large numbers of components. Such systems employ thousands of millions of transistors to perform combinations of thousands of interacting features. The design process for such systems involves creation of a functional architecture in which functionality at high levels is partitioned into components, and components are partitioned into more and more detailed sub-components through a series of levels down to the device level. At each level the same functionality is described, but at a different degree of detail. Such a functional architecture, if it existed in biological brains, would therefore be the basis for a scientific theory of consciousness as described in the previous paragraph. Design experience with electronic systems has demonstrated that unless a functional architecture exists and is simple in the sense that components on one level are roughly equal in size and require limited information exchange to perform their functions, the resulting systems are extremely difficult to build, repair, or modify. Coward (1990, 1997a) has argued that similar requirements result in natural selection exerting very strong pressures towards simple functional architectures in biological brains.

Commercial systems are designed by partitioning functionality into components which are conceptually instructions that generate commands to the system. To be able to generate system commands, all the information input to components must be meaningful and unambiguous. A critical distinction in system design is between global and local data. Global data is meaningful and unambiguous throughout the system. Local data is only unambiguous within one functional component and its sub-components. The terms local and global define logical data types, both types could have wide physical distribution within a system. To achieve a simple functional architecture, the design process for commercial systems optimizes the functional partitioning to minimize the need to convert local data to global data.

The unambiguous value of an element of global data could be required as input by any functional component. There is therefore a need for a reference copy of global data, which is generally stored in a subsystem called memory. Data which is unambiguous within a component and its sub-components but ambiguous outside the component will also be accessed by different sub-components via memory. If one component is operating on elements of global information, those elements are not unambiguously defined for other components. Components can therefore only access global information sequentially, and the currently active component is generally executed in a subsystem called processing. The memory, processing separation is therefore ubiquitous in commercial systems, and sequential execution can only be avoided if global data can be partitioned into orthogonal segments, each of which is adequate for a different functional component. The von Neumann architecture is an important instance of the instruction based functional architecture in which many of the instructions are regarded as unambiguous global data and recorded in memory.

The process of functional separation into components which exchange unambiguous information is a paradigm which is deeply embedded in electronic design. Even design using neural networks aims to produce modules which generate unambiguous outputs such as specific vectors for well defined cognitive categories. Dependence on exchange of unambiguous information between functional modules results either in memory, processing separation and sequential execution or in an inability to construct a system to perform a complex functionality. Coward (1990) proposed that the only way to avoid this constraint is to allow free exchange of ambiguous information between functional components. Such components are programmed to detect specific combinations of input information, but because the information is ambiguous, although not meaningless, the outputs of such components can only be system action recommendations rather than commands, and the recommendations must compete for control of system behavior. The specific combinations are not patterns in the full cognitive sense. The combinations of data are ambiguous, and therefore even if an approximately equivalent cognitive condition could be found, would not always repeat when the cognitive condition is present, and would sometimes repeat when it is not present. Such repetitions are ambiguous indications that a particular system response is appropriate. Consistent application of this paradigm results in a system with the recommendation architecture in which the major subsystem separation is into repetition similarity clustering and competition rather than the memory and processing found in instruction architectures.

Coward (1990) argued that the recommendation architecture was an important alternative to the instruction architecture for systems using large numbers of devices to perform a complex functionality, and that biological brains exhibit a striking resemblance to systems with the recommendation architecture. The understanding of consciousness in terms of physiology requires a consistent functional architectural approach to the conscious system as a whole. Such an approach must be based on an understanding of the architectural constraints which apply to any system performing very complex combinations of functionality.

Architectural Constraints on Complex Systems

The functionality of a system is the behavior which it generates using information derived both internally and from its environment. For example, an electronic system might take inputs from a keyboard, internal memory, and data communication links and perform a range of computing and display tasks such as word and graphics processing and e-mail. The problem in system design is to take this high level definition of the system functionality and create a description of a system which will perform as defined in terms of how its constituent devices (e.g., transistors) are connected together and organized. For many systems the functionality is extremely complex in the sense that many different but interacting functions are performed, and the number of devices required is very large. For example, a single telecommunications central office switch may require billions of transistors to provide the many interacting functions required to deliver reliable telephone service to 100 thousand users.

Any system which uses large numbers of devices to perform a complex functionality is subject to severe architectural constraints. To understand the nature of these constraints, imagine a design process in which (in a caricature of the process of biological evolution) a large number of technicians were given a large number of devices of different types and told to select and connect them at random. Periodically the result would be tested, and eventually a system found which performed as required. There are some severe problems with such a system. There are no blueprints which can guide the process of building another copy: the only option is to duplicate the original, device by device, connection by connection. If an error were made in such a duplication process a functional problem would result, but there would be no easy way to use the knowledge of the functional problem to identify and correct the error. Similarly, if a device failed during operation it would be very hard to identify which device was defective. Finally, device level changes would generate complex and unpredictable functional changes, and if there were a need to modify the functionality in a controlled fashion there would be no way to identify what device level changes would produce the desired functional modifications.

A practical system is therefore forced to adopt a simple functional architecture by these needs to build copies of the system, to recover from construction errors and component failures, to configure for individual system conditions, to economize on resources through sharing of subsystems across multiple functions, and to add new features (Coward, 1990, 1997a). In a system with a functional architecture, high level functionality is partitioned into components, components into subcomponents, and so on down to the functionality of the individual devices from which the system is constructed. In a simple functional architecture, each component at a given level of partitioning performs roughly the same proportion of the total functionality as the other components at that level, and on each level the functionality is divided up between the components to minimize the amount of information which must be exchanged between components as they perform their functionality. With a simple functional architecture it is possible to relate functionality described at a high level to the device functionality with which it corresponds. Such relationships make it possible, for example, to identify the device problems associated with a failure experienced at a system level and take appropriate repair action.

Design Process for Electronic Systems

Consider as an example a conceptual design process for a telecommunications switch. The highest level functional definition could be "handle the telephone service for a group of users which could number between 10 thousand and 100 thousand". Note that the functionality defined is implicitly an instruction. The next step is to imagine a partitioning of the system functionality into several subsystems and to define the functionality within each subsystem, which is then further partitioned. A possible initial partitioning could be that shown in figure 1. Each separation can be expressed as an instruction. The initial partitioning is tested by performing a series of scenarios such as the example in table 1 to determine the volume of information which needs to be passed between the subsystems as they perform their separate functions. Modifications to the partitioning are made to minimize this information volume while retaining roughly equal numbers of operations in each separation.

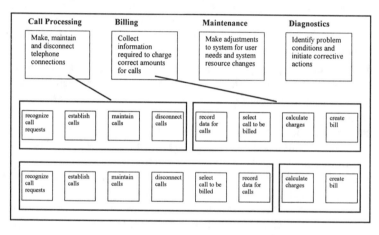

Fig. 1. Initial high level partitioning of functionality for a telecommunications switch. The initial partitioning is tested using scenarios of the type illustrated in table 1 and modified to retain roughly equal functional components but minimizing the need for information exchange between components.

In a commercial electronic system, each functional component receives data which is meaningful and unambiguous to the component, and generates outputs which are instructions, or commands of specific system actions. Such a component can be regarded as detecting pre-programmed combinations of information, or patterns, which are unambiguous from a system point of view. One component can of course be programmed with many patterns.

Table 1
Telephone Call Scenario

---

1. User indicates to system the desire to make a call.
2. System indicates to user it is ready.
3. User sends information on called party.
4. System records information on called party.
5. System finds physical location of called party.
6. System makes connection to called party.
7. System activated ringing of called party.
8. If called party answers, system establishes link.
9. System checks periodically, and if one party disconnects the resources are reassigned.
10. System records billing information.

In the partitioning in figure 1, the diagnostic subsystem cannot access information within call processing unless that information is expressed in a global system form. If the diagnostics subsystem as defined turns out to require high volumes of local call processing information, the effort to convert such information to globally meaningful form may be so large that is more effective to repartition the functionality between diagnostics and call processing. In the table 1 scenario, all the steps except the last would in the ideal case occur within the call processing function. An example of a global information requirement is for a database which relates all possible called numbers to a physical location. This database must be global because although it is used by call processing it is created and kept up to date by maintenance. Now consider the billing information in step 9. This billing information includes calling and called number, time of day and duration of call. If most calls are within a free dialing area and not billed to the customer, collecting this information and recording it in global form for every call would be an unnecessary drain on system resources. In such a case, it may be more effective to repartition functionality so that call processing makes the decision on whether to record the information, using a global database indicating destinations which are chargeable which would be kept up to date by billing. The process of design is thus one of rearranging the partitioning of functionality to achieve a tradeoff between even functionality and minimum information exchange. This design process is carried out at each more detailed level in turn until the device level is reached. At any level, a necessary repartitioning may affect much higher levels, in the worst case a separation at the highest level may prove to be impractical at the device level, forcing repartitioning at every level. Design is thus a process of reaching a compromise between equal sized functional components and minimized information exchange.

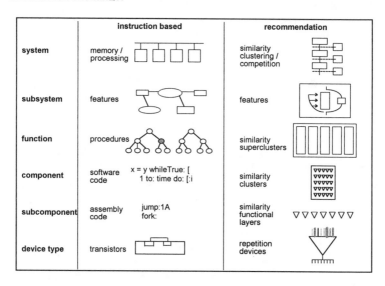

Fig. 2. Functional hierarchies for alternative functional element paradigms. In the instruction architecture, instructions are combined into higher level instructions. In the recommendation architecture, repetitions are combined into similarity clusters. At each level a part of the higher level is shown, in the greater detail of the lower level.

At the most detailed level of a typical functional architecture, devices execute very simple instructions (open or close the device gate). A number of these device level instructions are combined to form assembly code instructions (jump, branch). Assembly code instructions are combined to form software instructions (while x is true, do y). Software instructions are combined into procedure calls, procedure calls into features, features into major system functions. This hierarchy is illustrated in figure 2.

Ambiguous Information

If ambiguous information is exchanged between functional components, it is still possible to establish a simple functional architecture, but the form of that architecture is qualitatively different from that of the instruction architecture. Although the information exchanged can be ambiguous, it must be meaningful, the receiving component must have a partial context for the information. For example, imagine a simple calculator with two functional components, one of which receives two numbers from system input and multiplies them together, and the other displays an image based on the value of the product. The input to the first component is a pair of numbers, for example 33 and 26, which carry an unambiguous system meaning. Suppose that the first component multiplies the numbers by first calculating 33 x 20 = 660 and 33 x 6 = 198, then adding 660 + 198 = 858. The number 858 could be communicated to the second component and would be unambiguous, the second component could generate an instruction to display the appropriate image. However, consider the numbers 660 and 198 generated inside the first functional component. Such numbers are unambiguous within that component, and could be shared between subcomponents of that component, but would be ambiguous if received by the second component. If the information 198 were communicated to the second component, it is not meaningless, such a value could only occur for a limited range of answers, it could not occur if the answer were 825 for example. The presence of 198 is therefore an indication of a range of possible images to be displayed, and a component receiving such information could in principle generate a recommendation to display a particular image, but would need correlation with other recommendations to create a high integrity system action. When ambiguous information is the input to a functional component, the result generated by the component cannot be a system command, it can only be a recommendation which must compete with other recommendations for control of system action. The programmed combinations of data are not unambiguous system patterns but repetitions which can be extracted from the available ambiguous information and associated with action recommendations. In the functional hierarchy, repetitions detected at the device level are combined into clusters, which repeat if significant subsets of their component repetitions repeat. Superclusters repeat if significant subsets of their constituent clusters repeat. At the device level, the recommendations will be of the type "pay attention to this detected repetition", at higher levels the recommendations will be increasingly general behavior types. The functional clustering hierarchy is illustrated in figure 2, compared with the instruction hierarchy. Note that if the information exchanged were unambiguous, the repetitions and clusters would be cognitive patterns and categories.

It is important to emphasize that because functional components exchange ambiguous information, the repetitions programmed at every level are not well defined cognitive patterns. The programming identifies the repetition of conditions which in many cases but not in every case indicate that an associated behavior is appropriate. An individual component is programmed to extract a wide range of repetitions with similar but ambiguous functional significance. The algorithmic complexity can therefore become considerable, even at the device level. For example, a functionally useful repetition could include the particular time sequence in which a combination of information appeared. The algorithms to detect such repetitions would be very complex.

Inputs to a component could in principle be information derived from any other component at any level. However, to maintain a simple functional architecture the distribution of information must be limited, and only made available where it has the highest probability of providing functional value. Optimization of information distribution is a critical system function, and has to be maintained by special purpose functionality in the heuristically defined functional architectures discussed in the next section.

The output of a cluster at any level indicates the presence of a condition under which the action recommended by the cluster may be appropriate. Different functional components at the same level acting on the same information may produce different recommendations. There must therefore be competition between the alternatives to determine system action. This competition requires some criteria to determine the recommendation which will be selected. The available criteria are derived from the results of accepting similar recommendations under similar conditions in the past. This knowledge could be utilized by design (or for a biological system, by use of the results of past experience implicitly coded genetically) or heuristically from individual system experience.

A biological example of the separations into repetition similarity clustering and competition in such a system is illustrated in figure 3.

Coward (1990) argued that, as shown in figure 3, in mammal brains there was a first stage of clustering which extracted sensory independent repetitions from raw sensory inputs. Cognitive examples of such repetitions might correlate with object color independent of illumination, or object size independent of distance. However, useful repetitions may or may not correlate with simple cognitive interpretations, they are only repetitions which can be discovered within the mass of ambiguous input information, and because the information is ambiguous would only correlate partially with such a cognitive pattern. The first stage of competition is between sets of repetitions extracted from different objects. This competition corresponds with the attention function, and the repetitions extracted from the object selected as the focus of attention gain access to the second clustering stage. This second clustering stage contains a number of superclusters corresponding with recommendations of different types of behavior (aggressive, friendly, food seeking, sexual etc.). The information derived from a single object may generate outputs from any or all of the superclusters, corresponding with different types of action recommendation with respect to the object. The specific combination of outputs from a supercluster indicate the specific action recommended within the type. The alternatives compete in a second competition stage and the information representing the successful recommendation is allowed access to the third clustering stage in which the output clusters correspond with portfolios of muscle movements. Competition between the outputs of this third stage results in an integrated physical movement.

Architectures of Biological Brains

Although biological systems have not gone through a design process, they are also subject to pressures towards a simple functional architecture. Copies of biological brains must be constructed from DNA "blueprints"; there must be some ability to recover from construction errors and damage; and random mutations must sometimes result in significant functional changes. There is therefore strong selection pressure in favor of simple neural functional architectures. Heuristically associating information repetitions with behaviors is fundamental to the existence of life. At the simplest level the detection of the repetition of a genetically programmed chemical gradient generates behavior in bacteria. At higher levels the detection of complex combinations of repetitions indicates the presence of a familiar person and generates a wide range of alternative behaviors. In a universe in which nothing is ever repeated it is hard to imagine life dependent on learning from experience ever developing. Unambiguous information is typically not available to a biological brain, and Coward (1990) therefore argued that the recommendation architecture is ubiquitous in biological systems, and that the hierarchy of functional separations which therefore exists can be the basis for understanding psychological phenomena in terms of physiology.

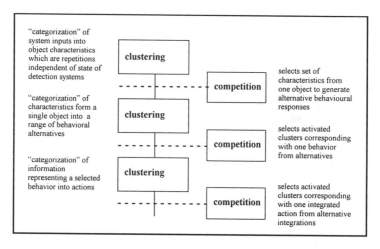

Fig. 3. The major functional separations of the recommendation architecture are repetition similarity clustering of information and competition between the outputs from activated clusters for control of action.

Changes to Component Functionality in a System with the Recommendation Architecture

A component in a functional architecture receives input information and generates output results. There are two types of result (Mira, Herrelo, & Delgado, 1997). One type is any output information generated, and the other is any changes to the combinations of input information which will generate output information in the future. Changes to future functionality require input information recommending that changes occur, and such information will generally derive from a higher functional level than the component being changed.

At the device level, there are four different ways in which programming can change. These four ways are illustrated in figure 4. When a combination of input information is imprinted, the presence of information derived from a higher level component plus a set of input information causes a device to be programmed to produce an output at the time and at any point in the future if the same set of input information repeats even in the absence of the higher level information. In the simple example illustrated in figure 4, a device with a large number of inputs is imprinted by disconnection of all inactive inputs. The level at which the device will fire in the future is set at or below its current total input level. The nature and source of the higher level information is discussed below. This imprinting concept was introduced by Coward (1990). In its simplest form a device is programmed at a single point in time with a single combination, and produces output if that combination repeats in the future. The programmed combination will be referred to as a repetition if the combination is made up of ambiguous information, and pattern if the combination is made up of unambiguous information. Models with multiple repetitions per device are discussed below. Imprinting can support instantaneously created, permanent declarative memory traces (Coward, 1990).

An example of tuning of combinations is the standard perceptron model for the neuron (Rosenblatt, 1961) in which the relative weights of different inputs are adjusted. An issue with many perceptron based neural network models, such as those based on backpropagation (Rumelhart, Hinton, & Williams, 1986), is the use of unambiguous information in the form of quantitative target answers. Use of such information will result either in an architecture which reduces to the sequential instruction architecture or a system which cannot scale up to handle very complex functionality. Tuning of combinations is important in the functional separations which competitively reduce the volume of data distributed to later clustering functions (Coward, 1990). The competitive algorithms discussed by Taylor and Alavi (1993) are applicable within such separations.

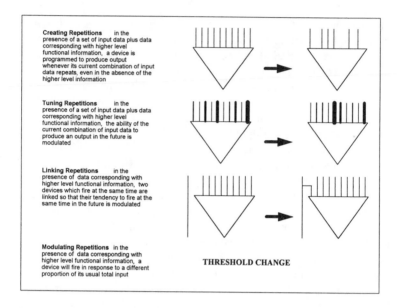

Fig. 4. Alternative ways in which the combinations of local data to which a device is programmed to respond can change.

Connecting combinations is a variation of the standard Hebbian mechanism (Hebb, 1949) in which the connection between two devices which frequently fire at the same time is strengthened. The variation is that a connection may be established if two devices frequently fire at the same time. As discussed below, this mechanism is important in maintaining the orthogonality of multiple repetitions imprinted on the same device, and Coward (1990) proposed that the mechanism is also important in managing the distribution of information, and in generating the self sustaining sequences of mental images which are one characteristic of human consciousness. All these types of combination changes depend at a more detailed level on mechanisms such as assignment or removal of devices; addition or deletion of single inputs; correlated addition or deletion of sets of inputs; changes in the relative strength of inputs; correlated changes in the strengths of sets of inputs; general changes in effective input strengths (i.e., threshold changes); and changes in the sensitivity to other parameters such as those which produce threshold changes.

Another qualitative aspect to changes in future functionality is the permanence of the changes, which can vary from change only while the controlling higher level functional information is present through limited time to long term after the controlling information is no longer present.

The particular combination of functionality changes appropriate to a device is determined by the higher level functional component within which the device is located.

Heuristically Generated Functionality in the Recommendation Architecture

In a system with the recommendation architecture, a cluster hierarchy can be established heuristically as a simple hierarchy of repetition. At all levels there is a search for repetition of sets or large subsets of information combinations which have occurred before. Frequent repetition results in the repetition being established as a component of similarity at its appropriate hierarchical level. Raw input information is searched for combinations which repeat, and any potentially useful repetitions are programmed into devices. These combinations are searched for combinations of combinations which repeat, and such combinations of combinations are programmed into clusters. Frequently repeating combinations of clusters are combined into superclusters and so on. The resulting similarity hierarchy can then be heuristically associated with behaviors. A similarity cluster can be provisionally associated with a particular type of behavioral recommendation, and if the results of accepting the recommendation are favorable, the association can be made permanent, otherwise it can be discontinued. The repetition imprinting mechanism thus makes it possible to define functionality heuristically on the basis of experience.

In figure 5, a cluster module composed of devices which can be imprinted with repetitions is illustrated conceptually. The cluster module is made up of a succession of layers of devices. As discussed later these layers are functional separations and in general the number of layers depends on the number of functional separations needed. A device has inputs corresponding with elements of information which are outputs from other devices, and is activated if a large enough proportion of its inputs are activated. Most inputs to devices within the module are from other devices in the module, and a high proportion of the inputs are from devices in the preceding layer. Lateral inputs and back projection inputs are also possible, but these inputs represent information from higher functional components, in this case layers. The first layer receives inputs from outside the module, and such inputs may be received by other layers for functional reasons such as maintaining information consistency as discussed later. Virgin devices are provided with a large number of randomly selected information inputs from the preceding layer, plus functional inputs from specific layers. Virgin devices will not fire unless both a significant number of information inputs are active and also a specific combination of functional inputs are present. If a virgin device fires once, it will fire unconditionally in the future if the same combination of information input repeats. In the model with one repetition programmed per device, the device is then called regular.

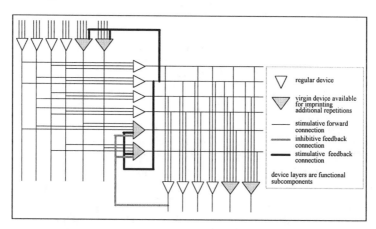

Fig. 5. Connectivity of a simple repetition similarity cluster module using the repetition imprinting mechanism at the device level. The layers perform similarity subfunctions as discussed in the text. Single examples of connectivity which performs required layer-to-device functionality are given, realistic functionality requires many more connections as discussed in the text.

Higher functional connectivity in the illustrated module is of two types. The first type is feedback from regular and virgin devices in the output layer to virgin devices in the output and all earlier layers of the cluster. This feedback is from a high proportion of output devices to all virgin devices, and inhibits imprinting. The second type is from regular devices in the middle layer to virgin devices in the same and all other layers, there are again a large number of such connections and the connections stimulate imprinting. To avoid confusion, examples of functional connectivity are portrayed rather than a realistic set as described in the text.

Suppose that the module in figure 5 has already been programmed to generate output in the presence of one (ambiguous) condition or object. Such programming would mean that input level regular devices are programmed with combinations of information extracted from the condition, regular devices in the second layer with combinations of input layer devices and so on, with the result that if information from the same condition were presented again, an output would result. Because two perceptions of the same object will not necessarily be identical, actual device activation would be a large subset of the total, but an output from the module would be generated. The inhibitive inputs to virgin neurons from those outputs dominates, and no imprinting would occur. Now consider what would happen if another condition very similar to the first were perceived. Many of the simple combinations of information in the early layers would repeat, but the very complex combinations close to output would not repeat. The stimulatory inputs to virgin devices would therefore be present, but not the inhibitive inputs from the output layer. Under these conditions, the number of active inputs from the preceding layer required to fire virgin devices is gradually lowered (for example, in proportion to the length of time the stimulate feedback has been present), and these devices begin to fire. The thresholds drop until enough virgin devices fire in the different layers to generate an output, at which point further imprinting is cut off by the inhibitive feedback. At first firing, a virgin device is imprinted so that any future repetition of a large proportion of the information combination will cause the device to fire, independent of the various feedback mechanisms. The new condition will therefore generate a module output whenever it is present in the future. Note also that the new repetitions imprinted by the new condition will contribute to triggering imprinting in future objects, and the definition of the cluster is thus generated heuristically. Because the input information is ambiguous, the outputs are ambiguous, in other words, because the recurrence of the same condition may not result in exactly the same inputs, and because other conditions may result in inputs similar to the original inputs, the output ambiguously correlates with the cognitive condition.

A condition which was not similar to the cluster definition would generate limited firing in the early layers, but insufficient to generate imprinting, and such a condition would have no effect on the cluster. A new cluster would be initiated by the experience of conditions which produced no response from any existing cluster. Devices in such a new cluster would be configured with large numbers of randomly selected inputs of appropriate types. The first subsequent condition which produced no response from existing clusters would force imprinting in the new cluster. The new cluster would then heuristically develop an internal similarity definition by experience of similar conditions.

One module being presented with information from various conditions is shown in figure 6. The connectivity is omitted, and five layers which are assigned different functional roles in later discussion are illustrated. For ease of explanation, initially a cognitive example implying the use of unambiguous information will be described and then the differences with ambiguous information explained.

Suppose that the functional cluster component is a category (i.e., unambiguous) associated with actions of the type "say that the painting is by Magritte". At the upper levels of the module, the devices detect patterns of relatively simple combinations of sensory data. The middle layers detect patterns of complex combinations of information which correspond with the 'style' of the painter. Close to output, very complex combinations are extracted which in general are unique to individual paintings. The exact combination of outputs can therefore be used to control the painting specific content of the action. If a painting by another artist is presented, there may be a limited extraction of patterns at the input levels and such weak extraction is ignored. If a new painting by Magritte is presented, there will be strong detection of patterns reaching deep into the module, but no output will be generated. Under these conditions, additional patterns are permanently imprinted until an output results. The new painting will be recognized in any future presentation because no significant imprinting will be required to produce an output. The additional patterns are additions to the category definition because they can contribute to triggering imprinting in response to future paintings.

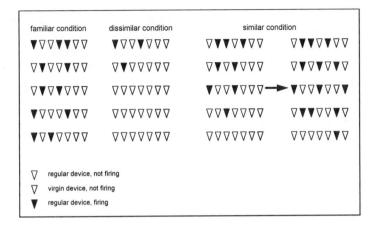

Fig. 6. Activation of one cluster module in response to information extracted from a condition which has been experienced before, a condition which is dissimilar from the objects which have defined the cluster in the past, a condition similar to past conditions at the moment the information is initially presented, and after imprinting. Devices in one layer are activated by programmed combinations of information, largely derived from activation of devices in the previous layer

Now consider the process with limitation to ambiguous information. Suppose the system is presented with a series of sensory experiences including experiences of a number of different painters. These experiences trigger the creation of a number of clusters corresponding with heuristically defined repetition conditions. These repetition conditions do not correspond with individual painters, but indicate the presence of similarity conditions in input information. Several clusters might produce output in response to a particular painter, not always all of the same clusters for a particular painting by that painter. Paintings by a different painter might produce outputs in different clusters, but sometimes the same cluster might produce outputs for different painters. The output of these clusters is therefore ambiguous, but can be used by a competitive function to generate high integrity behavior. For example, suppose there were five painters A through E, and the heuristic process generated seven similarity clusters one through seven. A recommendation to *say the name of painter A* could become associated by trial and error with strong outputs from cluster two, weak outputs from cluster four, and moderate outputs from cluster seven, a recommendation to *say the name of painter B* could become associated by trial and error with strong outputs from cluster four, weak outputs from cluster five, and moderate outputs from cluster six etc. A simple competitive algorithm could be designed which after an initial trial period would result in any novel painting by one of the five generating the appropriate response.

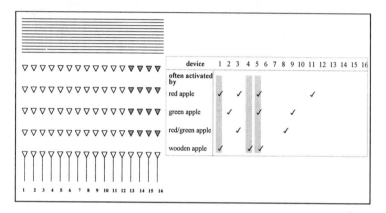

Fig. 7. Ambiguous information output by a cluster. Any output indicates the presence of a condition similar to cluster definition, and can be used as an action recommendation. The illustrated cluster could recommend eating behavior. The particular combination of output information is generally unique to a particular condition. The uniqueness can be used by the subsequent competition to manage the probability of future success of accepted recommendations. For example, the shaded device output, if removed from influence of behavior by pain following an attempt to eat an apple, would not remove the ability to respond to real apples.

There are a number of interesting properties of this type of clustering process. One property is that all the repetitions active at the time a condition is perceived are permanently programmed. If these combinations could somehow be activated again, the experience would be indistinguishable from the original exposure. Secondly, a permanent trace is instantaneously created which permits a clear distinction between conditions which have been experienced before and other conditions. Conditions not experienced before will require significant imprinting to generate an output, while conditions seen before will require no or much less imprinting. Thirdly, because the combinations are simply the weighted average of the presence or absence of a range of ambiguous repetition similarity clusters.

Electronic simulation has demonstrated that using the algorithms described in this section a system with the recommendation architecture can organize its experience into clusters without guidance, and the clusters can generate high integrity behavior through a competitive function after a small number of trials using only correct/incorrect feedback (Coward, 1996, in press).

Similarity Hierarchy in a System with the Recommendation Architecture

The next higher level of the similarity clustering functionality can be understood by consideration of figure 8. All perceived conditions (or objects) are sorted into clusters, with individual conditions being assigned to the clusters which generate the strongest familiarity indication as illustrated in figure 8. Initiation of a cluster is triggered by a single condition which does not generate output from any existing cluster. A new cluster module with large, random connectivity between device layers is forced to produce outputs in response to such conditions. Any subsequent condition which is sufficiently similar to the initial condition will generate imprinting in the same cluster, and the additional repetitions will refine the cluster definition. Correct/incorrect feedback can be used to guide the association between clusters and recommended behaviors. This functional separation is a key aspect of the architecture.

Note once again that if the information were unambiguous, the clusters would be categories. Clusters are ambiguous, and will therefore correlate partially but not exactly with cognitive categories. Neural network algorithms can achieve separation of input into categories. For example, Kohonen maps have demonstrated the ability to self organize to extract a reasonably small set of important features from input information (Ritter, 1995). However, Kohonen maps target unambiguous information as output, and even Kohonen's topological map scheme for unsupervised learning has been criticized on the basis that the patterns which are presented to the model must be preselected (Pfeiffer, 1996). Furthermore, gradual adjustment of weights has difficulty in accounting for the instantaneously created ability to recognize that an object has been seen before as discussed earlier.

repetitions of information which was present at the same tim
repetitions associated with one condition may include inforr
extracted from another condition which happened to be presen
infrastructure to support associative memory is thus establishe
side effect of the clustering process.

The process for establishing an heuristic association betwee
ters and behavior can be understood in more detail by considera
figure 7. Suppose that the illustrated cluster module is one of
which have heuristically acquired the ability to generate an ou
response to apple like objects. In principle it can be imagined t
outputs from such clusters could be distributed to functions dri
types of behavior. Suppose that one type of behavior were
Output from the module will then be interpreted as an action
mendation to eat. Now suppose that other clusters exist whicl
biologically valuable and biologically unfavorable conditio
output of a biologically valuable condition cluster is a recomme
to strengthen the connections from the clusters which recentl
control of behavior on to the recently active behavior type, the c
biologically unfavorable condition clusters is a recommend
weaken such connections or in extreme cases to disconnect an
from the source clusters.

An 'apple' cluster will generate outputs in response to ma
like objects, including apples of different colors, and even wo
ples and other objects with the right type of similarity to appl
ever, the particular combination of outputs are unique to i
objects. Hence the output of the clusters indicating the pr
biologically favorable or unfavorable conditions will result i
nection of recommendations in response to wooden apples wh
cing the strength of recommendations in response to real
module which has heuristically acquired the ability to genera
in response to generally inedible objects would be disconne
any access to eating behavior after experimentation. In system
repetition similarity condition detected by the cluster is not fu
valuable for recommending such a behavior. More complex c
algorithms which can use outputs to modulate behavior
general type recommended by the cluster are discussed below
output from similarity clusters has been associated throug
titive function to a behavior, the behavior will be associa
cognitive category, although the operational definition of the

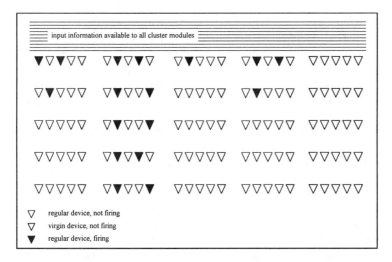

Fig. 8. Information repetitions extracted from a condition or object are presented to a range of clusters, and the clusters with the strongest activation imprint additional repetitions to produce an output. Conditions are thus heuristically sorted into clusters.

The primary issue with any similarity process for functional purposes is whether it can converge on a useful set of similarity clusters or categories. There are two problems to avoid. One is a proliferation of clusters or categories which at the extreme could reach one per object or even more. The second is the combining of many objects into a single grouping when the appropriate behaviors are not the same. Because there is scope for correction of the behavioral consequences of ambiguities through the separate competition process as discussed, it is not necessary that the clustering process even in principle be capable of perfect separation into cognitive categories, the requirement is that the resulting repetition similarity separation be practically useful. To put the same statement another way, a functional architecture made up of functional modules exchanging ambiguous information is able to generate appropriate actions. A further point to emphasize is that clean separation between clustering and competition is essential to achieve a simple functional architecture. The lack of this clean separation in neural networks is one reason that they cannot utilize ambiguous information in complex functional combinations.

Although the clustering can proceed without guidance, there are a number of parameters which must be defined, and feedback of the effectiveness of the clustering process can be used to tune the value of these parameters. These parameters include the number and configuration of virgin devices available for imprinting of useful repetitions; the balance between inhibition of imprinting by output and lateral stimulation; defining the level of lateral stimulation which will trigger imprinting; and duplication and proliferation of clusters. The critical issue is to ensure that the process of heuristic similarity clustering achieves a cluster separation which is useful in generating behavioral alternatives.

Feedback can be used to tune the parameters in a number of ways. For example, if a cluster produces recommendations which if accepted are sometimes followed by favorable conditions, sometimes unfavorable, a system management cluster detecting the conflicting results could generate recommendations to tighten the similarity definition, leading to more clusters. If multiple clusters frequently generated recommendations of the same type in response to the same object, other system management clusters could generate recommendations to merge the duplicate clusters. If within a cluster an object triggered imprinting but there were not enough combinations of the right type present to generate an output, this condition could trigger configuration of more or larger combinations. A tendency to proliferate clusters could be reduced by adjustment to the criterion for imprinting within clusters.

Some additional repetitions are in general imprinted at the device level whenever a cluster generates an output in response to a condition. An additional repetition is, in the one-repetition-per-device model, the active subset of the set of inputs which happen to be available on a device. The effectiveness of learning will therefore be influenced by the available combinations of physical inputs on such devices. These physical combinations must in general be configured in advance in a system dependent on physically wired connections. The configuration process could be random, but because useful new repetitions will frequently include new combinations of information elements which frequently occur in other repetitions in the same cluster, a bias in favor of inputs corresponding with such information will improve the effectiveness of learning. Such a bias could be achieved by activating all devices in proportion to the frequency of past activations and causing devices which will be programmed with additional repetitions to accept inputs which frequently contribute to firing other devices in their functional neighborhood. Such an activation would resemble a fast rerun of a mixture of past experience, and Coward (1990) proposed that providing this type of bias on connectivity was a primary functional role of dream sleep in biological brains.

This management of the information available at the device level is a specific example of an important architectural point. Although in principle a functional component at any level could accept input from any other component, the functional architecture is more simple if the information exchange routes are minimized. A compromise will be reached between the need for a simple functional architecture and the need for the most appropriate information to be available to each functional component. There is evidence that in biological brains the compromise is that each functional module at the cluster level receives input from about ten other modules and delivers output to about ten modules (Bressler, 1994). Selection of the information which will be used as input to a cluster is the function of the cluster input layer. Provisional inputs from other clusters would be accepted if those cluster outputs were frequently active at the same time as the receiving cluster was also generating outputs, provided the coincident outputs were more frequent overall than with other clusters. Dream sleep manages this information distribution function in a manner analogous with the device level information management described above.

A number of separate cluster subfunctions have been identified in the above discussion: managing inputs from other clusters; detecting the presence of enough activation to inhibit the creation of a new cluster; detecting the presence of enough activation to stimulate addition of the condition to the set which produce cluster output; detection of enough feedback from higher clusters to maintain activation; detection of enough output to inhibit additional imprinting; and generation of unique condition outputs. These separate functions can be separated in different module layers. The advantage of such a separation is that the functionality of one layer can be adjusted without introducing uncontrollable changes in the functionality of other layers.

Note that at every functional level, the clusters and repetitions which are programmed are simply combinations of information which have occurred once, and become potentially useful if a large subset of the combination occurs again.

Any domain of experience will be similarity clustered in order to associate different behavioral recommendations with different cluster combinations. Even continuously variable experience will be broken up into clusters in a system with the recommendation architecture. The experience of the forced separation of the continuous distribution of light wavelengths into the seven colors of the rainbow is an illustration of this effect.

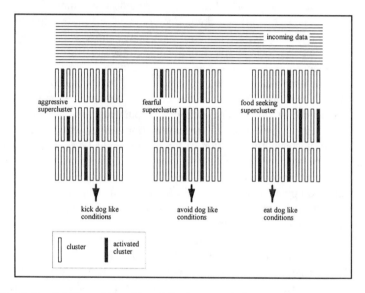

Fig. 9. Parallel hierarchies of heuristically created clusters generate alternative behavioral recommendations towards the same perceived object or condition. The activation of a set of clusters corresponds with the recommendation.

At a higher level in the functional hierarchy illustrated in figure 9, superclusters generate alternative general types of action recommendations. The superclusters correspond with alternatives such as aggressive, fearful, etc. Each supercluster contains a set of cluster modules to generate recommendations of the supercluster type towards any possible condition. Each of the active combinations in figure 9 could be regarded as "dog recognizing". A more accurate interpretation is that the different modules generate different action recommendations with respect to a similar but not necessarily cognitively identical "dog" cluster set. The supercluster separation also allows modulation of the different types of action recommendation depending on information about system needs. For example, extraction from internal sensory data of a cluster set which could be cognitively labeled "hunger condition" could correspond with an action recommendation to reduce thresholds of all devices in the food seeking supercluster. The duplication of clusters which could all be interpreted as "dog recognizing" means that local damage to the system cannot remove all the memory trace of a particular dog experience. The effect of damage would rather be to change the probable response of the system towards dogs. Such duplication could in principle be regarded as wasteful, but represents the solution to the requirement for a clear functional separation under conditions of ambiguous information usage.

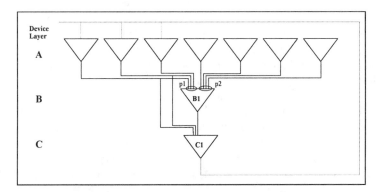

Fig. 10. Repetition orthogonality problem and solutions. If a device is programmed with multiple repetitions, its target devices must be able to distinguish between outputs due to relevant repetitions and irrelevant repetitions. One mechanism is to forbid sharing of inputs between different repetitions on the same source device and allow some of the inputs to the source to reach the target. A less restrictive mechanism is to use feedback to converge on a consistent set of device activations

The simple imprinting algorithm used implicitly in the above discussion can be modified to allow devices to be programmed to extract multiple repetitions imprinted at different times. Such a modification must solve the orthogonality problem illustrated in figure 10. How can a target device C1 in layer C which has been imprinted with a set of repetitions including B1(p1) in layer B be prevented from responding to the activation of B1(p2). The simplest solution is to require that multiple repetitions on a device like B1 do not have any inputs in common, and that their targets like C1 also receive some inputs from layer A which is the primary source for inputs to B1. This structure is still feedforward, but net repetition complexity increases somewhat more slowly from layer to layer than in the simple case. In practice this approach would probably sustain a practical degree of orthogonality even if there were a small degree of input sharing between different repetitions on the same device.

If the sharing becomes significant, an additional mechanism is feedback connections from C1 back to earlier layers such as A. Such feedback connections could be established at the time of imprinting of a repetition on C, and have the effect that an output from the recipient of the feedback would only continue if significant feedback were received. Such a mechanism would drive convergence on a consistent set of repetitions through many layers, the consistency being that the set have tended to be extracted at the same time in the past. In practice such feedback would be more useful if it extended from the more complex clusters to the simpler clusters illustrated in figure 9. Cauller (1997a) has proposed that the extensive feedback connectivity observed in biological brains has a predictive role and drives convergence of a dynamic system towards an attractor. The mechanism described here is functionally equivalent but expressed in recommendation architecture terms. Because a complex system with many components must employ either recommendation or instruction functional partitioning, under-standing of a system activation will be most accessible in the applicable functional paradigm. The tendency of the feedback circuitry described by Cauller to target a particular cortex layer reflects the same require-ment for functional separation within clusters discussed earlier.

The feedback mechanism allows simple separation of the function-ality to maintain orthogonality between the multiple repetitions imprin-ted on a single device. Higher level components can therefore use either the simple or more complex device functionality to achieve the same higher level functionality. The simple mechanism can therefore be used to understand the higher level functionality in device terms, the separate orthogonality mechanism can be added if required for system operating efficiency reasons.

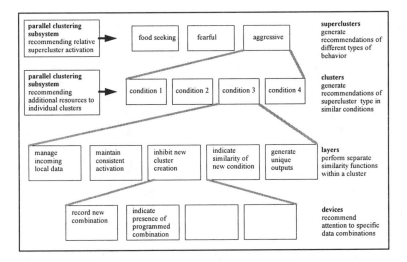

Fig. 11. A repetition similarity clustering hierarchy. Separate subsystems can exist with their own clustering hierarchy generating recommendations for management actions on the primary hierarchy. Separate competition functions will manage the access of these recommendations to the primary hierarchy.

The repetition similarity clustering hierarchy which results from the discussion of this section is illustrated in figure 11, using a biological example for illustration purposes. At the highest functional level illustrated, the superclusters correspond with broad behavioral types, and an output from such a cluster is a recommendation of a behavior of that type. Such an output is composed of outputs from a set of clusters within the supercluster. Such a set can be interpreted as an indication that an object or condition similar to a past condition is present and a similar behavior to one tried in the past is therefore recommended. The specific outputs can be used to specify the particular type of behavior within the general type. Within a cluster, layer subcomponents perform similarity subfunctions which are in turn made up of device level functions. An important architectural point is that if a set of information can be defined which is separate from the primary information set and can be used to generate a separate set of action recommendations, then it will be functionally simpler to establish a separate clustering, competition subarchitecture. Two such subarchitectures are illustrated in figure 11. One clusters information indicating system needs (e.g., hunger) and generates action recommendations to modulate the relative probability of a type of action (e.g., food seeking) by lowering the thresholds of a set of devices within the appropriate supercluster. Such a result could be achieved by distribution of an arousal neurohormone targeted at the supercluster (Coward, 1990). The other subarchitecture clusters information deriving from the effectiveness of the clustering process and individual cluster activity and generates resource assignment recommendations including assignment of additional resources to clusters demonstrating high imprinting rates. Such a function would contain implicit information about the time sequence of experience which could be used for behavior recommendation generation.[1]

If a totally novel type of condition were perceived, then new clusters would be established in all behavioral superclusters. Devices in the new clusters would be made sensitive to the appropriate arousal neurohormone. The information used as input to the clusters would be biased towards information which has generally proved useful in the past in generating behavior of the supercluster type. Behavior towards such a totally novel condition would be experimental, with many different types being tried. In a mature brain, most conditions would have some similarity to past experience and could generally be accommodated with an additional cluster in an existing set. It is also possible for a new supercluster to be defined heuristically. Such a supercluster would have a different general arousal sensitivity, perhaps a sensitivity to a combination of primary neurohormones. Clusters would be heuristically established within the supercluster. An example could be game playing or sport, where neurohormone sensitivity could include combinations of cooperative and aggressive and other sensitivities.

Within the similarity clustering based functional architecture, memory as experienced by the system has a number of meanings. Firstly, if an object is perceived and little imprinting is required to generate an action recommendation, the object will be experienced as familiar. If significant imprinting is required to generate action recommendations, the object will be experienced as unfamiliar. Perception of the degree of imprinting required to generate behavioral recommendations is thus the device level basis for the instantaneous creation of a permanent trace giving the ability to recognize familiarity. Although there is some resemblance between the mechanism for similarity triggered learning described here and the adaptive resonance algorithms (Carpenter & Grossberg, 1988) there are substantial differences. ART tunes patterns using correlated firing of devices in the neighborhood. The imprinting mechanism (Coward, 1990) uses similar information to manage the creation of repetitions. A key difference between the imprinting algorithm and adaptive resonance is that a single exposure to an object results in a permanent record, and a clear difference is established between the experience of an object which has been seen before and an object which is novel. A further difference is that ART targets output of unambiguous category vectors and ART modules therefore cannot be combined in a recommendation architecture.

Secondly, the immediate experience of a perceived object is the activation configuration generated, made up of device activation across the alternative recommendation type superclusters. This activation can be imagined as a set of parallel cascades of device firing, corresponding with alternative behavioral recommendations. As long as a path from input to behavioral recommendations is activated, or is in an aroused state for which a small proportion of original input will reactivate, the recommendations can be regenerated and the object experience maintained. The aroused state is the basis for short term memory, during which the partial mental state induced by an object can be maintained.

Thirdly, the repetition recording mechanism at the device level imprints the currently active combination of inputs. Actual imprinted repetitions will therefore depend upon whatever physical inputs happen to be available. Even with the biasing provided by dream sleep some physical inputs to devices in clusters activated by the perception of a dog would be activated by the perception of, say, a cat or a tree. If such objects happened to be present when new information combinations are imprinted by a novel dog, then some information from such extraneous objects could be included. As an example, the perception of a dog chasing a cat up a tree could result in some cat and tree information being included in repetitions imprinted in dog related clusters. Some of the set of cat related clusters could even be shared with the set of dog related clusters. A later perception of a dog and a tree could result in a weak associative activation of a cat related behavioral recommendation. This activation is the basis for associative memory, which is the way in which images and behaviors appropriate for objects which are not present can be generated. Unless amplified in some way, such a weak associative activation would be negligible compared with the primary activations. The means by which such an amplification could occur is discussed later.

Fourthly, the use of the imprinting mechanism means that within the similarity clustering function all the information combinations activated at the time of an experience are permanently recorded, although only a small subset are actually recorded during the experience, the majority are repetitions of combinations recorded in earlier experiences. Hence if associative activation were able to activate the complete set, the experience would be indistinguishable from the original perception. In practice as discussed below, in reminiscence the activation is always of a subset which in particular excludes repetitions close to sensory input. One qualification on this argument is that if repetitions which never or extremely rarely repeated were eventually deleted to save resources and simplify the functional architecture as proposed by Coward (1990), then such repetitions would no longer be available.

Because similarity clustering is heuristic, and therefore strongly influenced by the type and order of experience, it will vary between different individuals, and individual behavior will be strongly influenced by individual experience. Furthermore, the repetitions programmed in an individual brain are determined partly by what connectivity options happened to be available. Hence the activations in two brains in response to the same experience will vary both because of differences in experience and because of accidental connectivity factors. Experience of a specific external input, say the color blue, is the activation of an assembly of repetitions created in the course of a wide range of individual experiences of the color blue in conjunction with other experiences. These repetitions are unique to individual experience, and the experience *blue* is therefore unique to the individual.

Different types of component output information can be the basis for an additional functional separation. For example, the presence or absence of an output can indicate the presence or absence of a recommendation, the modulation of that output (e.g., device firing rate) could indicate the strength of the recommendation, and the second order modulation (e.g., rate of change of device firing rate) could indicate the input data population from which the recommendation derived. The second order modulation could thus be the functional basis for object binding as proposed by Llinas, Ribary, Joliot, and Wang (1994).

Competitive Reduction of Local Information

The above discussion of heuristic association between clusters and behavior included a simple mechanism by which information output by a cluster could be eliminated from consideration by a management mechanism using simple pleasure and pain type feedback.

A practical architecture requires more sophisticated means to reduce the volume of information. Similarity clustering of input information can generate a large volume of ambiguous information corresponding with action recommendations of different types. In the early stages these recommendations can be interpreted as "pay attention", at later stages interpretations are more specific system actions. In the multi-stage reduction suggested as a model for the mammal brain in Coward (1990), the first stage is a competition between domain outlines which are ambiguous equivalents of the primal sketches described by Marr (1982). This mechanism is more completely discussed in Coward (1997a), and the result of the competition is access for the information originating within the domain defined by the primal sketch to more detailed clustering generating alternative behavioral recommendations. The second competitive stage as described in Coward (1990) is illustrated in figure 12. Recommendations from different superclusters enter different but parallel pipes, with cross inhibition between pipes which is modulated to achieve the exit of not more than one recommendation from the structure. The success of a recommendation allows the corresponding information access to a further clustering into body movements. Coward (1990) suggested that the first competition corresponds with the thalamus structures, the second with the basal ganglia, and offered supporting physiological evidence.

Cluster Management in a System with the Recommendation Architecture

The process of imprinting of repetitions at the device level can support a range of cluster management functions in addition to the basic similarity clustering of experience described earlier. For example, once the cluster structure to generate a set of behavioral recommendations has been heuristically defined, there may be advantages in accelerating the speed with which a response can be generated in the presence of its programmed information. Such an acceleration could be achieved by reducing the number of device layers through which information must pass in the cluster hierarchy, at a cost of reducing its ability to evolve heuristically in the future. Such a reduction could be achieved by setting up a parallel but simpler cluster structure, providing that structure with the same input and output populations as the primary structure, imprinting paths through the simpler structure only when the primary structure was producing outputs, and imprinting the outputs of the secondary structure to the targets of those primary outputs.

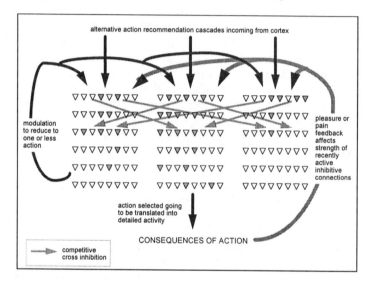

Fig. 12. A possible competition structure. Active information representing alternative action recommendations of different types enters separate pipe like paths. The recommendation in one path inhibits the transmission in all other paths. If more than one recommendation approaches output, a feedback loop damps down all paths. Feedback on the consequences of an accepted recommendation changes the strength of recently active inhibitive connections in the successful path and thus modulates the probability of similar actions in the future.

The process described is essentially one of cloning an existing cluster structure for the same function. It is also possible to clone a cluster structure for a different function. For example, consider a system which had already established the cluster structure to play table tennis, which is required to acquire the capability to play tennis. At some level of clustering there is some similarity between the two activities. If the clusters developed for table tennis are forced to generate behavioral recommendations for tennis, partially usable recommendations will result, with imprinting of additional repetitions. The new repetitions will incorporate information more appropriate for tennis, and the outputs will become heuristically associated with behaviors more appropriate for tennis. The newly imprinted repetitions will be the seeds of clusters fully appropriate to tennis. Creation of a cluster hierarchy from scratch would require a much longer and more resource intensive process.

Another application of the cloning process is suggested in figure 13. If clusters have developed which generate action recommendations appropriate to certain shapes being in particular relative position, their inputs will be information relevant to the presence of the shapes and their relative positions. Now suppose that information on the relative time sequence of perception of the objects is available, for example as a side effect of a process which assigned neuron and connectivity resources to clusters on an as-received basis (see note 1). If simultaneous reminiscent activation of the perception of the three shapes occurred, then much of the input information which generally produced outputs from the corresponding clusters would be present, although not necessarily the relative position information. However, information indicating relative time sequence could be active. In some situations appropriate behavior could depend on the time sequence in which the shapes were experienced. If time sequence information happened to be incorporated as input to the relative position clusters by the biased random correction process selection process, cluster outputs would begin to discriminate between conditions on the basis of time sequence and thus gain functional value. Such functional value would reinforce the inclusion of such inputs. Because the imprinted repetitions would include time sequence related information and not spatial information, two populations of imprinted repetitions would develop for spatial related and temporal related behavioral recommendations. The temporal cluster would have been cloned from the spatial cluster. This cloning scenario suggests that there would be a spatial basis for our thinking about time. Jaynes (1976) has emphasized the pervasiveness of spatial models and vocabulary in our thinking and speech about temporal relationships.

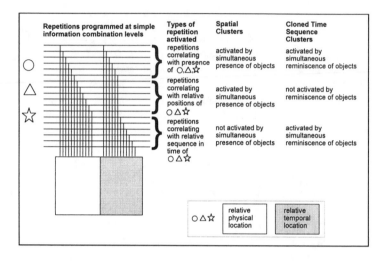

Fig. 13. Cluster cloning to support time sequence dependent action recommendations. Clusters which detect the repetition of conditions in which objects are aligned in space have as input much of the information needed for clusters detecting time sequence repetitions. Additional information is required on relative time sequence in which repetitions were recorded. Such information could be derived from the resource map discussed in the text. If such information happened to be available at the space module, weak similarity could lead to imprinting, but because the new repetitions contained time information they would develop into a separate population cloned from the space population.

Given the heuristic process for associating clusters with behavior it is also possible to see how a useful cluster could be adopted in another function. For example, clusters which frequently generated appropriate behavior in the food seeking supercluster could be used as a template in the speech generation supercluster. A new cluster template would be established with the appropriate neurohormone sensitivities. The information which frequently generated outputs in the existing clusters would be connected as inputs to the new clusters. Outputs would be speech related behaviors and could include both experimental phoneme activation and pseudo-sensory input activation. Imprinting would be triggered in the new clusters whenever the existing clusters generated an output recommendation, and the outputs from the new clusters could be heuristically guided to appropriate behaviors.

The Recommendation Architecture in Biology

For the reasons discussed earlier, biological brains must experience strong selection pressures in favor of simple functional architectures. However, biological brains do not exhibit the memory, processing separations of systems with the instruction architecture and do not functionally resemble the instruction based operations of such systems. The evidence that biological brains have adopted the recommendation architecture is extensively discussed in Coward (1990) but can be summarized in three areas: functional evidence; structural evidence; and evidence from the functional effects of damage.

The functional evidence includes the ubiquitous role of categorization in animal (Lorenz, 1977) and human (e.g., Harnad, 1987) cognition. Further evidence is the existence of heuristic definition of functionality. The major requirement for management of the distribution of information in a heuristically defined functional architecture is consistent with the operations of dream sleep.

Physical evidence is based on the structures of a system with the recommendation architecture reflecting the constraints of that architecture, just as memory and processing structures appear in any instruction system. Figure 14 indicates how major physiological structures in the brain can be understood as clustering and competition structures. At a more detailed level, cortex columns correspond with cluster modules (Coward, 1990; Tanaka, 1993). The strong layering observed in the cortex is as expected from the functional separations within clusters discussed earlier, with functional separations such as management of incoming information, indication of requirements for new clusters, indication of cluster membership, maintenance of repetition orthogonality, and maintenance of sufficient diversity in cluster outputs to indicate different conditions within the cluster definition differently etc., leading to physical layering. De Felipe (1997) has described strong cross connectivity of spiny stellate cells in layer IV of the cortex, and inhibitive back projection by bouquet cells. This connectivity would be the type required to implement the cluster membership subfunctions discussed earlier (see figure 5), with the cross connectivity detecting repetition of a significant subset of the information combinations defining the cluster and stimulating imprinting of additional combinations, and the inhibitive backprojection preventing imprinting in the presence of already significant output.

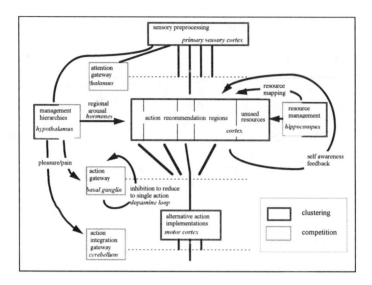

Fig. 14. Major physiological structures in the brain can be mapped into similarity clustering and competition subsystems with an architecture resembling figure 3 plus subsystems as illustrated in figure 11. Information generated by an initial clustering in the primary sensory cortex is competitively reduced through the thalamus structures. The remaining information is reclustered in the cortex to generate alternative action recommendations. These alternatives compete in the basal ganglia structures, and the information making up one alternative is allowed to proceed from the cortex to the cerebellum where it is reclustered to specific muscle movements. Parallel similarity clustering subsystems manage major system management functions.

Another example is backward projections, for example from the higher to the lower areas of the primary sensory cortex which terminate in layer I (Cauller, 1995) and which I have argued above are associated with maintaining repetition orthogonality under conditions of multiple repetitions per device. The observation that the typical cortex neuron has about 100 thousand inputs and fires if about 75 of them are active (Cauller, 1997b) indicates that neurons are programmed with multiple repetitions. Similarity clustering by detection of information repetitions requires that primary connections are stimulative, although connections managing local recognition of similarity may be inhibitive. This requirement is consistent with observations that long range cortex connectivity is mainly stimulative, but a proportion of local connectivity in inhibitive (Douglas & Martin, 1991).

In figure 14 there are a number of subsystems, also with the clustering, competition structure, which perform system management subfunctions. One of these subfunctions modulates the relative arousal of behavioral superclusters in response to perceived need. For example, within the subsystem, clusters take inputs indicating internal body states and generate behavioral recommendations to lower device thresholds in a food seeking supercluster. Such subsystem clusters would roughly corresponding with the cognitive category/recommendation *low blood sugar/feel hungry*. Clusters roughly corresponding with *threat to self or property/feel angry* could increase the probability of aggressive action recommendations. Clusters correlating with perception of attractive member of the opposite sex could generate sexual arousal recommendations increasing the probability of courting behavior. Following Coward (1990), the hypothalamus is identified as the structure which performs this function within the mammal brain. Another key subsystem clusters information about resource usage by cluster modules and generates recommendations to assign additional resources. Coward (1990) argued that this function is performed by the hippocampus using a map of cortex resources to assign additional resources as required.

The evidence from damage is particularly striking. In general, the types of functional deficits which can and cannot result from physical damage are a strong indication of system functional architecture. The heuristic similarity clustering process means that information extracted from a single experience will be recorded in numerous clusters located in a number of behavioral superclusters. Physically localized damage to the similarity clustering function is therefore unlikely to remove all such information, the effect of such damage will be reduced ability to generate recommendations of one or some types. This exactly corresponds with the observation that local damage to the cortex does not remove event memory, but may produce behavioral shifts (the classical reference is Harlow, 1868). Damage affecting the management subsystem which assigns resources for recording repetitions may result in time sequence deficits if the damage interferes with access to a block of resources assigned over a period of time. Coward (1990) has pointed out that the deficits associated with Korsakov's syndrome, including loss of a time block of memory and the inability to create new memories, are exactly as expected from damage to the communication between a cortex performing the clustering function and a hippocampus performing the mapping function outlined above. A further example is damage to a competitive reduction function. Coward (1990) has argued that the symptoms of Tourette's syndrome, including rapid behavioral shifts, are consistent with a failure of the competitive system to reduce behavioral alternatives to one or less, and the dopamine function which is associated with Tourette's syndrome plausibly plays the role of damping down the number of alternatives in the basal ganglia.

The recommendation architecture supports a plausible evolutionary sequence by which cognition evolved. The scenario identifies a sequence of small physiological changes, each of which generates a change to system functionality which is of value to the system without any of the subsequent changes. In the scenario, the neuron emerged first within a multicellular organism with the ability to drive a response from combinations of sensory inputs including internal physiological conditions. Genetically programmed hierarchies of neurons developed to manage choices among complex motor response alternatives. Neurons extracting repetitions from internal physiology took on the role of tuning genetically hard wired neuron hierarchies to details of individual body development. This tuning was an early hierarchy management role and eventually evolved into pleasure and pain. Networks of randomly connected neurons were added which allowed repetitions extracted from individual experience to be used to generate a wider range of potential behavioral responses to a given situation. Pleasure and pain extended their functions to manage the selection probabilities of alternative behaviors. Dreaming put statistical bias on the random connectivity resulting in better use of resources. Speech allowed communication of internally generated clusters, and as a side effect made internal feedback possible, which allowed more extensive searching of individual memory to develop better behavioral responses in complex social situations. This feedback is experienced as self awareness (Jaynes, 1976), and the search process is experienced as the explosion of associative images we call consciousness. More detail of the later cognitive developments is given in Coward, 1997b, and below.

The recommendation architecture paradigm thus demonstrates considerable explanatory power for the behavior of biological brains. A number of further experimental tests of the existence of the recommendation architecture in biological brains were proposed by Coward (1990). These tests apply to instances of the architecture which exhibit heuristic definition of functionality (i.e., mammal brains). One test is the existence of the imprinting mechanism as described earlier as a primary plasticity mechanism in mammal cortex neurons. A second test is the existence of the neuron connectivity changes resulting from the information distribution management function of sleep. A third test is at the phenomenological level deriving from the information management function. The prediction is that under conditions of dream sleep deprivation accompanied by waking experience which is intensive with significant novel content in some behavioral domains where there is a biological need to take action, and minimal in other behavioral domains, then behavior in response to the intensive experience will shift towards types of behavior appropriate to domains which have not been stimulated. The reason is that imprinting resources are required to generate action, especially if some novelty is present. Dream sleep renews these resources where they have been depleted. If such resources are depleted in the most appropriate superclusters and a need to respond is present, less relevant superclusters will be used resulting in less appropriate behavior.

High-level Functional Definition of Consciousness

The term consciousness is used to label phenomena ranging from the simple ability to respond to a stimulus to the ability to experience and talk about a constant succession of mental images generated largely independently of sensory input. These mental images can include objects never directly experienced. Images of self acting and experiencing can be generated, with either an internal or an external view-point (the "I" and "me" in Jaynes, 1976). In Jaynes' example, we can generate a mental image of ourselves running to the lake shore and diving into the water, and also a mental image of the feel of our body swimming, the splashing of water on our face. The first of these images is generally not part of our direct sensory experience.

From a functional point of view, four levels of consciousness can be distinguished (Coward, 1990), with each level including all the lower levels. At the lowest level 1 is the ability to respond to a stimulus, which does not require a nervous system. Indications of favorable or unfavorable conditions are simply stimuli, not a separate pleasure and pain system as is used at higher levels. Level 2 is the ability to develop complex, appropriate responses to complex combinations of stimuli. Level 2 requires a nervous system but does not require recording of individual specific experiences. A primitive separate pleasure and pain system may be used to tune the genetically programmed nervous system to variations in individual body growth. Level 2 is typical of insects and reptiles. Level 3 includes the ability to record the state of the brain during an individual experience and to partially reactivate that state in later, similar experiences as an aid to generation of behavior. Simultaneous activations of various combinations of individual specific memory traces correspond with alternative action recommendations. The choice between alternatives is managed by an extended pleasure and pain system which influences the probability of future action selections. Level 3 is typical of mammals. Level 4 adds to the ability to generate multiple behavioral alternatives the ability to generate from an alternative a set of pseudo-sensory inputs as if the alternative had been accepted and carried out. Additional alternatives are generated by the combination of actual and pseudo-sensory inputs, which can in turn result in further pseudo-sensory inputs and yet more behavioral alternatives. The process is experienced as a constant succession of mental images, and greatly extends the range of individual specific memory which can be searched for behavioral guidance in a given set of circumstances. Level 4 consciousness requires that a representation of a behavior be created and communicated to a point at which pseudo-sensory input corresponding with self performing the behavior can be generated (Coward, 1990). This generation of a mental image by a symbolic representation strongly resembles speech, and both Jaynes (1976) and Dennett (1991) have argued that speech plays an important role in consciousness. Following Jaynes' phenomenological discussion, Coward (1990) suggested that physiological paths internalizing the route from utterance to hearing are the basis for level 4 consciousness. A process by which this internalization could have occurred is outlined in Coward, 1997b. From this point in the paper, the term consciousness without a level qualification will mean only level 4 consciousness.

Consciousness Models

Lorenz (1977) proposed that the phenomena of human consciousness derive from a number of capabilities which exist in other animals or have developed from such capabilities. The major change between other animals and human beings is in the way in which these capabilities interact. These capabilities are the abilities to extract constant objects from sensory input; to maintain mental models of relative positions; to treat every object as biologically relevant in order to find objects which are genuinely significant (i.e., curiosity); to compose complex actions from a vocabulary of muscle movements; to try past behaviors in new situations; and to imitate behavior. Humans have added the abilities to represent time with spatial models and to imitate behavior by indirect instruction. Lorenz does not directly address the source of the constant stream of mental images, or discuss any neurophysiological mechanisms. The capabilities which Lorenz identifies are all typical of a recommendation architecture exhibiting heuristic definition of functionality. For example, the capability to extract constant objects from sensory input reflects the search for information combinations which repeat, which may require the inclusion of information about the state of sensory organs. Curiosity reflects the need to establish a set of similarity clusters which can generate outputs in response to all conditions.

Jaynes (1976) offers a well developed psychological theory of consciousness along with some controversial ideas on the evolutionary and historical origins of consciousness. In Jaynes' view, as we interact with an object we perceive the object in many different ways over a succession of instants in time. These different ways Jaynes labels percepts. An object is represented in consciousness by a reactivation of a percept. A conscious image is thus the reproduction of one of the instantaneous mental images which occurred during direct perception of the object in the past. New objects are assimilated into existing categories developed to define behavioral responses. Mental objects are arranged in a spatial framework called a mindspace. This mental arrangement is used to represent relationships in space, in time, and in emotion (e.g., containing or letting out anger). Central to Jaynes' theory are the concepts of analog I and metaphor Me, which are conscious representations of self acting and self experiencing. The ability to tell stories is the basis for arranging events in a sequence and thus to modeling causal relationships. Consciousness for Jaynes is thus a linguistic invention, developed in response to a need for behavioral responses to extremely complex social situations. Implicit in Jaynes' theory is the recommendation architecture concept of development of repetition similarity clusters to define behavioral responses, and the behavioral role of consciousness in developing behavior in complex social situations developed in detail in this paper is the functional role originally proposed by Jaynes.

Baars (1988) has proposed a phenomenological theory of consciousness around the concept of the global workspace, and has begun (1994) to develop the corresponding physiological theory. According to Baars, the contents of consciousness are the contents of a global workspace located in the primary sensory projection areas of the cortex (e.g., VI for the visual sense). A set of input processors generate visual images, inner speech etc., which compete through structures like the brainstem reticular formation and the nucleus reticularis for access to the global workspace. The contents of the global workspace are distributed widely to specialty unconscious processors including perceptual analyzers, output systems, action systems, syntax systems, and planning and control systems.

In Baars' model, the function of consciousness is to provide overall access to unconscious brain knowledge. This includes auto-biographical memory, the lexicon of natural language, automatic routines that control actions, and, by way of sensory feedback, the detailed firing of neurons and neuronal populations. The primary difference from the recommendation architecture approach is that there does not appear to be a clearly articulated view of the partitioning of behavioral functionality in Baars' model. Concepts like perceptual analyzers, output systems, action systems, planning and control systems are von Neumann concepts implying the use and generation of unambiguous system information. However, the input processors postulated by Baars have a functional resemblance to clusters in the sense that they generate alternative activation recommendations which compete for implementation.

Coward (1990) modified Jaynes' phenomenological theory of human consciousness in a number of areas and provided a physiological model of consciousness based on recommendation architecture theory of brain architecture. The first modification to Jaynes' theory is that direct perception is by extraction of a set of combinations of information from the perceived object, most of the combinations being repetitions of combinations created by perception of previous, similar objects, and a small set being created by the immediate process of perception. A mental image is the reactivation of a subset of the repetitions within a set of repetition similarity clusters frequently activated by similar objects. The second modification is that overlapping mental images can activate a set of pseudo-sensory repetitions which are frequently present during the perception of additional objects, which can in turn generate a mental image of the additional objects. These pseudo-sensory activations are developed and communicated using mechanisms similar to those used to generate speech, but are not themselves necessarily oral. The third modification is that perceptions and images of objects are functionally action recommendations, and multiple action recommendations for the same object result from the object being assigned to multiple sets of repetition similarity clusters which may be similar in sensory terms but separate functionally. The relative strength of action recommendations derived from the same object is modulated by feelings and emotions such as hunger, anger, and fear. Such feelings and emotions are themselves modulated by action recommendations. The fourth modification is that selection of action is functionally separate from generation of action recommendations, and only the latter can enter consciousness. The 1990 model is developed in more functional detail in the body of this paper.

Metzinger (1996) has defined a set of components which need to be specified at both the psychological and physiological level in any integrated, systematic theory of the phenomenal content of consciousness. These include the smallest unit of phenomenal content; the smallest representable unit of content; object constitution, or binding; temporal relationships; spatial relationships; a hierarchy of relationships derived from spatial; self representation; first-person and other perspectives; and global modeling of reality which is not recognized as a model. This chapter attempts to define a complete set of components of consciousness and their interactions at both the psychological and physiological levels within a recommendation functional architecture and addresses all the functions called for by Metzinger.

Architecture of a System Delivering Consciousness

The highest level functional separations in a system delivering level 3 consciousness are shown in figure 3 (following Coward, 1990). An initial similarity clustering extracts sensory system independent repetitions from raw sensory input. A competition between sets of repetitions from different sensory domains results in the repetitions from one domain proceeding to further clustering. This first competition is the attention process. The second clustering generates parallel activations corresponding with recommendations of different types of behavior (aggressive, fearful, sexual, food seeking, cooperative, etc.).

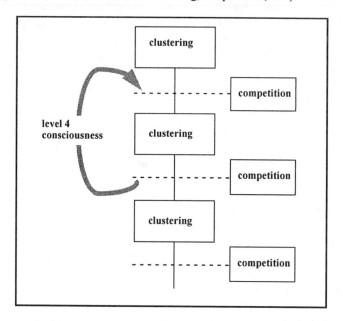

Fig. 15. The functional feedback loop which makes possible the activation of mental images independent of direct sensory input.

A competition between the different recommendations results in selection of a behavior. The activations corresponding with the selected behavior are further clustered into a portfolio of action sequences which compete to generate an integrated action.

The comment of Lorenz (1977) on the importance of the animal capability to extract constant objects from sensory input, and Jaynes' (1976) observation that most mammals assimilate slightly ambiguous perceived objects into previously learned schemas are both reflections of a functional architecture based on similarity. The importance of categorization in human cognition also reflects the recommendation architecture with sets of clusters operating through a competitive function to define cognitive categories.

The transition to level 4 consciousness depends upon the introduction of an additional functional mechanism, which is derived from signaling capabilities and illustrated in figure 15.

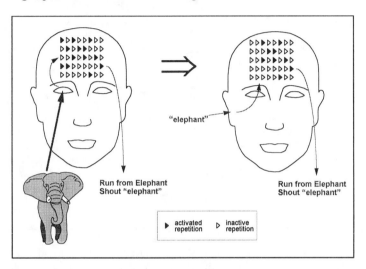

Fig. 16. Signaling depends upon the signal being able to activate a significant subset of the local information which would be activated by the object signaled, and thus generate the same action recommendations

To demonstrate the development of this capability, consider how signaling achieves its behavioral effect in a recommendation architecture as illustrated in figure 16. The presence of an elephant results in a population of repetitions being generated which in turn generates a set of behavioral recommendations, including flight. If one of the behavioral recommendations can be to shout "elephant!" the value of the signal is its capability to generate flight or other appropriate behavior in the absence of direct sensory input. The simplest way to achieve this is if the sensory input of the word activates many of the intermediate level repetitions activated by direct perception. These pseudo-sensory repetitions are then clustered into the same behavioral recommendations as would result from direct perception. An appropriate point in level of complexity for these pseudo-sensory repetitions to be activated by signals would be more complex than raw visual repetitions but prior to the attention competition. Entry at that point would minimize the processing of information but allow independent decision on whether to pay attention to the signal.

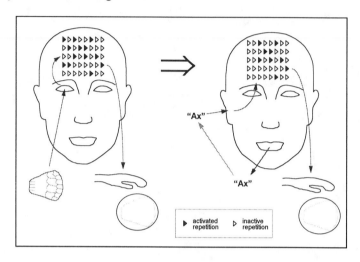

Fig. 17. The set of active repetitions generated by looking at a tool are an important part of the information which generates the sequence of action recommendations to make a new tool. Once a word for a tool is available, the spoken name can generate the same set of active repetitions and generate the sequence of action recommendations to make a new tool in the absence of an example. The same mechanism makes it possible for an individual to accept oral commands. The words of the command generate the activated repetitions representing the commanded action, which can drive the action recommendations to carry out the action.

The creation of the associations which activate the pseudo-sensory repetitions from the word can be a Hebbian type mechanism. Provided that the appropriate functional architectural framework is available, connections in the recipient brain for activation of the appropriate pseudo-sensory repetitions could be established heuristically by simultaneously seeing the object (i.e., activating the appropriate sensory level repetitions) and hearing the word (i.e., activating the appropriate auditory repetitions) and establishing connections between functional components which are frequently active at the same time.

However, there is a side effect of this mechanism. If the word "elephant" is spoken, it has the capability to activate pseudo-sensory repetitions in the mind of the speaker as if the elephant were being perceived, a feedback loop has been established. The simplest result of this side effect is that sensory images can be prolonged after the original stimulus has disappeared. A commonplace example is when we speak aloud to ourselves a telephone number we have just read, long enough to drive the motions of dialing. Coward (1997b) has argued that use of spoken signals in an analogous manner was important in making early human tool making less dependent on the copying of physical models (figure 17). The recommendation to speak the name of a tool could derive from associative activation from combinations imprinted when the tool had been used in the past, hence the recommendation to make a tool could be activated from conditions in which a tool was needed. The need conditions activate a mental image of the tool, which drives the tool making behaviors.

There is an important functional value gained if internal physiological routes replace the external spoken route, as illustrated in figure 18. When image activation is dependent on speech, the only images which can be evoked are those for which a word exists. In figure 18, a supercluster exists which generates recommendations to activate pseudo-sensory repetitions which have frequently occurred in the past when its component clusters have been producing outputs. Again, the connectivity to support the functionality could be established using a Hebbian type mechanism, and in general activation would be as a result of associative overlap. However, the internal function has the advantage that images of parts of the tool which have no name can be evoked and generate more detailed action recommendations. Much more detailed tools can be made, and furthermore the sustaining of images becomes easier, sometimes occurring without actual tool making. Because imprinting occurs when images are activated, whether or not actual tool making occurs, the additional repetitions will lead to more variability in the tools made. Greater variation in tools would therefore be expected from image driven tool making, and can explain the explosion in new types of tools observed in human archaeology in the 40,000 b.c. to 15,000 b.c. period (Jaynes, 1976).

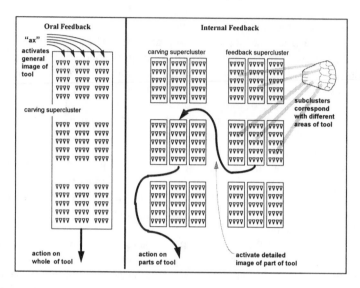

Fig. 18. Comparison of orally controlled and internally controlled feedback. Words can only activate images for which there is a word. Internal feedback loops can activate subclusters for which there are no verbal labels but which can generate more detailed action recommendations. The internal feedback clusters are initially activated by associative overlap.

Such an internal feedback system can be the basis for a new function. As discussed earlier, the same sensory information will in general result in multiple alternative behavioral recommendations. For example, the result of attention being focused on a dog is the generation of recommendations of the friendly, aggressive, speech generation etc. types. If the feedback system is also applied to the friendly, aggressive etc., behavioral recommendations, the result will be activation of a set of pseudo-sensory repetitions which were frequently active in the past when such recommendations were accepted, and could include repetitions imprinted by past internal body information as well as past external environment information. Such activations could therefore be experienced as self actions. Clusters developed from observation of other individuals could be cloned if such cloned clusters proved valuable in directing activation feedback. The activation of such cloned clusters would be experienced by the system as observation of self taking an action, viewed from outside of self. The result would be to activate an additional set of clusters and therefore generate additional behavioral recommendations, and the functional role is therefore to search a more extensive range of individual specific memories for behavioral guidance.

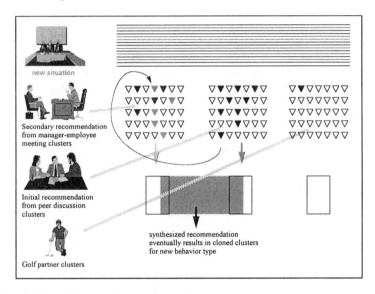

Fig. 19. Initial action recommendations are derived from the most similar of previously defined cluster sets. Activation of simple repetitions frequently active when the higher order repetitions corresponding with the recommendation have been active in the past activates a wider range of recommendations. An action recommendation representing a synthesis results. Imprinting in all active cluster sets results in cloning a new cluster set for the new behavioral type.

As Jaynes (1976) has argued, the primary value for this process lies in generating behavior appropriate in complex social situations as illustrated in figure 19. In that figure the brain has developed clusters which generate action recommendations when experiencing one particular individual in different circumstances. When this individual is experienced in novel circumstances, the first recommendation generated is one appropriate to the most similar of the programmed circumstances. This recommendation results in activation of pseudo-sensory inputs as if the action had been taken, generating enough repetitions to activate a recommendation appropriate to a second programmed circumstance. The overlap of the recommendations results in a somewhat different accepted recommendation, and the imprinted repetitions form the starting point for a set of clusters appropriate to the new circumstances. The feedback driven activation process results in repetition imprinting or even new cluster creation just as in activation by direct experience, and these virtual memories can also become resources for future behavioral guidance.

The feedback functionality is derived from speech and can therefore be expected to be unique to human beings, and the physiological location of the functionality would also be expected to be unique. Two possibilities are the inferior parietal lobe (Coward, 1990) or the anterior cingulate cortex (a different interpretation of results discussed in Cotterill, 1995).

When the feedback capability is combined with the associatively generated activations discussed earlier, weak associative activations can be recommendations to generate the full activations of the clusters usually activated by the associatively activated object. Such full activations can themselves give rise to further weak activations amplified in turn by feedback, resulting in the system experiencing a series of states similar to those resulting from a series of actual perceptions. The system thus experiences a series of images decoupled from direct sensory input.

The psychological-level description of the experience of sequences of images decoupled from direct sensory input thus corresponds with a physiological-level description in which several sets of active repetitions overlap and generate further repetition sets as illustrated in figure 20. An important issue is how to identify the repetition set to which a particular repetition belongs. The functional need is to ensure that appropriate behavioral recommendations can be generated with respect to individual objects, but also that it be possible for activation sets for multiple objects to overlap and generate activation sets for additional objects, which must themselves be distinguished from their sources. This is essentially the binding problem and a widely discussed solution uses coherent modulation of firing rate across populations of activations (see Llinas et al., 1994). A more general solution is that the repetitions associated with a particular object are tagged with a particular firing modulation frequency in the 40 Hz range, the primary object of attention is identified by the main frequency, and other objects can be identified by modulation frequencies offset from the main frequency.

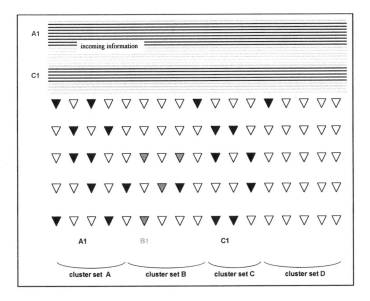

Fig. 20. Local information extracted from objects A1 and C1 is introduced simultaneously into a similarity clustering function. Confusion between the objects is avoided because their information is tagged by different rates of change of neuron firing rate, and recommendations generated are similarly tagged. The simultaneous presence of repetitions from the two objects activates a set of higher complexity repetitions extracted in the past from objects in cluster sets B, which have frequently been present at the same time as objects in cluster sets A and C. This set can be an action recommendation to activate the simpler repetitions which have frequently been present at the same time. Acceptance of the recommendation would activate an image of the object B1

The experience of the images of consciousness can then be under-stood as follows. There is a competition as described in Coward (1997a) between the ambiguous equivalent of the primal sketches pro-posed by Marr (1982) from which the winner gains access for all the repetitions extracted within the domain defined by the sketch into the behavioral recommendation generation function. All repetitions derived from the winning domain are tagged by the main modulation frequency, and it is output repetitions with that frequency which form the exter-nally directed behavioral recommendations. Secondary objects may gain some access, but repetitions extracted from within their domains are tagged with a frequency offset from the main frequency. Output activation sets composed of offset frequency repetitions can only be recommendations to activate pseudo-sensory activations. Such recommendations, if accepted, will generate activation sets tagged with a single modulation frequency. This frequency could in some cases be the main frequency, as when an imagined object drives behavior, for example when writing a paper.

A critical capability is therefore the number of independent modulation frequencies which can be supported in the alternative behavioral generation function. The number is likely to be small, and defines the number of independent objects which can be imagined at the same time. The capability is only relevant for sustaining the feedback activation of images, and can therefore be expected to be limited to the human beings among Earth species.

Options for Similarity Cluster Functionality

At this point it is useful to revisit the range of possible functions which a similarity cluster can fulfill. A cluster is any set of repetitions which can have a useful internal or external function, with the proviso that if the distribution of information between clusters becomes too complex, the system will become difficult to construct and maintain and the organism possessing such a brain will probably become extinct.

The functional role of a cluster is to generate behavioral recommendations. However, recommendations can also be directed at the system itself. A cluster composed of an appropriate set of repetitions can drive necessary system functions. Useful clusters could include detection that a particular activation set is driven by internal feedback and does not correspond with any current external object. Such clusters could recommend against certain types of behavior. Another type of cluster could detect that recommendations corresponding with similar sets of cluster activations sometimes produced favorable results, sometimes unfavorable. Such clusters could recommend addition of input information to generate additional outputs which could discriminate between the apparently similar conditions. An example could be if the same behavior towards a particular individual produced different results at different times, and activation of 'contradiction detection' clusters resulted in adding information such as time of day or mood indications to the inputs utilized and adding cluster outputs which incorporated the additional information.

The capability to refine the definition of repetition similarity when similar behavior in apparently similar conditions produces inconsistent results, has clear behavioral advantages. Physiological mutations in favor of such a functionality would therefore be selected in evolutionary terms. However, once such a functionality exists in combination with the ability to sustain multiple independent mental images, the functionality which will tend to generate consistent belief systems such as history, philosophy, and science is in place. To understand why this is the case, consider the scenarios illustrated in figure 21.

A human visits London, Paris, and New York. In London he sees the Houses of Parliament, and the sensory input generates the behavioral recommendation to say "London, the birthplace of liberty". The same individual visits Paris, sees the sites of the Revolution, and again the sensory input generates a behavioral recommendation, in this case to say "Paris, the birthplace of liberty". Finally, the same individual visits New York and sees the Statue of Liberty, and yet again the sensory input generates a behavioral recommendation, in this case to say "America, the birthplace of liberty". Note the similarity with early classical Greeks who could place the birthplace of Apollo at the sites of a number of different cities without apparent awareness of a problem (Johnson, 1987). Now suppose that associative activation of secondary images, the ability to sustain multiple images, and inconsistency clusters are in place. When the individual says or thinks "New York, the birthplace of liberty" the 'birthplace of liberty' content may activate repetitions imprinted at the times when he has said the same things about the other places. These activations simultaneously generate recommendations to say the three contradictory statements. Detection of the contradiction generates a recommendation to recluster the input information towards a set of clusters which generate consistent statements, the first step towards a consistent historical view.

Other management clusters could detect repetitions correlating with the inability of a supercluster to produce output recommendations, either because individual clusters lacked imprinting resources or because input conditions were insufficiently similar to any existing clusters. Such management clusters could generate recommendations to add imprinting resouces, add clusters, or modify the similarity criteria of existing clusters.

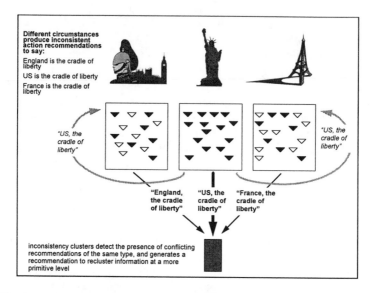

Fig. 21. Without feedback, a brain can generate recommendations in different situations which would be contradictory if generated at the same time. Feedback results in the recommendation to say "the US is the cradle of liberty" in one situation activating enough simpler information to activate "England is the cradle of liberty" and "France is the cradle of liberty" recommendations at the same time. The simultaneous generation of conflicting recommendations of the same type is a condition which activates clusters with output recommendations to recluster the information at the simple level.

The Dynamic Experience of Consciousness

At any instant in time, sensory input is directed to two parallel similarity clustering functions. One function extracts repetitions which indicate the presence of coherent objects in the external environment ("primal sketches"). The other extracts repetitions indicating the presence of object characteristics (e.g., object color independent of illumination). Outputs from the first function are action recommendations to *pay detailed attention to this sensory domain* or *carry out programmed action* with respect to the primal sketch. Programmed actions include rapid response behaviors such as ducking, grabbing, etc. A *pay detailed attention* recommendation, if accepted, results in repetitions extracted by the second function from sensory input within the domain defined by the primal sketch gaining access to a further similarity clustering which generates alternative action recommendations with respect to the primal sketch. The tagging of such repetitions with a single modulation frequency overlaid on the neuron firing rates which indicate the presence of the repetitions is the mechanism which indicates to later functions that all the repetitions derive from one primal sketch. As discussed earlier, all the repetitions derived from one image activation recommendation are similarly tagged by a (different) common modulation frequency.

The alternative action clustering function is subdivided into superclusters which generate behavioral recommendations of different types. Each supercluster contains a hierarchy of clusters. Types of behavior include aggressive, fearful and food-seeking for example. The relative probability of action recommendations of different types is modulated by a separate clustering function which clusters a combination of inputs including a significant proportion of inputs derived from within the body. For example, repetitions indicating body strength and external threat increase the probability of aggressive behavior, inputs indicating low blood sugar increase the probability of food seeking behavior. This modulation function underlies the experiences of emotion. Within one supercluster, recommendations can include shifting the focus of attention, for example to subdomains within the current primal sketch (e.g., pay attention to the mouth and teeth areas of a dog). Recommendations could also include to increase the arousal of the supercluster itself (e.g., to become more angry).

One supercluster within the alternative action clustering function can generate speech recommendations, including in the simplest case to speak the name of the primal sketch. Note that as discussed earlier, a set of ambiguous clusters acting through a competitive function form the operational definition of a cognitive category. Another supercluster generates recommendations to activate inputs which were frequently present in the past when the current outputs were present. Such recommendations generated by pseudo-sensory input compete with *pay detailed attention* recommendations generated from current sensory input, and if accepted result in an activation state similar to the state resulting from sensory conditions in the past which contributed to imprinting of the currently active outputs. This feedback process underlies the experience of mental images independent of current sensory input. Such images can be distinguished from activations created by current sensory input both by different modulation frequencies and by the absence of the repetitions closest to sensory input.

Feedback from clusters imprinted by conditions including past conditions of the body generates mental images of self separate from actual current sensory input from the body, and may include images which could not be generated from any actual input (e.g., self viewed from outside). Mental images of self can include self conditions such as anger or fear.

As active assemblies decay, new assemblies can be activated by action recommendations derived either from a primal sketch or from feedback of an associative activation generated by the currently active assemblies. The combination of currently active assemblies is the current content of perception, and thus evolves under the influence of both sensory input and associative activation. Once an assembly has fully died away, it can only be reactivated by appropriate sensory input or appropriate pseudo-sensory input generated by assembly overlap. Some assemblies may not be accessible in a given situation.

What are the content limitations of consciousness? To answer this question it is important to appreciate both how the contents of consciousness are activated and how those contents can be determined by an outside observer. Baars (1996) offers a practical definition of human consciousness in terms of abilities such as answering questions and reporting perceptual events. This definition is consistent with level 4 consciousness but only addresses how the contents can be determined. Consider how split brain patients can be shown (right hemisphere only) an embarrassing picture, and respond with embarrassment while being unable to explain the actual cause, often inventing reasons to account for their reaction. The physical breakdown is that information about the picture has not been able to reach the speech centers of the left hemisphere, and we typically conclude that there is no consciousness of the picture, although repetitions derived from the picture must be active in the right hemisphere and split brain patients exhibit apparently normal consciousness in less constrained conditions. Any mammal with level 3 consciousness has a set of repetitions activated by a sensory experience which are a mental image which can even generate communication recommendations in some cases. The distinctive property of level 4 consciousness is the ability to generate action recommendations to create pseudo-sensory inputs as if a non-perceived condition were present. The brain function which can generate such recommendations is derived from the function generating speech recommendations and both functions are located within the clustering function which generates all action recommendations. An accepted image generation recommendation produces pseudo-sensory inputs to that same clustering function, which could in turn generate speech recommendations to communicate current content. Image generation recommendations cannot directly generate pseudo-inputs to any competitive function or to the initial sensory preprocessing clustering function, and these functions cannot generate speech recommendations. The contents of these functions are therefore outside of the scope of consciousness.

Consider the state of the brain when paying attention to a coffee mug. An assembly of parallel cascades of neuron firing extends through the cortex from visual input to action recommendations such as 'pick up and drink'. Imagining a mug uses a recommendation generated internally by assembly overlap to activate by feedback an assembly of neuron firing which extends for part of the length of the assembly generated by viewing a real mug. If the point at which the feedback initiates the assembly is close to the senses, the image generated is strongly visual. If further away the image is more abstract. If one of the parallel cascades generates a speech action recommendation, we can verbalize the content of the assembly at that point, such as an action recommendation to 'pick up the mug'.

Consider now the process of molding a mug out of clay. An assembly generated by paying attention to the clay is followed in attention by an assembly made up of repetitions extracted from past mug experiences which is generated by feedback of an associative activation. Repetitions activated by overlap of the two assemblies generate action recommendations to manipulate the clay. Other associatively generated activations are action recommendations to focus attention on detailed parts of the mug, say the handle, and so generate action recommendations which affect the appropriate area of the clay. Activation of unrelated assemblies during the molding process or when thinking about it may influence the repetitions activated and thus the result. Imprinting of additional information combinations in the course of generating action recommendations makes it possible to regenerate the action recommendation in the future and experience reminiscence.

Suppose now that assembly overlap, associative activation, recommendation acceptance and feedback generate a set of activations characteristic of a chimpanzee soon after a mug assembly. Repetitions activated by the overlap of the succession of mug and chimpanzee assemblies generate the associative activation of a relationship: chimpanzee throwing mug. Feedback generates an assembly corresponding with actual observation of the action. If similarity clusters corresponding with "I" were activated close to this time, overlap could generate pseudo-sensory input of self throwing the mug, along with an action recommendation to do it. Within a ball-playing supercluster this could be a strong recommendation. However, feedback of "I" taking the action generates an assembly which inputs to clusters constructed from social experience. Alternative action recommendations of 'put the mug down carefully' are generated along with 'inhibit throwing the mug' from clusters extracting inconsistencies. In addition, generation of pseudo-sensory representations of "me" experience during an action of this type could be fed back to generate the repetitions associated with attention on my internal experience associated with such an action, generating additional positive and negative action recommendations. In complex social situations, this process of extraction and feedback may continue through many cycles of attention, supplemented by action recommendations to 'become angry' etc., which change the type of action recommendations generated. Clusters recording a wide range of experience are searched, with additional repetitions imprinted, until an action recommendation is accepted and implemented.

There is no qualitative difference between direct sensory experience and reminiscence and stream of consciousness, all are constructed from the activation of widely shared repetitions. However, direct experience activates repetitions close to sensory input which are generally not activated in imagined images. Clusters indicating the absence of such repetitions could generate recommendations to behave accordingly, enabling a behavioral distinction between direct experience and reminiscent experience.

In dream sleep the interaction of assemblies to generate action recommendations, and thus create a permanent record, is non-normal, as demonstrated by the relative rarity of remembered dream compared with total dream. Dream sleep has the function of limiting the distribution of information between functional components at every level but making it available where it has the highest probability of being functionally relevant. At the device level this role consists of programming additional information combinations to be capable of imprinting the appropriate subsets to enable activations in response to new objects and experiences in subsequent wake periods. Actual imprinting is therefore turned off during this preparation period. A fast rerun of past repetition activations is used to identify combinations of information frequently activated at the same time, which become potential additional repetitions or distribution routes. The anomalous nature of the impressions created when imprinted (and therefore rememberable) sets of repetitions are created in dreaming is because the acceleration results in combinations of activated information which would not occur in regular waking experience, but recorded if mid-dream waking turns on imprinting.

The Functional Components of Consciousness

As discussed earlier, Metzinger (1996) has defined a set of components which need to be specified at both the psychological and physiological level in any integrated, systematic theory of the phenomenal content of consciousness. These include the smallest unit of phenomenal content; the smallest representable unit of content; object constitution, or binding; temporal relationships; spatial relationships; a hierarchy of relationships derived from spatial; self representation; first-person and other perspectives; and global modeling of reality which is not recognized as a model. In terms of the recommendation architecture model described in this paper, the smallest units of phenomenal content are the imprinted repetitions at the device level which can be activated by feedback of associative activations. The smallest representable units of content are sets of clusters which can generate recommendations to activate the population of repetitions which most often are present when the cluster set is activated. Object binding is indicated by a common modulation of firing rate shared across a population of activated device level repetitions. Any temporal or spatial relationship is a cluster or set of clusters with an associated type of behavioral recommendation. Self representation occurs when a set of clusters created by imprinting of information combinations occurring in past experience of self are activated, plus clusters cloned from experiences of other individuals. Activation of these clusters has the functional role of generating pseudo-sensory information as if a behavioral recommendation had been implemented, in order to search a more extensive range of individual specific memory for further behavioral recommendations. Global modeling of reality which is not recognized as a model corresponds with the hierarchy of clusters heuristically created in the course of experience which search for repetitions in current experience to generate behavioral recommendations. The hierarchies of clusters are an implicit model of reality, but activations within the "model" are driven by information derived from the current environment and directly generate recommendations for action on that environment. The "model" is not a parallel path which can be compared with reality and thus is not experienced as a model.

The functional theory as described is radically different from content focused models such as the global workplace theory proposed by Baars (1988), because Baars' model incorporates paradigms based upon the use of unambiguous information. In Baars' model the output from a wide range of specialized processors competes for access to a small global workspace, and the contents of that workspace are widely distributed throughout the brain. Only a limited number of specialist processors can broadcast global messages via the workspace because different messages may be contradictory. The contents of consciousness are the contents of the global workspace and become conscious by being broadcast. In the theory outlined here, there is no small "executive" workspace or working memory. The contents of consciousness are the currently active information repetitions wherever they are physically located in the alternative behavioral recommendation function (which includes a large proportion of the cortex). There is competition between different sets of information for access to the behavioral generation function, but the winner of this competition is not the content of consciousness, it drives the activation of more complex repetitions which are the contents. Because multiple parallel behavioral recommendations are generated in response to any winning information combination, and in general these parallel recommendations include recommendations to speak, it is possible to talk about the current configuration of activations. Some clusters are in a sense specialist processors which compete for access, but there are two major types. One type is primal sketch clusters which like Baars' processors are outside of consciousness. The other type is clusters corresponding with recommendations to activate information in the alternative behavioral generation function. These clusters are within the potential contents of consciousness. As an example on the psychological level, I can sometimes be aware of and speak about an inclination to activate an image before or at the same time as activating it.

Baars' model places emphasis on internal consistency as a key restriction in determining which combinations of specialized processors gain access, but does not address the mechanisms which would enable consistency to be achieved. In the model described here, consistency is imposed because the only repetitions which will be activated by the input information are ones which have frequently occurred together in the past, and feedback loops cause the system to converge on a self consistent set.

Baars' model does not address the issue of how qualia arise from the information processing in the brain. The explanation in the proposed model can be understood by considering how the experience of the color red develops. Repeated experiences of objects with the color red in different situations will result in heuristic definition of clusters. The heuristic process searches for information repetitions. The profile of light wavelengths reaching the retina will not repeat even for the same object because of differences in ambient light. Repetitions will occur if combinations of information from both ambient light and object light are included, and clusters will develop on this basis. The experience of red corresponds with these clusters being activated. There could of course be some genetically controlled bias in initial cluster connectivity which favors development of useful clusters, particularly in the sensory preprocessing clustering function, but because the clusters are created at least partially heuristically, they will incorporate information extracted from experiences which included the color red, and the activation of such information can lead to activation of other clusters activated in such experiences by the feedback process. Such activations can therefore in some cases become part of the experience of the color red.

Conclusions

There are only two possible qualitatively different types of simple functional architecture, the instruction architecture based on consistent use of instruction functional elements exchanging unambiguous information, and the recommendation architecture based on consistent use of repetition/action recommendation functional elements exchanging ambiguous information. Systems with the recommendation architecture can have the ability to heuristically define their own functionality. A theory has been described that biological brains have been constrained by selection pressures to adopt simple functional architectures of the recommendation type, and the hierarchy of functional separations which exists as a result can be the basis for understanding cognitive phenomena in terms of physiology. The existence of a simple recommendation based functional architecture means that the human experience of a constant succession of mental images, including self images, independent of sensory input can be understood at higher levels as the experience of a function which activates potentially relevant information recorded from an extensive range of individual experience for behavioral guidance in complex situations. Such a function can activate a wider range of information than the information activated directly by sensory input. The operation of this function can be traced through a hierarchy of functional separations at increasing levels of detail down to the operations of individual neurons. To be effective in understanding cognitive functions, functional modules must be components in a recommendation architecture. Physiological structures can be understood in terms of major functional separations, and patterns of neural activation such as sleep with dreaming understood in terms of the execution of recommendation architecture functions. The relationship between physical damage and defects and the resulting system deficits can be understood through the functional hierarchy. Philosophical theories can be evaluated for consistency with the underlying biological architecture. Electronic systems with phenomenology very similar to human psychology could be designed and built using the recommendation architecture paradigm.

Notes

[1]The repetition similarity conditions of clusters are defined by the accumulation at repetitions recorded on neurons. Because these cluster-level conditions are defined heuristically, the connectivity and neuron resources for a particular cluster must be assigned as required. Coward (1990) proposed that the hippocampus manages this assignment process in a manner which results in an implicit map of the time sequence in which repetitions were imprinted.

References

Baars, B .J. 1988. *A cognitive theory of consciousness.* Cambridge: Cambridge University Press.

―――. 1994. A neurobiological interpretation of global workspace theory. In *Consciousness in philosophy and cognitive neuroscience,* edited by A. Revonsuo and M. Kamppinen. New Jersey: Erlbaum.

―――. 1996. Understanding subjectivity: Global workspace theory and the resurrection of the observing self. *Journal of Consciousness Studies* 3: 3.

Bressler, S. L. 1994. Dynamic self-organization in the brain as observed by transient cortical coherence. In *Origins: Brain and self-organization,* edited by K. Pribram. Hillsdale, NJ: Erlbaum.

Carpenter, G. A., and Grossberg, S. 1988. The ART of adaptive pattern recognition by a self-organizing neural network. *IEEE Computer* 3:77-88

Cauller, L. 1995. Layer I of primary sensory neocortex: Where top-down converges with bottom-up. *Behavioural Brain Research* 71:163-170

―――. 1997a. NeuroInteractivism: Explaining emergence without representation. Manuscript submitted for publication.

―――. 1997b. Private communication.

Cotterill, R. 1995. On the unity of conscious experience. *Journal of Consciousness Studies* 2:290-311.

Coward, L. A. 1990. *Pattern thinking.* New York: Praeger.

―――. 1996. Understanding of consciousness through application of techniques for design of extremely complex electronic systems. (From *Towards a Science of Consciousness 1996 "Tucson II",* Tucson, Arizona.)

―――. 1997a. The pattern extraction hierarchy architecture: A connectionist alternative to the von Neumann architecture. In *Biological and artificial computation: From neuroscience to technology,* edited by J. Mira, R. Morenzo-Diaz, and J. Cabestanz. Berlin: Springer.

―――. 1997b. Unguided categorization, direct and symbolic representation, and evolution of cognition in a modified connectionist theory. In *Proceedings of the international conference New trends in cognitive science,* edited by A. Riegler, and M. Peschl. Vienna: Austrian Society of Cognitive Science.

―――. in press. A functional architecture approach to neural systems. *International Journal of Systems Research and Information Systems.*

De Felipe, J. 1997. Microcircuits in the brain. In *Biological and artificial computation: From neuroscience to technology,* edited by J. Mira., R. Morenzo-Diaz, and J. Cabestanz. Springer: Berlin.

Dennett, D. C. 1991. *Consciousness explained.* Boston: Little John.

Douglas, R. J., and Martin, K. A. 1991. A functional microcircuit for cat visual cortex. *Journal of Physiology* 440:735-769

Harlow, T. M. 1868. 'Recovery from passage of an iron bar through the head. *New England Medical Society* 2:327-46

Harnad, S. 1987. Category induction and representation. In *Categorical perception: The groundwork of cognition*, edited by S. Harnad. New York: Cambridge University Press.

Hebb, D. C. 1949. *The organization of behaviour*. New York: Wiley

Jaynes, J. 1976. *The origin of consciousness in the breakdown of the bicameral mind*. Boston: Harvard.

Johnson, D. M. 1987. The Greek origins of belief. *American Philosophical Quarterly* 24:319-27.

Llinas, R., Ribary, U., Joliot, M., and Wang, X.-J. 1994. Content and context in temporal thalamocortical binding. In *Temporal coding in the brain*, edited by G. Buzsaki, et al. Berlin: Springer.

Lorenz, K. 1977. *Behind the mirror*. New York: Methuen.

Marr, D. 1982. *Vision*. New York: W.H. Freeman.

Metzinger, T. 1996. Towards the neural and functional correlates of phenomenal content. *ASSC Electronic Seminar.*

Mira, J., Herrero, J. C., and Delgado A. E. 1997. A generic formulation of neural nets as a model of parallel and self programming computation. In *Biological and artificial computation: From neuroscience to technology*, edited by J. Mira, R. Morenzo-Diaz, and J. Cabestanz. Springer: Berlin.

Pfeifer. R. 1996. Symbols, patterns and behavior: Beyond the information processing metaphor. *Encyclopedia of Microcomputers* 17, 253-75, New York: Marcel Dekker.

Ritter, H. 1995. Self-organizing feature maps: Kohonen maps. In *The handbook of brain theory and neural networks*, edited by M. Arbib. Boston: MIT Press

Rosenblatt, F. 1961. *Principles of neurodynamics: Perceptrons and the theory of brain mechanisms*. Washington D.C.: Spartan

Rumelhart, D. E., Hinton, G. E., and Williams, R. J. 1986. Learning internal representations by error propagation. In *Parallel distributed processing: Explorations in the microstructure of cognition: Volume 1*, edited by D. E. Rumelhart, and McClelland, J. L. Cambridge, MA: The MIT Press.

Tanaka, K. 1993. Neuronal mechanisms of object recognition. *Science* 262:685-88.

Taylor, J. G., and Alavi, F. N. 1993. Mathematical analysis of a competitive network for attention. In *Mathematical approaches to neural networks*, edited by J. Taylor. North Holland: Elsevier.

Chapter 7

Common Unconscious Dynamics Underlie Uncommon Conscious Effects: A Case Study in the Iterative Nature of Perception and Creation

Cees van Leeuwen
Ilse Verstijnen
Paul Hekkert

When perceiving a work of abstract, visual art, we experience balance, order, complexity, and (in)congruity. These phenomenal qualities are the effects of structural properties that, according to the Gestalt tradition in perception, "pop up" spontaneously in a perceiver's awareness. Data from the field of experimental aesthetics indicate that while these properties constitute necessary conditions of aesthetic appreciation (Hekkert, 1995), they are not sufficient. Only when they occur in a manner or context that is, in some sense "striking", or "surprising", will we find aesthetic appraisal for the work. It seems to be the case therefore, that a novel, unanticipated synthesis of perceptual structure is involved in this uncommon conscious effect.

Consequently, one might ask, what kind of skill does an artist have who is able to synthesize what is perceived spontaneously, in a manner that cannot be anticipated? By putting the question this way, the creative process is depicted as a supreme kind of seeing. The making of art is subject to the myth of the spontaneous, immediate inception of structure, superb and seen by no one else before.

Creative individuals involved in abstract art-making have nourished this myth themselves, as did, for instance, Picasso, with his well-known dictum: "I don't search, I find." The myth conveys the belief that the right image falls to mind in a moment of divine inspiration. In an attempt to characterize such beliefs, Margaret Boden (1990) distinguished between inspirational beliefs, reflecting a Platonian notion of insight as the discovery of an aeternal ideal (see also Rothenberg & Hausman, 1976), and romantic beliefs, stressing the uniqueness of artistic and scientific talents.

We would like to substitute the more realistic belief that the creative process of even the most gifted artist is often painstaking and far from instantaneous and, in this respect, far from unique. Creative processes, both of designers and innovative scientists, evolve slowly (Ippolito & Tweeny, 1995). It may therefore be considered useful to choose a notion of artistic production in which its temporal characteristics are emphasized. Such a characterization may provide a faithful description of art making as often involving an iterative process of imagining, sketching, and evaluating the aesthetic quality of the sketch in perception. Since the artist herself continuously monitors the evolution of her products, the creative process draws heavily on the same resources that are involved in the aesthetic apprehension of a completed work of art.

Understanding the dynamics of aesthetic production will therefore require a view of aesthetic perception. Even though the conditions for aesthetic appreciation of abstract art are relatively well-known, knowledge of such conditions alone is not sufficient for an understanding of aesthetic awareness in a dynamic theory of art creation. In particular, the Gestalt notion of spontaneous inception of structure is too static. Contrary to what Gestalt psychology assumed, the perception of structural properties does not always occur spontaneously. Sometimes it takes effort (Rock & Mack, 1994). Thus, the properties that give rise to aesthetic experience will not be objective, time-invariant qualities of the work of art itself. Instead, they will have to be understood as situated in the conscious and unconscious interactions between the perceiver and the work of art, in which structures evolve as a function of time. In short, the reliance of aesthetic creation upon aesthetic perception requires a theory of the perceptual micro-dynamics that produce aesthetic sensation. Such a dynamic theory of perception will allow us to entertain the notion that perception and creation in visual art share common dynamical characteristics that (1) are a function of time, yet function at different time-scales, and (2) are largely unconscious. These "common unconscious" dynamics stand in contrast to the "uncommon conscious" effects they produce, the latter term referring to the artist's struggle to produce figures that suggest a maximum of hidden structure (i.e., *surplus* structure), and the observer's aesthetic experience of finding such surplus structures. Given these distinctions, the present paper will propose a theory of perception and creation which claims, essentially, that the dynamic struggle for structure occurring during perception, recapitulates itself in the dynamic interactions between imagery and sketching that occur during the act of creation. Such a theory of perception and creation will serve to integrate the fields of perceptual processing and aesthetic apperception, while simultaneously shedding light on why it is the creative process often involves an interactive relationship between imagining, sketching, and evaluating the result of the sketch (Anderson & Helstrup, 1993a, 1993b; Verstijnen, van Leeuwen, Goldschmidt, Hamel, & Hennessey, 1998a Verstijnen, van Leeuwen, Hamel, & Hennessey, submitted). Such a clarification is important, for composers are frequently said to hear the music "in their inner ear" before writing it down without the need of correction. Such accounts lead one to the assumption that an artist should be able to perform the creative process in imagery until the created product reaches a definitive stage, at which point it can be produced in one final, sublime solution—the artist should find, not seek! Though this may be the case in some forms of creation, the presently-proposed account will make it clear that the quest to produce aesthetic apperception in visual art, via the generation of surplus structure, *necessitates* an iterative relationship between imagining, externalization (i.e., sketching), and perceiving.

Surplus Structure

A work of abstract art usually will not invoke aesthetic experience immediately. Aesthetic experience will occur after prolonged viewing, which allows the work to reveal its hidden regularities, or *surplus struc-*

ture. Such structure is perhaps best described as a tension between the pattern's component structure (local structure) and the integral, relational aspects of the pattern (global structure). The task of the artist may therefore be described as the production of a pattern in which local and global structure coexist. To achieve this result, the artist may, for example, combine powerful overall regularities with interesting hidden detail (noticeable also in figurative art, see for example Jeroen Bosch; Bouleau, 1963). Or, he may present an unexpected solution in the way in which components are joined into a global whole (as in Maurits Escher's work, in which locally correct stairs are joined into a globally impossible staircase). In what follows, we will examine (1) the role of surplus structure in aesthetic appraisal, (2) the perceptual dynamics that underlie the aesthetic response to surplus structure, (3) the interactions among imagery, analysis, and synthesis that take place during the creation of surplus structure, and (4) the contribution of sketching to this creative process.

Studies of Aesthetic Appraisal

The artist produces his work, among other reasons, to elicit aesthetic appraisal. Predominantly in abstract art, aesthetic appraisal of a painting or drawing will be elicited by its structural or organizational properties. Hekkert and van Wieringen (1990), for instance, demonstrated that beauty ratings of non-categorizable (i.e., abstract), cubist paintings were significantly related to complexity scores, whereas ratings of figurative paintings were not. In accordance with a prediction derived from Berlyne's (1971) psychobiological theory of aesthetics, the relationship between beauty and complexity was of an inverted U-shape. This indicates that increased complexity raises the beauty rating, until an optimum level is reached, with increased complexity beyond this level leading to a decrease of aesthetic preference.

Berlyne's theory of aesthetic appraisal (1966, 1971) is founded on the assumption that humans seek out stimulation and information to either gratify their curiosity (specific exploration) or to simply overcome boredom (diversive exploration). Visual patterns, such as works of art, can satisfy this need in that they afford a certain amount of novelty, complexity, or ambiguity. These 'collative' properties contribute to the arousal potential of a pattern (i.e., the amount of attention or excitement that a pattern can produce). Berlyne's theory initiated a considerable amount of research on the relationship between preference and arousal potential, the latter variable often being operationalized in terms of one of the collative variables (i.e., complexity). Beauty or preference is hypothesized as being related to arousal potential in an inverted U-shaped manner. However, in addition to evidence supporting the predicted inverted U-shaped function (see Berlyne, 1971, pp. 181-213 for a review), a number of other studies reported U-shaped, monotonic, and bimodal relationships among these variables (see Boselie & Leeuwenberg, 1985, for a review of these studies).

Berlyne's model can be conceived of as a version of the famous 'unity in variety' principle (Walker, 1980). This principle holds that the greatest pleasure or beauty is arrived at by utilizing as much variety, novelty, or complexity (arousal inducing variables) as possible, counteracted with a maximum of unity, lawfulness, or order (arousal reducing variables). Various previous attempts to mathematically express beauty (M) by some function of order (O) and complexity (C), such as $M = O/C$ (Birkhoff, 1933) or $M = O * C$ (Eysenck, 1942), however, had failed to predict the rated beauty for polygons (e.g., McWhinnie, 1968). Following on these attempts, Boselie and Leeuwenberg (1985) also adopt the unity-in-variety principle, but relate it to another of Berlyne's collative variables (i.e., ambiguity).

Like complexity, ambiguity is often held to be responsible for exploratory behavior (Berlyne, 1971). Ambiguous patterns induce a response conflict and thereby invite the perceiver to prolonged, active viewing to resolve the conflict. Nicki, Lee, and Moss (1981), for instance, showed that viewing behavior increased with the ambiguity of cubist paintings. Ambiguity in works of art can therefore be regarded as a powerful means by which to ensure that a perceiver actively explores a work of art. There are however various ways in which a pattern can be made ambiguous and not all of these types will be conducive to preference or beauty. When a pattern has several alternative meanings, disjunctive ambiguity concerns the case where the meanings are mutually exclusive (Attneave, 1971; Kaplan & Kris, 1948). Disjunctive ambiguity can be described as the existence of two mutually exclusive global structures, between which perception alternates. This type of ambiguity is for instance observed in the Necker cube depicted in figure 1. The two rivalling interpretations are globally consistent orientations of a 3D cube. That disjunctive ambiguity is caused by switching between alternative global structures, is suggested by Attneave (1971), who showed that groups of Necker cubes do not reverse independently of each other, but do so simultaneously. At each moment any one of these interpretations will dominate, leading to a stable, but uninteresting percept. Disjunctive ambiguity is therefore often regarded as detrimental to the beauty of a pattern (e.g., Boselie, 1983; Hochberg, 1978).

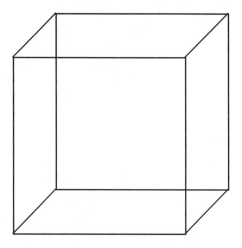

Fig. 1. Disjunctive ambiguity: Necker Cube with two rivalling global interpretations, referring to alternative views from below and from above, which are mutually exclusive.

The focus of Boselie and Leeuwenberg's (1985) model was, however, on conjunctive ambiguity. This type of ambiguity is arrived at when separate meanings are jointly effective for the interpretation of a pattern, as is exemplified in figure 2. Conjunctive ambiguity must be understood as the co-existence of a local and a global structure in the percept. If the local organization is predominant perceptually, the global organization is sensed as providing additional consistency to the figure. If the global organization predominantes, the local structure will add richness in detail. Whichever of the two interpretations is predominant, that one yields additional regularities that can be perceived without weakening the other (Boselie & Leeuwenberg, 1985). This hidden order or 'surplus structure' contributes to the aesthetic appeal of the pattern, and conjunctive ambiguity is therefore regarded as conducive to aesthetic preference (e.g., Arnheim, 1974; Berlyne, 1971; Gombrich, 1959).

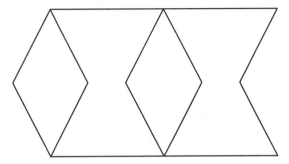

Fig. 2. Conjunctive ambiguity. The figure can be perceived in different ways, of which the most likely to be perceived initially is the mosaic of hour-glasses and diamonds. Only later a 3-D orientation will be seen in the figure (2 cubes, viewed from above). Hence, the 3D organization is a global surplus structure of the local mosaic.

In addition to conjunctive ambiguity, time itself seems to play a critical role in aesthetic appraisal. To be sure, there are those who have modeled aesthetic appraisal without making reference to the contribution of time. Boselie and Leeuwenberg (1985) for example, based on a coding theory of perceptual structure, adopted a description of order, complexity and surplus structure, which completely ignored the contribution of time. It might be the case however, that they were able to ignore the contribution of time because they restricted themselves to simple polygonal figures in which all structure is almost instantaneously transparent. Real works of art, on the other hand, will often hide a greater number of additional regularities, and whether an observer actually perceives the surplus structure will depend upon aesthetic insight. Perceptual repetition (i.e., prolonged active inspection and exploration) prepares this insight. Thus, a considerable amount of active viewing may be necessary before the surplus structure of a piece of art emerges. The inception of an aesthetic insight could be equated to the perceptual reorganization that appears to occur under prolonged, active inspection of a visual structure.

The time course by which surplus structure becomes conscious may therefore be relevant to aesthetic appraisal. For this reason, a theory of perceiving art should take into account the dynamics of perceptual reorganizations that occur during prolonged active viewing. The following conjecture on the dynamics of art appreciation could be proposed: a work of art must, on a first inspection, reveal a structure that invites prolonged, active viewing. This could be achieved if the structure initially perceived has conjunctive ambiguity. The conjunctive ambiguity leads to aesthetic appraisal when, as a consequence of prolonged active inspection, the surplus structure is detected. Then, the aesthetic appreciation provides an intrinsic reward for the effort invested. Berlyne's principle of 'arousal jag' (Berlyne, 1971) refers to a situation in which a temporary rise in arousal—viewing effort—is pursued for the sake of the pleasurable relief that follows.

Surplus structure, in the presently proposed view, is not a static stimulus characteristic but is understood in relation to perceptual reorganization. This notion does not provide a recipe for how to provoke the perceptual reorganizations that lead to aesthetic appraisal. It could safely be assumed, however, that the artist has intuitive knowledge of these processes, way beyond the best characterization any present theory could provide. Introspective reports by artists are, however, notoriously uninformative regarding the nature of such knowledge and on how it is applied. This is what the Dutch painter K. Appel had to say on this subject: "I just mess around." This makes it likely that the artist relies on what he sees and on the processes of creative imagery, rather than on goal-directed metacognitive rules. The knowledge applied is therefore unlikely to show up in think-aloud protocols (Ericsson & Simon, 1980). Rather than using stored declarative knowledge, the artist will exploit the capacity of the perceptual and imagery systems to reorganize. A study of the processes involved in making abstract art, will therefore have to consider the dynamics of perception and imagery.

The Perception of Structure

To create conjunctive ambiguity, an artist must create a pattern in which independent local and global structures coexist. How are these structures to be described? The notions of local and global as used here in the domain of perceptual structure, differ from those often used in the information processing literature (e.g., Navon, 1977). The notions found in the information processing literature refer to the relative size aspects of local and global. These, however, are insufficient for understanding how parts and wholes of a visual object are perceived (Pomerantz, 1983). For this reason, *functional* notions of local and global are required (see van Leeuwen, 1998). These notions allow for the distinct functional roles of wholes in a visual object and their component parts; wholes being determined primarily by global, and parts by local, structure.

The Gestalt Approach. The Gestalt psychologists were the first to deal with this problem. The Gestalt principles of organization, such as the laws of proximity, similarity, good continuation and closure (see figure 3) describe the spontaneous, direct experience of structure. These descriptive notions were explained by the theoretical principle of Prägnanz. This principle was radically holistic; Prägnanz is a property of a global visual field. In other words, such a principle may be useful to describe global structure, but will have difficulty in explaining the nature of local structure. Holistic concepts are notoriously hard to define. In the heydays of Gestalt psychology, electrostatic field theory was the only approach available. It was easy to disprove a role for electrostatic brain fields in visual field organization, and this discredited the whole approach.

Too holistic an account of perception ultimately implies that immediate context prescribes what we see in a situation. This isn't always the case; even within a single object, perceivers may selectively attend a component and neglect its relations with other parts of the figure (Peterson & Hochberg, 1983). The notion that components of a local or global structure can be attended separately, runs against the radical holism of the Berlin school of Gestalt psychology. At least one branch of Gestalt psychology, called the Graz school (Von Ehrenfels, Meinong, Benussi, Metelli, Kanizsa), never committed itself to the radical holism of the Berlin School (e.g., Kanizsa, 1994; von Ehrenfels, 1890). If the time has come to rehabilitate Gestalt psychology (Epstein, 1988), Graz school notions will have to be among the first to be considered as allowing for strategic influences on perceptual organization phenomena.

The presently proposed account of local and global structure (see figure 4) therefore, dates back to the original notion of Gestalt qualities (von Ehrenfels, 1890). In this approach, wholes and component parts are perceptual qualities for which underlying structural properties are required. The global structures required for perception of a whole have a primary status in perception, independent of local component parts.

And vice versa, the local structures are independent of the global structures that constitute the whole. For the global structure, the component parts of a whole are subject to strong coherence constraints from the whole. But from the local structure, the components appear independently of the whole. Local structures differ from global ones, in that the whole imposes weak coherence constraints upon the component parts. The absence of these constraints in the local structure facilitates piecemeal perception (Peterson & Hochberg, 1983). Perceivers, therefore, will experience wholes when global structure predominantes and piecemeal perception when local structure does so.

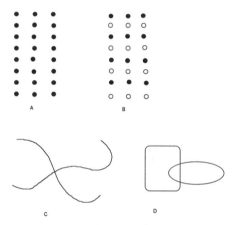

Fig 3. Illustrations of Gestalt principles of organization. Proximity (A), Similarity (B), Good continuation (C), and Closure (D).

Given that attention to components results in an overall *piecemeal* mode of perception, which is characterized by a loose integration of parts having lots of room for inconsistency between them, Kanizsa (1970) demonstrated that perception is often more local than Gestalt psychologists, at least those of the Berlin school (Koffka, Köhler, Wertheimer), would have expected. In figure 5 (adapted from Kanizsa, 1970), the global structure is a checkerboard, of which one square is colored black. This regularity is not experienced perceptually. Instead the local structure, a black cross in a checkerboard, is seen.

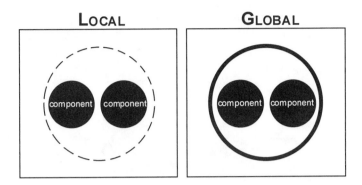

Fig. 4. The notions local and global according to von Ehrenfels. In a local structure the components are separately perceived or show a loose binding, whereas in a global structure the components are integrated.

Fig. 5. Kanizsa figure: a cross instead of a square occludes the checkerboard.

The strategic, attentional character of local versus global perception can be experienced even in figure 5, which Kanizsa had designed to show the contrary. By attending the diagonals, the global structure in figure 5 is reinforced and can in fact become dominant. Spatially and functionally, local and global coincide in this example because atten- tion is given to regions which are segmented on the basis of *spatial* proximity (Compton & Logan, 1993; Van Oeffelen & Vos, 1982). If another criterion for functional organization is used, for instance trans- parency or symmetry as in figure 6B, spatially and functionally, local and global are dissociated. For instance, figure 6A is spatially more glo- bal than 6B, but functionally more local. For the discussion of structure in art, as well as in general for issues regarding the perception of structure, the functional notion of local and global is considered of more importance than spatial characteristics, even though spatial scale itself can sometimes be a constitutive aspect of a work of art (e.g., Cleas Oldenburg).

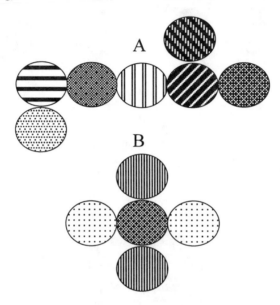

Fig 6. The upper configuration (A) is spatially more global than the lower one, because the upper one is larger. The lower configuration (B) is functionally more global than the upper one, because the regularity of the whole binds the components strongly to their functional role in the configuration.

Instantiating Global-Local Perceptual Dynamics. The functional notions of local and global belong to a broader processing distinction, which also includes processing strategies and styles. These are usually distinguished in terms of analytic versus holistic processes. Analytic strategies and styles imply the perception of separable components, intraconceptual relationships or serial structure. More in general, we find on the analytic side, sharpening of categories, verbal coding, high conceptual differentiation, and serial processing. Holistic processing implies the perception of global Gestalt structure, integral dimensions, family resemblance, interconceptual relationships (Drews, 1987), and more generally, leveling of categories, visual codes, low conceptual differentiation, loose analogies, and intuitive judgement (Miller, 1987). The construct validity of the analytic-holistic distinction is widely acknowledged (Beyler & Schmeck, 1992; Koller, Rost, & Koller, 1994). Beyler and Schmeck (1992), for example, compared several potential measures of the analytic-holistic construct compiled from surveys and questionnaires. Studies show a convergence of these measures, and a divergence of others.

Underlying these functional distinctions, a distributed neural representation system is often assumed. In such a system, representational structures are formed by dynamic binding of activated units (Von der Malsburg & Schneider, 1986). Under such generic constraints, perceptual structure is likely to grow from loose, independent components, to a coordinated, global activation pattern. The autonomous dynamics of perception are therefore likely to be local-to-global in nature (Sekuler & Palmer, 1992). Most authors today consider a general principle for such dynamics impossible. Because of computational complexity considerations (Tsotsos, 1993), most rely on domain-specific, specialized mechanisms, such as those proposed for shape-from-shading (e.g., Ramachandran, 1990), symmetry (Wagemans, 1995), color, etc. This approach reflects a constructivist approach to perceptual processing (e.g., Gregory, 1981; Hochberg, 1978). According to this approach, perceptual structure is synthesized from elementary sensations. Perception, in this view, is predominantly involved in the creation and maintenance of global perceptual structure. This does not imply that global perceptual structures are always predominant in perception (Peterson & Hochberg, 1983). Global perceptual structures require the involvement of memory schemes (Hochberg, 1978). These schemes are not specific to certain combinations of sensory features. Rather they are to be regarded as abstract classificatory mechanisms. In other words, the perceptual schemes of constructivism are global and abstract, and contrast with the specific and local sensory patterns.

There are reasons to assume that the identification of local and global with sensory stimulation and schematized classification, respectively, is not useful for the study of abstract art. By its very definition, abstract art defies object classification and for this reason, it appears better to associate the notion of global structure with dynamic self-organization, rather than with stored schemes.

There are other, more important reasons why a dynamic approach appears able to deal with the perception of structure in art better than a constructivist account. According to a constructivist view, all formation of structure would be a process of synthesis. In synthetic processes, either components are joined to form a global whole, or the whole is retrieved as a scheme from memory. During this process, there is no reconsideration of the components. Once a stable global structure is formed by a constructive synthesis, perception is complete, and component structure is not altered.

Yet, perception does not appear to be as stable as constructivist accounts presume. If perceptual activity is prolonged after a global structure has been found, a phenomenon may occur, which resembles what occurs when an ambiguous figure is presented. After a certain time, the percept reverses spontaneously. It seems to be the case therefore, that perception does not exclusively involve synthesis processes, but also involves processes that lead to the destruction of a given structure and the subsequent transformation of its components, which may lead to the distinction of novel components. These processes have been called *analysis* (Verstijnen, 1997) or *restructuring* (Verstijnen et al., 1998a). Synthesis alone, therefore, does not provide a sufficient account of the formation of global structure in perception. Rather, the formation process entails both holistic and analytic processes. The combination of these processes provides perception with intrinsic instability.

According to this approach, what is perhaps best known as *Hologenesis* (van Leeuwen, 1998; van Leeuwen & Bakker, 1995), the intrinsic instability of perception has functional significance. Too much stability would make perceptual systems inflexible (i.e., unlikely to perceive new structure spontaneously; Grossberg & Mingolla, 1985). Too little stability would make it impossible for the perceptual system to detect structure in a dynamically evolving environment. In dynamic systems, such as neural network models of perception, it is possible to implement a subtle interplay between those forces which approach and those which diverge from stable perceptual patterns (cf. Skarda & Freeman, 1987). Due to these opposing forces, even a simple line drawing can only lead to an apparently stable image for a certain, restricted time (Kelso, 1995; van Leeuwen, Steyvers, & Nooter, 1997). The global structure seems to dissolve, giving rise to an alternative organization, which sometimes leads to the discovery of new and unanticipated global structure. Perception, therefore, is best characterized as an ongoing process that is driven by the opposing tendencies to create global structure and to destroy it via analysis.

Findings in the field of aesthetics are in overall agreement with the notion that perceptual attractiveness entails an interaction among two opposing forces or tensions (e.g., Apter, 1984; Arnheim, 1974; Berlyne, 1970, 1971; Kreitler & Kreitler, 1972; Martindale, 1981). One of these forces is equated to relaxation, the search for a stable image in perception. This tendency emphasizes familiarity, stability, and reduction of complexity. The other tendency is a tension-heightening striving for novelty or complexity which precludes habituation and enables the processing of incongruous or novel stimuli (Hekkert, 1995). The notion of dynamic interactions among these two tendencies is, of course, consistent with the interaction between synthesis and analysis proposed in the hologenic theory of perception. Such an account allows for a unique description of the interaction between perception, imagery, and sketching in the generation of surplus structure. Specifically, if imagery produces global structure, the purpose of the sketch is to create local structure. Sketching in abstract art may therefore have the role of creating local from global structure, as is required for the perception of surplus structure.

Imagery, Analysis, and Synthesis

The manipulations involved in the creative process could be understood as a sequence of transformations on a mental image (Finke, 1990, 1993). In principle, it is observed, creative inventions can be made in imagery and require no externalization at all. Nevertheless, we shall argue, the making of sketches and their evaluation by the artist are an essential part of the pursuit of surplus structure because certain of the processes available in perception, are not available in imagery.

Imagery and synthesis. Synthetic processes, in which components maintain their structure, are easy in imagery. Some of the synthetic processes could be called creative, in the sense that a figural combination results in a new, unanticipated *configuration*. Finke and his colleagues (Finke, 1990; Finke & Slayton, 1988) asked subjects to synthesize elements into a recognizable object before their inner eye. For example, a letter "J" and a letter "D" can form an umbrella. Finke showed that subjects were not only able to create familiar objects but were also able to discover new, unanticipated, creative ones. A newly synthesized object, however, respects the local structure of its original components; the "J" and the "D" are preserved as components in the newly established configuration.

A synthesis in which the parts are joined could easily be imagined in the reversed order; removing the "D" from the umbrella leaves the "J". This process maintains the original components and does not lead to novel ones. The notion of *creative synthesis* is therefore exclusively used to refer to processes in which initially separate objects are joined to form a new configuration.

Imagery and analysis. Certain transformations on mental object representations are particularly difficult in imagery. These are the *analytic* (Verstijnen, 1997; Verstijnen et al., 1998a) or *restructuring* processes referred to in the hologenic theory of perception, and their name is meant to indicate that such transformations involve the properties of underlying structure (Verstijnen, van Leeuwen, Hamel, Goldschmidt, & Hennessey, 1998b). For example, despite the claims of celebrated inventors, and Finke's claims notwithstanding, Chambers and Reisberg (1985) showed that subjects were unable to reverse an ambiguous figure (e.g., duck/rabbit) and detect the alternative interpretation during imagery. Subsequent investigations (Hyman & Neisser, 1991; Peterson, Kihlstrom, Rose & Glisky, 1992) with a similar paradigm also observed that discovery performance remained strikingly low during imagery. These results suggest that there are certain forms of discovery that cannot easily be performed in imagery.

Reed and Johnsen (1975) have shown that imagery is constrained in reinterpreting images, as compared with visual perception. These authors used a component detection task. Whereas discovery of parts coinciding with the global structures of the pattern was performed in imagery and perception equally well, performance in imagery was worse if the part did not belong to the global structure of the pattern.

The opposing conclusions of Finke (1993) versus Chambers and Reisberg (1985), and Reed and Johnsen (1975) could be reconciled on the assumption that two types of discovery exist, which are of different breed. Verstijnen et al. (1998b) argued that, whereas Finke's figural combination task predominantly involves synthesis, and leaves component structure intact, the tasks used in both Chambers and Reisberg (1985) and Reed and Johnsen (1975) involve the identification of novel components. Subjects are required to restructure their image in a way which involves new, unanticipated components. This is, of course, the process of analysis (Verstijnen, 1997).

Finke's figural combination task does not require analysis (i.e., the initial structure of the elements stays intact when the synthesis is made). In the umbrella example this means that the component structure of each letter "J" and "D" is not violated. Finke's experiments, therefore, are in accordance with the suggestion that whereas synthesis is easy in imagery, analysis is difficult.

Since perception and imagery share resources (Kosslyn, 1980), one might assume that the processes involved in the former should also reside in the latter. But the ease and difficulty with which synthesis and analysis are accomplished in imagery, respectively, indicates that the processes of imagery constitute a subset of the perceptual processes (Verstijnen et al., 1998a, 1998b). The processes that are part of perception, but not of imagery, are the analytic processes (Verstijnen, 1997). They involve the modification of existing component structures and the creation of new ones. An example of this process can be seen in figure 7. Putting two components of a mosaic together in a manner that preserves their separate structures is an example of synthesis. Processes that do not preserve the separate figures and result in their breakdown, constitute an example of analysis, and such analysis is difficult in imagery (Verstijnen et al., submitted), because it requires the production of unanticipated components.

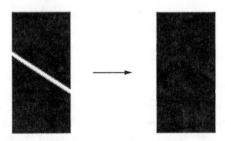

Fig. 7. If two components of a mosaic are joined, this is regarded as a synthetic transformation which is easily performed in imagery. If, however, the components are transformed, or completely disappear in the structure, this is considered an analytic transformation, which is difficult in imagery.

In the case of figure 7, it could be disputed whether the bringing together of the components (synthesis), or the transformation in shading which leads to the dissolving elements (analysis), is the decisively creative step. Probably, both are needed to be creative. There are clear cases, however, in which the analysis constitutes the creative process. This is the case when analysis is involved in the detection of novel components. Novel components are obtained if the component structure of an image is transformed. For instance, in figure 8, two hourglasses will, on analysis, be shown to consist of two overlapping parallelograms. This process is called novel decomposition. Like the earlier-discussed form of analysis, novel decomposition is expected to be difficult in imagery, because it involves transformation of the components.

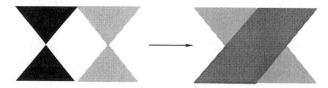

Fig. 8. Novel decomposition as a form of analytic transformation which is hard to perform in imagery. The leftmost figure, initially synthesized from two hourglasses, requires a novel decomposition in order to be seen as two overlapping parallelograms.

Sketching

The fact that synthesis in mental imagery can be useful as a source for creative discovery raises the question of why artists sketch. If imagery is such a powerful tool for creative discovery, why do artists and other creative people have to externalize their images, and what contributions do these sketches make to invention? According to the theory of hologenesis, it is assumed that perceptual processes have the tendency to continuously revolt against established structure and reassemble components in different ways, thereby spontaneously producing different forms of local and global structure (van Leeuwen et al., 1997). This hologenic process may provide a key to understanding the need for sketches in creative art, in that creative processes involve synthesis as well as analysis. Perceptual processes meet no obvious difficulties in switching between alternative structural interpretations, thus perceptual processing seems to have a larger proportion of analytic processing.

This may be related to the fact that images are stored in memory as global wholes (Hardcastle, 1995). During a sketch, the analytic visual qualities of the figure can be restored from the global representation. If, for instance, the Kanizsa figure (figure 5) is sketched from memory, the sketcher will begin drawing the checkerboard from the global structure and color one square black. Despite this fact, once it is sketched, the local structure of the Kanizsa figure could be perceived. The sketch adds surplus structure to the image: if the image has retained only the global structure, sketching restores the local structure. Sketching is a form of interactive imagery (Goldschmidt, 1991), which allows one to combine the synthetic abilities of imagery with the analytic abilities of perception. In general, this may be the reason why creative processes are facilitated by externalization.

This hypothesis was put to the test in two series of experiments. The first series used a Reed-like component detection task (Verstijnen et al., submitted), the second series used Finke's figural combination task (Verstijnen et al., 1998b). In both series expert sketchers were used as subjects. The results of these experiments could be summarized in a diagram (figure 9). It may be concluded that synthetic processing is easy and frequent in imagery and cannot be enhanced by sketching. Analytic processing, by contrast, is difficult in imagery and benefits from sketching.

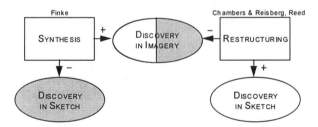

Fig. 9. Model showing the possible transformations that can lead to production of creative structure and the possibility of performing these in imagery. Analysis is difficult to perform in imagery. These processes are performed better with the aid of externalization, such as sketching. The shaded areas are those for which imagery is easy and frequent and can be obtained without benefit from sketching.

Results of these experiments and the studies of aesthetic appraisal and visual perception, converge on a description of the role played by sketching in the making of art. From the field of aesthetic appraisal it was concluded that a sequence of sketches should reveal the aim of the artist to create surplus structure by means of conjunctive ambiguity. This ambiguity implies that multiple structural interpretations have to be created. Both synthesis and analysis are likely to be involved in the creation of these structures.

Imagery can perform synthesis, and therefore does not require support of sketching. But the creation of local structure requires sketching and perceiving the result of the sketch as an interactive activity. Perception and imagery have complementary roles in this process. The end-results of synthetic processing in imagery will be reflected already in the first sketch made. Subsequent sketches will reflect the analytic changes in component structure that give rise to surplus structure.

The Time Course of Surplus-Structure Creation

Creation of surplus structure is a long-term process, when compared to perceiving surplus structure. Therefore, not only microdevelopment of structure will occur in the making of art, but also development over a larger time scale may take place. Goldstone and Medin (1994) and van Leeuwen, Buffart, and van der Vegt (1988) described the evolution of perceptual structures and categories as a result of practice. Practice in imagery-alone conditions was studied by Bethel-Fox and Shepard (1988) and by Heil, Roesler, Link, and Bajric (1998). All these studies deal with the development of perception and imagery during episodes roughly identical to those in which works of art are created. These processes showed a development from an early preference for local structure, to a later preference for global structure. A similar development is expected for sketching. That is, the earlier sketches will have more local structure and the later ones, more global structure as a result of the accumulation of synthesis of global structure in creative imagery. In the course of sketching, imagery produces increasingly global structure. For this reason, the analytic transformations used in the early sketches will differ from those used in the later ones. As a result, different forms of surplus structure will be observed in subsequent sketches. In what follows, we will first focus on these different forms of surplus structure and how they can be produced in sketching. We will then examine these dynamics at work in a series of sketches created by P. Kleijne

Various Forms of Surplus Structure

The first sketches will reflect the result of a primitive synthesis. The formation of a mosaic out of loose components (see figure 10) could be understood as such a primitive synthesis. That mosaic interpretations are the result of a primitive synthesis is suggested from perception studies. Sekuler and Palmer (1992) presented occluding figures (figure 11A) for short durations (50-400 ms) before interrupting viewing by presenting the next figure. The occluding figures were perceived as a mosaic (figure 11B) for the shorter durations (below 200 ms) and as an occlusion (figure 11C) for longer ones. The earlier mosaic interpretations are more local than the later occlusions, which are often completed according to their global structure. The early occurrence of mosaics in imagery synthesis could therefore parallel the early occurrence of mosaics in the microevolution of a percept.

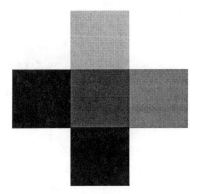

Fig. 10. A synthetic process of combining figures in a mosaic leads to the formation of a new configuration

During this process, individual features change: what were corners of a shape in the initial mosaic in figure 11A lost this function on emergence of the occlusion interpretation of figure 11B. The creation of an occlusion interpretation from a mosaic can, therefore, not be understood entirely from synthesis, but requires analytic processing as well. Analysis is less likely to occur in imagery, and will require externalization. The transition will therefore be observed in a sequence of sketches. In producing these sketches, the artist will attempt to create surplus structure, equilibrium between alternative local and global structures. In this stage of the creative process, this will involve the local mosaic and the global occlusion. For that reason, the first type of surplus-structure will involve a mosaic-occlusion ambiguity (type-1 surplus structure).

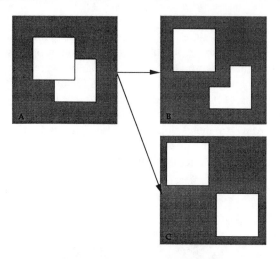

Fig. 11. The figure synthesized in A has surplus structure of type 1: besides the mosaic interpretation depicted in B, the occlusion interpretation depicted in C is possible.

As an illustration of how type-1 surplus structure could be realized in an occlusion interpretation, consider figure 12. Once an occlusion interpretation has been recognized, it can be further strengthened, for instance by another analytic transformation, which makes the elements of the occlusion more consistent.

The second form of surplus structure will arise after an occlusion interpretation has already been formed, and is thus expected to emerge later than type-1 surplus structure. Van Lier, van der Helm, and Leeu-wenberg (1995) studied occlusion interpretations. They investigated the controversy whether completions are made according to local or global perceptual structure. Whereas on the one hand Kanizsa and Gerbino (1982) suggest that perceptual completions be performed locally (i.e., they are performed on the basis of the principle of good continuations), Buffart, Leeuwenberg, and Restle (1981) have argued that the global structure of the figure determines the completion.

Fig. 12. Surplus structure of type 1 is created. The occlusion interpretation of the mosaic is strengthened by making its components more consistent with each other with respect to location, shade, and size.

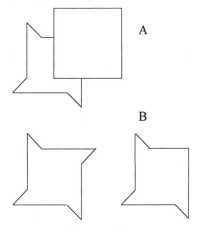

Fig. 13. Alternative, global (A) and local (B) completions.

In figure 13, alternative possible completions of a figure are shown. The completion in figure 13A is in accordance with the global regularity of the component; the one in figure 13B is in accordance with local component structure. Using a formal simplicity metric to calculate the complexity of alternative patterns, van Lier et al. (1995) obtained a reasonable prediction of the preference for a local or a global completion, depending on the relative simplicity of either structure. From this result, it could be concluded that occlusion interpretations are not exclusively made according to local or global structure, but that it depends on the relative simplicity of both. This implies that in occlusion interpretations, local and global structure can occur as rivals if their structures are equally simple. The importance of this result for our present considerations is that surplus structure can also be realized by manipulating the relative simplicity of alternative local and global completions.

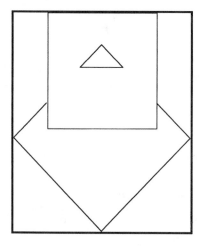

Fig. 14. Surplus structure of type II is created by a modification on a global occlusion interpretation.

In figure 14, it is illustrated how a figure can establish surplus structure by an analytic transformation on a (global) occlusion. Originally, the structure consists of two occluding squares. The occlusion interpretation has lost its original consistency as a result of the transformation to restore the global occlusion interpretation; it must now be assumed that the background figure peaks through a slit in the foreground. By bringing a part of the background square to the front, a small triangle will occur. A novel component is formed, with which there is local structure rivaling the global occlusion interpretation. This suggests the interpretation of a local occlusion. The existence of a local occlusion interpretation, independent of the global one is a new form of surplus structure, called surplus structure of type II. Examples of this kind of ambiguity can be found in Penrose and Penrose (1958), in the early work of Reutersvärd (1985) of course, and in the work of Maurits Cornelius Escher.

Examination of Series of Sketches by P. Kleijne

Two types of surplus structure have been distinguished. We now turn to the work of the artist Paul Kleijne, who will be shown to use these surplus structures. Moreover, he uses them in the predicted order of type I before type II. Figure 15A shows the first sketch. It contains a main square with four surrounding triangles. This sketch is clearly a mosaic, although some overlap may exist of the main square on the darker M-shaped form at the bottom of the sketch. The surrounding triangles have different shades and imprecise locations with respect to the main square and therefore could be said to be aligned to the main square independently. The presence of a mosaic structure corresponds to the primitive synthesis expected to occur in the earliest stage of imagery and sketching. The aligned triangles may already seem to suggest a second square occluded by the main square. This occlusion interpretation is not yet very strongly represented in the first sketch, and therefore this sketch does not show much surplus structure. In having a mosaic, however, it fulfils one of the preconditions for surplus structure of type I.

In the next sketches (figures 15B and C), we observe that the occlusion interpretation is successively strengthened. In this process, an analytic transformation is observed, in which the individual triangles dissolve: in figure 15B they are given an identical shading (as in figures 7 and 12). At the same time these triangles are more precisely located with respect to each other, which further enhances the suggestion that they form a square, occluded by the main square. On top of the main square a parallelogram (A) is introduced, which further enhances the depth of occlusion. Also, the darker M-shaped form at the bottom of the sketch has become an occluded figure. Parallelogram 'A', interpreted as being on top of all other forms, seems to be aligned as a mosaic to a figure in the background, the darker rectangle 'B'.

(A)

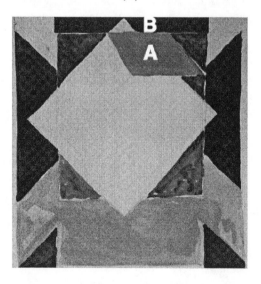

(B)

Fig. 15. Sketches A and B.

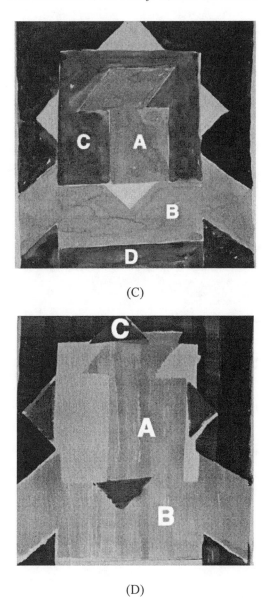

(C)

(D)

Fig. 15. Sketches C and D.

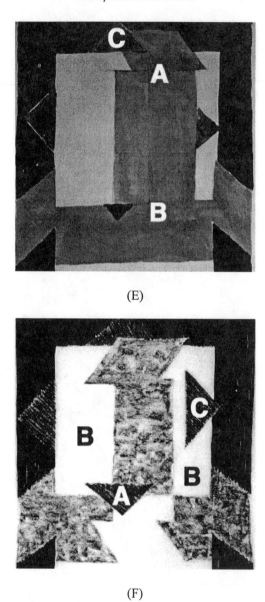

(E)

(F)

Fig. 15. Sketches E and F.

(G)

(H)

Fig. 15. Sketches G and H.

(I)

Fig. 15. Sketch I.

Surplus structure of type I could be said to be approached in figure 15B. Occlusion dominates, but the sketch combines independent mosaic and occlusion interpretations. The sketch in figure 15C maintains these aspects of type I surplus structure. In addition, the first signs of surplus structure type II begin to appear. This form of surplus structure was identified as a conjunctive ambiguity between a local and a global occlusion interpretation. Because the global occlusion would normally be predominant, it is weakened by analytic transformations, making it inconsistent. We distinguished three analytic techniques used by the artist to establish this impression:

1. The suggestion of continuity through fusing the shading of a form on top with a form in the back.

2. The suggestion of continuity through continuation of a form underneath a second form that's not adjacent in depth.

3. Through moving a part of a form, that is currently partly covered by other forms, to the front (already introduced in figure 14).

The first two techniques can be observed in figure 15C. The sketch in figure 15C introduces a new form, labeled 'A'. Through fusing of rectangle 'A' on the foreground with the M-shaped form 'B' in the background, a globally inconsistent occlusion is introduced, according to the first technique. The second technique is applied in the introduction of form 'D' in figure 15C. Because of its width and shading, it seems as if form 'D' is an extension of 'C' and seems to peek out underneath 'B', although this is impossible because 'C' seems to be on top of 'B'.

The sketches in figures 15D and 15E illustrate the third technique. Form 'C' being a part of the (suggested) dark square underneath the light square, is being moved to the front, and now overlaps the front form 'A'. In figure 15D this is done somewhat hesitantly, but in figure 15E, this overlap clearly shows. Both sketches also show a stronger conjunction of form 'A' and 'B' than in figure 15C. The first technique to obtain type II surplus structure, which started with figure 15D, continues to be applied in these sketches, gradually extending in force. The gradual extension of the conjunction across figures 15D-F suggests a slowing down in approaching the critical, equilibrium point.

Nevertheless, the attempt to obtain type II surplus structure appears to be unsatisfactory to the artist. Figure 15G shows an attempt to reintroduce elements from the first sketch; for instance the flanking edges of the initial sketch reappear. But these later sketches do not show conjunctive ambiguity any more. For his central structure, the artist seems to have passed beyond conjunctive ambiguity. Instead, the central figure now shows a recursive hierarchic structure. The global, recursive structures that predominate in his last sketches (figure 15G-I) have a sterile appearance. Before he gives up, the artist makes one attempt to save this line of work. This attempt is quite drastic in terms of the dynamics. He returns to elements from his first sketch (the flanking structures) and aligns them to the central figure in a mosaic. The similarity with his initial sketch is striking. The artist thereby attempts to add the most local structure of his repertoire, to compensate for the global character of his central figure. But going back to the initial mosaic doesn't succeed in creating surplus structure with the central figure. The central figure is too strong and too self-contained a global structure to form an occlusion with the flanking figures any more. As a result, there is no occlusion that could rival the mosaic. In other words, it is too late for an attempt to save the sketch by trying type I surplus structure. Not even the attempt to mix the two, by adding little copies of the main figure to the flanking context, as in figure 15I, has effect. The result is boring. The artist decides to give up working on this sequence. Figure 16 gives an overview over the series.

Conclusion

Recent developments in the fields of experimental aesthetics, perception, and imagery supply converging evidence for a proposed account of creative art production. All these fields have shown interest in the processing of functionally local and global structures. Aesthetic appreciation of abstract art results from the apprehension of surplus structure. Surplus structure becomes apparent by prolonged active inspection of a work of art, and its detection is facilitated by conjunctive ambiguity. Conjunctive ambiguity implies the coexistence of local and global structure in perception. Studies in the perception of structure have shown that two processes could be distinguished; synthesis, involved in the creation of global structure and analysis involved in its destruction and replacement by new, unanticipated forms. Imagery studies demonstrate that the same processes of synthesis that operate in perception are also involved in discovery in imagery.

Despite the similarities of these functions in the three different fields, certain contrasts were observed. Whereas synthetic processing is as unconstrained in imagery as in perception, analytic processing in imagery is severely reduced. This contrast provided the major impetus for studying a series of sketches by an artist. These sketches were made in order to overcome the limitations of imagery in creating surplus structure.

In perception, both synthesis and analysis were involved in the production of global structure. In order to obtain a global structure, some features must acquire a new meaning. This phenomenon was exemplified in the transition from a mosaic to an occlusion interpretation during the microgenesis of a percept (Sekuler & Palmer, 1992). Creation of global structure will therefore require analytic processing in perception.

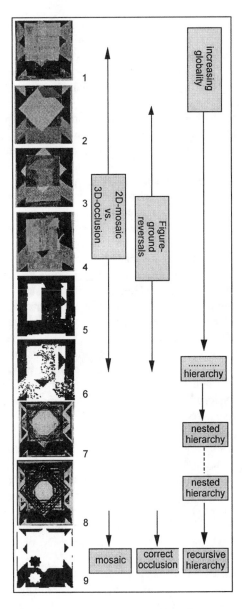

Fig. 16. Review of the iterative processes taking place across sketches.

That analytic processing in perception is easy and frequent can be shown from the spontaneous reversal of ambiguous figures, which requires the breaking up, and subsequent reorganization, of an existing global structure. Such processes of analysis also occur under prolonged perception of a work of abstract art, allowing for the detection of surplus structure.

In imagery, synthesis can be involved in the creation of both local and global structures. Synthesis leads to local structures, for instance when two separable components actually become separated by a mental transformation. Synthesis can give rise to an unanticipated global structure, when separated components are combined in imagery (Finke, 1993). Creative synthesis processes are considered to be involved in creating global structures in imagery.

Analytic processing occurs much-less frequently in imagery than in perception. The detection of novel components by an analytic transformation is very difficult in imagery (Verstijnen, 1997). Therefore, creative processing in imagery will mainly involve the creation of global structure. In perception, the detection of local structure by creative analysis can compensate for the constraints of imagery. The creative processing of local structure is left to perception (Reed, 1974; Verstijnen et al, submitted).

Creative imagery can therefore be enhanced by externalization (e.g., sketching) if the creative process requires analytic processing. This is the case in the production of abstract art, if surplus structure is to be interpreted as a form of ambiguity between a more local and a more global alternative perceptual organization.

The artist, using sketching as a resource to create surplus structure, will operate within the constraints of the creative process. Because creative processing in imagery implies predominantly the production of global structure, a long-term tendency in creative production can be observed. Early creative synthesis in imagery will produce more local structures than later creative processes in imagery. As a result, different techniques to obtain surplus structure could be detected in sketching, depending on whether sketches are made early or late during the creative process.

Early strategies will appeal more to the local structure, and will involve the production of type I surplus structure. This type of surplus structure was identified as a conjunctive ambiguity between a mosaic and occlusion interpretation for a pattern. Later strategies will appeal to type II surplus structure. This type of surplus structure was specified as a conjunctive ambiguity between a local and a global occlusion interpretation for a pattern. In the sequence of sketches produced by the artist Paul Kleijne, type I surplus structure was produced in earlier sketches and type II in later ones as was in accordance with the prediction.

The question could be raised what could be made of Picasso's dictum; "I do not search, I find." In light of the previous discussion, the suggestion can be made that at the moment synthesized mental products are externalized, the unanticipated new information that can be taken from the sketch, comes much to the surprise of the artist. Also, in experimental settings (Verstijnen et al. submitted) many subjects reported this kind of AHA-experience.

This suggestion would imply that an artist does not experience the quantum jump often reported by celebrated scientists such as, for example, Kekulé. Although parallels can be drawn between artistic and scientific discoveries—both are insightful and considered creative—differences can also be noted.

In the first place, scientific discoveries are instantiated by inconsistencies in scientific theorizing. This inconsistency sets the boundaries to the solutions, and thus makes it a clear-cut problem. For example, for Kekulé, the kernel for his discovery of the benzene ring was the detection of a molecule with an impossible ratio of elements, as contemporary theories prescribed the string form for organic molecules. In contrast, artists have the freedom to set their own boundaries, and even if set by the environment, considerable freedom remains.

In the second place, most scientific discoveries are not reported to pop-up after some form of externalization. Kekulé reported that he was seated before his fireplace, and was half-asleep. He certainly was not sketching at that moment. Artists get frustrated if they are withheld from externalization, like the subjects (Designers) in the non-sketch condition of the reported imagery experiments (Verstijnen et al., submitted).

Some of the anecdotal reports, however, allow for the possibility that external factors have served as an external trigger to drop certain structures. For example, Kekulé reported to see snakes in the fire. One snake was biting its own tail, hinting Kekulé to reconsider the organic-molecules-can-only-exist-in-strings-rule, and extend it with an option for ring-structures. Also Archimedes, sitting in bath, discovered a way of measuring the girth of an irregular object, by seeing the water-level rise through his own volume. But not all discoverers report such an external perceptual factor. Penrose, for example, was reportedly taking a bus for a geological trip. Although external perceptual factors might have caused him to find the solution to a mathematical problem that bothered him for a long time, he does not report so.

It could be the case that analytic processes can take place in imagery without external support, but take a long time to develop, as is suggested by the duration of supposed "incubation periods." In light of the present paper however, it can be suggested that it is useful to consider the role of perceptual cues in these processes, whether they are used purposefully as in the sketches by the artist Paul Kleijne, or accidentally, as in Kekulé's story (Verstijnen, et al., 1998a). If we do so, and keep the observed differences between perception and imagery in mind, an interesting integrative observation can be made: there are still reasons to claim similarity in creative production and aesthetic experience, and these similarities reside within the dynamics by which structures are apprehended—namely, the struggle for aesthetic structure in creativity and the mining for surplus structure in perception. In our conscious efforts to create, we rely on the unconscious processes of perception; without realizing it we use the conscious products of our perceptual processes to monitor the creative process.

References

Anderson, R. E., and Helstrup, T. 1993a. Visual discovery in mind and on paper. *Memory & Cognition* 21(3):283-293.

———. 1993b. Multiple perspectives on discovery and creativity. In *Imagery, creativity and discovery: A cognitive perspective*, edited by B. Roskos-Ewoldsen, M. J. Intons-Peterson, and R. E. Anderson. Amsterdam: North Holland.

Apter, M. J. 1984. Reversal theory and personality; A review. *Journal of Research in Personality* 18:265-288.

Arnheim, R. 1974. *Art and visual perception: The new version*. London: Faber & Faber Limited.

Attneave, F. 1971. Multistability in perception. *Scientific American* 225:63-71.

Berlyne, D. E. 1966. Curiosity and exploration. *Science* 153:25-33.

———. 1970. Novelty, complexity, and hedonic value. *Perception and Psychophysics* 8:279-286.

————. 1971. *Aesthetics and psychobiology*. New York: Appleton-Century-Crofts.

Bethel-Fox, C. E., and Shepard, R. N. 1988. Mental rotation: effects of stimulus complexity and familiarity. *Journal of Experimental Psychology: Human Perception and Performance* 14:12-13.

Beyler, J., and Schmeck, R. R. 1992. Assessment of individual differences in preferences for holistic-analytic strategies: evaluation of some commonly available instruments. *Educational and Psychological Measurement* 52: 709-719.

Birkhoff, G. 1933. *Aesthetic measure*. Cambridge, Mass.: Harvard University Press.

Boden, M. 1990. *The creative mind: Myths and mechanisms*. London: Weidenfeld and Micolson.

Boselie, F. 1983. Ambiguity, beauty, and interestingness of line drawings. *Canadian Journal of Psychology* 37:287-292.

Boselie, F., and Leeuwenberg, E. 1985. Birkhoff revisited: Beauty as a function of effect and means. *American Journal of Psychology* 98:1-39.

Bouleau, C. 1963. *The painter's secret geometry: A study of composition in art*. New York: Brace and World.

Buffart, H., Leeuwenberg, E., and Restle, F. 1981. Coding theory of visual pattern completion. *Journal of Experimental Psychology: Human Perception and Performance* 7:241-274.

Chambers, D., and Reisberg, D. (1985). Can mental images be ambiguous? *Journal of Experimental Psychology: Human Perception and Performance* 11:317-328.

Compton, B. J. and Logan, G. D. 1993. Evaluating a computational model of perceptual grouping by proximity. *Perception and Psychophysics* 53(4): 403-421.

Drews, E. 1987. Qualitatively different organizational structures of lexical knowledge in the left and right hemisphere. *Neuropsychologia* 25:419-427.

Ericsson, K. A. and Simon, H. A. 1980. Verbal reports as data. *Psychological Review* 87:215-251.

Epstein, W. 1988. Has the time come to rehabilitate Gestalt psychology? *Psychological Research* 50:2-6.

Eysenck, H. J. 1942. The experimental study of the 'Good Gestalt': A new approach. *Psychological Review* 49:344-364.

Finke, R. A. 1990. *Creative imagery: Discoveries and inventions in visualization*. Hillsdale, NJ: Erlbaum.

————. 1993. *Mental imagery and creative discovery*. Amsterdam: North Holland.

Finke, R. A., and Slayton, K. 1988. Explorations of creative visual synthesis in mental imagery. *Memory & Cognition* 16(3):252-257.

Goldschmidt, G. 1991. The dialectics of sketching. *Creativity Research Journal* 4:123-143.

Goldstone, R. L., and Medin, D. L. 1994. Time course of comparison. *Journal of Experimental Psychology: Learning, Memory and Cognition* 20:29-50.

Gombrich, E. H. 1959. *Art and illusion. A study in the psychology of pictorial representation.* London: Phaidon Press.

Gregory, R. L. 1981. *Mind in science.* London: Weidenfeld.

Grossberg, S., and Mingolla, E. 1985. Neural dynamics of form perception: Boundary completion, illusory figures and neon color spreading. *Psychological Review* 92:173-211.

Hardcastle, V. G. 1995. *Locating consciousness.* Amsterdam: John Benjamins.

Heil, M., Roesler, F., Link, M. and Bajric, J. 1998. What is improved if a mental rotation task is repeated—the efficiency of memory access, or the speed of a transformation routine? *Psychological Research* 61:99-106.

Hekkert, P. 1995. *Artful judgements: A psychological inquiry into aesthetic preference for visual patterns.* Unpublished doctoral dissertation, Delft University of Technology.

Hekkert, P., and Wieringen, P. C. W., van. 1990. Complexity and prototypicality as determinants of the appraisal of cubist paintings. *British Journal of Psychology* 81:483-495.

Hochberg, J. 1978. Art and perception. In *Handbook of perception* (Vol. X), edited by E. C. Carterette and M. P. Friedman. New York: Academic Press.

Hyman, I. E., and Neisser, U. 1991. *Reconstruing mental images: Problems of method.* (Emory Cognition Report #19). Atlanta, GA: Emory University.

Ippolito, M. F. and Tweeny, R. D. 1995. The inception of insight. In *The nature of insight*, edited by R. J. Sternberg and J. E. Davidson. Cambridge, MA: MIT Press.

Kanizsa, G. 1970. Amodale Ergänzung und Erwartungsfehler des Gestaltpsychologen. *Psychologische Forschung* 33:325-344.

———. 1994. Gestalt theory has been misinterpreted, but has also had some real conceptual difficulties. *Philosophical Psychology* 7:149-162.

Kanizsa, G. and Gerbino, W. 1982. Amodal completion: Seeing or thinking? In *Organization and representation in perception*, edited by J. Beck. Hillsdale, NJ: Erlbaum.

Kaplan, A., and Kris, E. 1948. Esthetic ambiguity. *Philosophy and Phenomenological Research* 3:415-435.

Kelso, J. A. S. 1995. *Dynamic patterns. The self-organization of brain and behaviour.* Cambridge, MA: MIT Press.

Koller, O., Rost, J., and Koller, M. 1994. Individuelle Unterschiede beim Lösen von Raumvorstellungsaufgaben aus dem IST-bzw. IST-70-Untertest "Würfelaufgaben" (Individual differences in solving "cube tasks" of the IST and IST-70. *Zeitschrift für Psychologie* 202:65-85.

Kosslyn, S. 1980. *Image and mind.* Cambridge, MA: Harvard University Press.

Kreitler, H. and Kreitler, S. 1972. *Psychology of arts.* Durham: Duke University Press.

Martindale, C. 1981. *Cognition and consciousness*. Homewood, Illinois: The Dorsey Press.

McWhinnie, H. J. 1968. A review of research on aesthetic measure. *Acta Psychologica* 28:363-375.

Miller, A. 1987. Cognitive styles: An integrated model. *Educational Psychology* 7:251-268.

Navon, D. 1977. Forest before trees: the precedence of global features in visual perception. *Cognitive Psychology* 9:353-383.

Nicki, R. M., Lee, P. L., and Moss, V. 1981. Ambiguity, cubist works of art, and preference. *Acta Psychologica* 49:27-41.

Penrose, L. and Penrose, R. 1958. Impossible objects: A special type of visual illusion. *British Journal of Psychology* 49:31-33.

Peterson, M. A. and Hochberg, J. 1983. Opposed-set measurement procedure: A quantitative analysis of the role of local cues and intention in form perception. *Journal of Experimental Psychology: Human Perception and Performance* 9:183-193.

Peterson, M., Kihlstrom, J., Rose, P., and Glisky, M. 1992. Mental images can be ambiguous: Parts, wholes, and strategies. *Memory & Cognition* 20:107-223.

Pomerantz, J. R. 1983. Global and local precedence: selective attention in form and motion perception. *Journal of Experimental Psychology: General* 112(4):516-540.

Ramachandran, V. S. 1990. Interactions between motion, depth, color, and form: the Utilitarian theory of perception. In *Vision: Coding and efficiency*, edited by C. Blakemore. New York: Cambridge University Press.

Reed, S. K. 1974. Structural descriptions and the limitation of visual images. *Memory & Cognition* 2:329-336.

Reed, S. K., and Johnsen, J. A. 1975. Detection of parts in patterns and images. *Memory & Cognition* 3:569-575.

Reutersvärd, O. 1985. *Omöjliga figurer I färg*. Lund (Sv): Daxa AB.

Rock, I., and Mack, A. 1994. Attention and perceptual organization. In *Cognitive approaches to human perception*, edited by S. Ballesteros. Hillsdale, NJ: Erlbaum.

Rothenberg, A., & Hausman, L. R. 1976. *The creativity question*. Durham, NC: Duke University Press.

Sekuler, A. B., and Palmer, S. E. 1992. Perception of partly occluded objects: a microgenetic analysis. *Journal of Experimental Psychology: General* 121:95-111.

Skarda, C. A. and Freeman, W. J. 1987. How brains make chaos to make sense of the world. *Behavioral and Brain Sciences* 10:161-195.

Tsotsos, J. K. 1993. The role of computational complexity in perceptual theory. In *Foundations of perceptual theory*, edited by S. C. Masin. Amsterdam: North Holland.

van Leeuwen, C. 1998. Visual perception at the edge of chaos. In *Systems theories an a priori aspects of perception*, edited by J. S. Jordan. Amsterdam: Elsevier.

van Leeuwen, C., and Bakker, L. 1995. Stroop can occur without Garner interference: Strategic and mandatory influences in multi-dimensional stimuli. *Perception & Psychophysics* 57:379-392.

van Leeuwen, C., Buffart, H. and van der Vegt, J. 1988. Sequence influence on the organization of meaningless serial stimuli: Economy after all. *Journal of Experimental Psychology: Human Perception and Performance* 14:481-502.

van Leeuwen, C., Steyvers, M., and Nooter, M. 1997. Stability and intermittency in large-scale coupled oscillator models for perceptual segmentation. *Journal of Mathematical Psychology* 41:319-344.

van Lier, R., van der Helm, P., and Leeuwenberg, E. 1995. Competing global and local completions in visual occlusion. *Journal of Experimental Psychology: Human Perception and Performance* 21:571-583.

van Oeffelen, M. P., and Vos, P. G. 1982. Configurational effects on the enumeration of dots: Counting by groups. *Memory and Cognition* 10:396-404.

Verstijnen, I. M. 1997. *Sketches of creative imagery.* Unpublished doctoral dissertation, Delft University of Technology.

Verstijnen, I. M., van Leeuwen, C., Goldschmidt, G., Hamel, R., and Hennessey, J. 1998a. Sketching and creative discovery. *Design Studies* 19:519-546.

Verstijnen, I. M., van Leeuwen, C., Hamel, R., Goldschmidt, G., and Hennessey, J. 1998b. Creative discovery in imagery and perception: Combining is relatively easy, restructuring takes a sketch. *Acta Psychologica* 99:177-200.

Verstijnen, I. M., van Leeuwen, C., Hamel, R. and Hennessey, J. M. (submitted) What imagery can't do and why sketching might help.

Von Ehrenfels, C. 1890. "Über Gestaltqualitäten". *Vierteljahresschrift für Wissenschaftliche Philosophie* 14:249-292.

Von der Malsburg, C. and Schneider, W. 1986. A neural cocktail-party processor. *Biological Cybernetics* 54:29-40.

Wagemans, J. 1995. Detection of visual symmetries. *Spatial Vision* 9:9-32.

Walker, E. L. 1980. Berlyne's theoretical contributions to psychology. *Motivation and Emotion* 4:105-111.

Implicit Models of Consciousness

Chapter 8

Is the Dialogue over the Nature of Consciousness Limited by Its Own Terms?

Lawrence Souder

In the year 2001 it will be reported, according to Arthur C. Clarke (1968), that a famous computer uttered these words: "I am a HAL Nine Thousand computer Production Number 3. I became operational at the HAL Plant in Urbana, Illinois, on January 12, 1997." Thus was born one of the most famous computers, real or imagined. So famous is HAL that just last month Urbana hosted Cyberfest '97, a virtual birthday party for this computer. Apart from the entertainment value of this science fiction character, however, Clarke seems to be offering us a kind of experiment for us to execute to explore the answers to a what-if scenario. Clarke seems to be provoking us to ask such questions as: What if a computer had the powers of HAL? Would it be conscious (as HAL seemed to be)? Would it be capable of evil (as HAL seemed to do)? What does the power of HAL say about human powers? Are we any different from HAL?

The movie *2001: a Space Odyssey* was a sophisticated production even by today's standards, but its portrayal of HAL is engaging for rather subtle, unsophisticated reasons. We can't fail to be struck and perhaps intimidated by certain clearly human but understated aspects: HAL communicates via human-like voice, HAL can recognize faces and even read lips, and HAL refers to itself in first-person singular pronouns. What are we to make of all this? Should we fear displacement by computers as their powers continue to outstrip our own? Should we feel diminished in our humanity as so many aspects of human consciousness become duplicated, or at least simulated, in silicon? Such is the power of Clarke's invention that it can provoke us to fathom these deep issues.

As it turns out, such experiments are not found strictly in science fiction. It is common in philosophical discussions over topics like personal identity, consciousness, and ethics to offer hypothetical examples that provoke an interlocutor to imagine a scenario and grapple with its underlying issue. Such examples are called philosophical thought experiments.

Thought experiments are a common sight on the landscape of Anglo-American philosophy. They are a curious hybrid of science fiction and hard-nosed rationalism. Moreover, those who use them often seem schizophrenic about them. The typical objection to the use of philosophical thought experiments is Wilkes' (1998). She contends that because philosophical thought experiments rely so heavily on intuitions, imagined cases are wide open to interpretations, so, she says, "opinions diverge sharply and the strength of intuitions on each side, being equally balanced, helps not at all" (p. 17). On the other hand, philosophers seem to find it hard to resist offering and responding to thought experiments, perhaps because, as Jackson (1992) observes, the thought experiment "provides ample scope for the exercise of ingenuity in the usually arid confines of academic writing" (p. 528). Nevertheless, their use can not be dismissed, for their place in philosophy in general seems well established. Brooks (1994) notes, "Thought experiments seem too integral to philosophy since Plato's cave for us to abandon them" (p. 71).

I propose that thought experiments in discussions over topics like consciousness are common because relevant empirical data is not always available so that interlocutors are forced to fabricate their own. This role of the thought experiment has been the object of another criticism. Thomas Kuhn (1997) asked rhetorically on behalf of all empiricists, "How, then, relying upon familiar data, can a thought experiment lead to new knowledge or to a new understanding of nature?"

(1977, p. 241). Even more troublesome perhaps is that their fictive nature has made some thinkers wary of the persuasive effects of thought experiments. Sorensen (1992) says, "Thus, we worry whether the lovely thought experiments of Nietzsche, Einstein, and Judith Thomson charm us into conviction" (p. 266).

My contention is that thought experimenters use terms in the construction of their scenarios that not only attempt to convince but also both reflect a philosophical position and constrain it. I will illustrate my thesis with two sets of examples of thought experiments: one set that samples a variety of thought experiments in the literature of the philosophy of mind from Locke to the present and another set that evolved from John Searle's (1980) Chinese Room. For all these examples I try to show that form and content mutually constrain each other. In view of the constraining effects of terms, I will conclude with a radical proposal for the conduct of future investigations over the nature of consciousness.

Methodological Aspects of Thought Experiments

One of the earliest examples of thought experiment in the philosophy of mind is perhaps John Locke's (1975). To support his belief that consciousness is a matter of continuity of memory he speculates:

> Had I the same consciousness that I saw the ark and Noah's flood, as that I saw an overflowing of the Thames last winter, or as that I write now; I could no more doubt that I who write this now, that saw the Thames overflowed last winter, and that viewed the flood at the general deluge, was the same self. (p. 45)

Locke's first-person report here is a practice typical of British empiricists and perhaps imitative of Descartes. During the author's account of his own introspection, the reader is expected to replicate the author's line of thinking and to arrive at the same conclusions. In short, the author's "I" becomes the reader's "I". This ploy is not merely an undisguised rhetorical device but a way to endorse introspection as the proper way of studying the phenomenon of consciousness.

When introspection yields to logical empiricism as a methodology, thought experiments seem to stress a need for empirical foundations and attempt an appeal to experimental rigor. In advancing an empirical concept of the soul Anthony Quinton (1975) once offered the following thought experiment as a counterexample to the claim that certain character traits require the possession of certain bodily characteristics:

> It would be odd for a six-year-old girl to display the character of Winston Churchill, odd indeed to the point of outrageousness, but it is not utterly inconceivable. At first, no doubt, the girl's display of dogged endurance, a world-historical comprehensiveness of outlook, and so forth, would strike one as distasteful and pretentious in so young a child. But if she kept it up the impression would wear off. (p. 60)

Notice that this account is reported in the 3rd person as is even the representation of the observer.

Some philosophical thought experiments are derivative of actual experiments. Derek Parfit (1984), for example, in his attempt to refute the necessity of the unity of consciousness, offers an invented example built around Roger Sperry's experiments with commissurotomy.

> suppose that I have been equipped with some device that can block communication between my hemispheres. Since this device is connected to my eyebrows, it is under my control. By raising an eyebrow I can divide my mind. In each half of my divided mind I can then, by lowering an eyebrow, reunite my mind. This ability would have many uses. Consider [that] I am taking an exam, and have only fifteen minutes left in which to answer the last question. It occurs to me that there are two ways of tackling this question. I am unsure which is more likely to succeed. I therefore decide to divide my mind for ten minutes, to work in each half of my mind on one of the two calculations, and then to reunite my mind to write a fair copy of the best result. (p. 246)

Parfit says of such examples "[their] impossibility is merely technical (p. 252)." He believes that given enough time and resources such an experiment could be conducted. By relating his experiment in the first-person, Parfit seems to have it both ways methodologically, introspectionist and objectivist.

Phenomenological Aspects of Thought Experiments

The thought experiments offered so far seem to use language, especially pronouns, in a way that reflects a methodology. In this next group I hope to show that the choice of terms reflects a view of the phenomenon as well. In effect I want to illustrate how aspects of form are manipulated in ways that both reflect a philosophical position and constrain it.

Thought experiments are notorious for eliciting responses in kind. Perhaps the most notable in this regard is John Searle's (1980) Chinese Room. The literature, in fact, contains a plethora of examples that attempt to clarify or modify Searle's original scenario in order both to refute and to affirm his argument. It is in the dialectical tension between the original thought experiment and its variation that the significance of the choice of terms becomes evident.

The Chinese Room thought experiment is John Searle's counterexample to the strong AI thesis that a computer could ever instantiate human intelligence. Searle's account starts out as the first-person report of a man in a room with a pile of Chinese symbols and a translation manual:

> Suppose that I'm locked in a room and given a large batch of Chinese writing. Suppose furthermore (as is indeed the case) that I know no Chinese, either written or spoken, and that I'm not even confident that I could recognize Chinese writing as Chinese writing distinct from, say, Japanese writing or meaningless squiggles. To me, Chinese writing is just so many meaningless squiggles. Now suppose further that after this first batch of Chinese writing I am given a second batch of Chinese script together with a set of rules for correlating the second batch with the first batch. The rules are in English, and I understand these rules as well as any other native speaker of English. They enable me to correlate one set of formal symbols with another set of formal symbols, and all that 'formal' means here is that I can identify the symbols entirely by their shapes. Now suppose also that I am given a third batch of Chinese symbols together with some instructions, again in English, that enable me to correlate elements of this third batch with the first two batches, and these rules instruct me how to give back certain Chinese symbols with certain sorts of shapes in response to certain sorts of shapes given me in the third batch. Unknown to me, the people who are giving me all of these symbols call the first batch a 'script,' they call the second batch a 'story,' and they call the third batch 'questions.' Furthermore, they call the symbols I give them back in response to the third batch 'answers to the questions,' and the set of rules in English that they gave me, they call the 'program.' Now just to complicate the story a little, imagine that these people also give me stories in English, which I understand, and they then ask me questions

in English about these stories, and I give them back answers in English. Suppose also that after a while I get so good at following the instructions for manipulating the Chinese symbols and the programmers get so good at writing the programs that from the external point of view—that is, from the point of view of somebody outside the room in which I am locked—my answers to the questions are absolutely indistinguishable from those of native Chinese speakers. (p. 355)

While it is true that Searle's prose style has a reputation for being casual, maintaining as he does here an informal, first-person stance, his choice of first person verbs in the Chinese room example is, I believe, more than just a matter of consistency of style. The emphasis on the first person singular seems central to Searle's argument. Elsewhere in a related discussion Searle makes a case for the subjective nature of consciousness. The upshot of this subjectivity is that the mental is "an irreducibly first person ontology" (1994, p. 95). As a result consciousness is not accessible to all observers in the same way. So by keeping the account of the Chinese room in the first person, Searle keeps the subjective aspect of the mental implicit and thereby encourages the reader to do likewise by running the simulation in his own mind. Searle's purpose here seems to be to segregate consciousness from other phenomena with respect to the way they can be studied, where the Cartesian distinction between res cogitans and res extensa is usually assumed. A first-person point of view serves to reinforce the subjective nature of the mental and so confers a certain epistemic privilege on itself.

David Cole's (1991) amended version of the Chinese room does not cooperate with Searle's expectation that the readers will act as simulators of Searle's place in the scenario. Instead Cole takes a third person perspective and treats the scenario as one to be observed rather than simulated. In Cole's variation the insistence on the third person is almost tedious:

Suppose, for example, a person (Searle, in the original statement of the argument) who does not know Chinese sits in a room with instructions written in English (a 'program') that tell one in detail how to manipulate Chinese symbols, producing strings in response to the strings given to one ... Since the instructions tell one what to do entirely on the basis of formal or syntactic features of the strings, without ever mentioning (or revealing) meaning, one can generate Chinese sentences without any understanding. (1991, p. 400)

Cole begins his critique of Searle's conclusion (i.e., one can generate Chinese sentences without understanding them) by noting: "Searle's self-report of incomprehension of Chinese in his scenario conflicts with other evidence, notably the response in Chinese to Chinese questions" (p. 401).

As in Searle's original account, Cole's choice of person may seem a matter of stylistic consistency. But it seems too strategically connected with his philosophical commitments. Cole is an avowed functionalist; at the end of his argument he has optimistically declared, "Finally, it might even become possible to replace entire damaged neurons by functionally equivalent silicon-based electronic devices" (p. 411). Such sentiments are often accompanied in the AI debate by a rejection of introspection as a method of studying consciousness and an insistence instead on the importance of an analysis of environmental inputs and behavioral outputs. In view of these commitments Cole's insistence on the third-person perspective and his skeptical regard for "Searle's self-report" seem strategic.

Yet another mode of representation is possible: a second-person account. Here the use of the pronoun you seems to suggest something intersubjective about consciousness; there is a need for agreement among interlocutors about what consciousness is and who has it. This perspective seems at the core of behaviorism. Here is a variation on the Chinese room by Sharples, Hogg, Hutchinson, Torrance, and Young (1989), that hints at this:

> If you directly ask the person inside the Chinese Room what all these symbols mean, the answer is likely to be: "Search me—they're just a bunch of meaningless squiggles to me." If you ask the system, which the operator is operating, whether it understands Chinese, the answer will come back, in Chinese: "Of course I do, what do you think I'm speaking now?" (pp. 295-6)

Conclusion

I've limited my analysis of discourse over consciousness to the personal pronouns. I've done so because these are basic words that don't so much name things as they suggest relationships. As Martin Buber (1970) noted about the second person, "Who says you does not have something ... but he stands in relation" (p. 55). So it is with all pronouns; they show our relation to something. And that relation is always limited by the particular pronoun we choose. The limits of pronouns seem evident in the variations on the Chinese Room thought experiment. These same limits become part of the limits of the whole methodology behind consciousness studies.

Many Western thinkers have asserted a strictly linguistic character of human experience. Charles Sanders Peirce (1958) has stated, "My language is the sum-total of myself" (p. 313). Ludwig Wittgenstein (1953) said, "It is only in language that one can mean something by something" (p. 18). And, Hans-Georg Gadamer (1976) said, "Human experience is essentially linguistic" (p. 19). The language of the Chinese Room thought experiments to the contrary seems to suggest that any choice of terms will yield an incomplete account of consciousness.

For this reason I propose an approach to consciousness studies that will seem paradoxical coming from a rhetorician. Consciousness studies need to follow the example set by this symposium, viz., to let the methodology be as broad-based as the phenomenon of consciousness itself. The most complete account of consciousness will emerge from an interdisciplinary perspective, one that incorporates not just language, but art, dance, music, sports, etc. Let our accounts of consciousness be informed by executing a pas de deux or eating an oyster, as well as by reporting a mental state.

References

Brooks, D. H. M. 1994. The method of thought experiment. *Metaphilosophy* 25: 71-83.

Buber, M. 1970. *I and Thou*. Translated by Walter Kaufmann. New York: Charles Scribner's Sons.

Clarke, A. 1968. *2001: A space odyssey*. New York: New American Library.

Cole, D. 1991. Artificial intelligence and personal identity. *Synthese* 88: 399-417.

Gadamer, H. G. 1976. *Philosophical hermeneutics*. Berkeley: University of California Press.

Jackson, M. W. 1992. The gedankenexperiment method of ethics. *The Journal of Value Inquiry* 26: 525-535.

Kuhn, T. S. 1977. *The essential tension*. Chicago: The University of Chicago Press.

Locke, J. 1975. Of identity and diversity. In *Personal identity*, edited by John Perry. Berkeley: University of California Press.

Parfit, D. 1984. *Reasons and persons*. Oxford: ClarendonPress.

Peirce, C. S. 1958. *Collected papers of Charles Sanders Peirce*, edited by C. Hartshorne, P. Weiss, and A. Burks. Cambridge: Harvard University Press.

Quinton, A. 1975. The soul. In *Personal identity*, edited by J.Perry. Berkeley: University of California Press.

Searle, J. R. 1980. Minds, brains, and programs. In *The mind's I*, edited by D. Hofstadter and D. Dennett. New York: Bantam. First published in *The Behavioral and Brain Sciences* 3:417-457.

————. 1994. *The rediscovery of mind*. Cambridge: MIT Press.

Sharples, M., Hogg, D., Hutchison, C., Torrance, S., and Young, D. 1989. *Computers and thought: A practical introduction to artificial intelligence*. Cambridge: MIT Press.

Sorensen, R. A. 1992. *Thought experiments*. Oxford: Oxford University Press.

Wilkes, K. V. 1988. *Real people: Personal identity without thought experiments*. Oxford: Clarendon Press.

Wittgenstein, L. 1953. *Philosophical investigations*. New York: Macmillan.

Chapter 9

One Model, Diverse Manifestations: A Paradigm of Consciousness in Twentieth-century Art

Charlotte Stokes

By their very nature the visual arts should be able to afford us with eloquent models of the artistic consciousness, but the works created during the twentieth century are so disparate. To whom do we look for this model of modern artistic consciousness? Pablo Picasso or Grant Wood? However varied, the form and content of twentieth-century art are based on a conception of consciousness that is unique to our century. Modern art could not exist without this model of human awareness, which lies behind the works that on the surface are very different from one another.

Our model of artistic consciousness is a combination of widely-shared assumptions: that modern art is a highly personal—even idio-syncratic—exercise; that artistic activity is derived from the physical (rather than the spiritual) nature of the brain, knowledge of which has come from scientific, especially medical, research; that artistic consciousness is politically or artistically revolutionary; that "creativity" is the eruption of some special, non-rational forces within the artist; and, last, that "talent" is the unstable combination of such factors as mental abnormality and eye-hand coordination. The irony of such ideas is that with one hand we give artists special, even supernatural, powers, but with the other, make artists slaves of their mental instability.

Our uniquely modern conception of how artists think and work affects our perceptions of art from more traditional cultures and from the history of western Europe. A closer look at manifestations of the artistic consciousness from more traditional times establishes a baseline from which to examine our contemporary views of art and artists.

Thirteenth-century Italian altarpieces, such as Cimabue's *Madonna Enthroned with Angels and Prophets,*[1] have the appearance of traditional icons. They were based on a very different set of assumptions concerning the nature of art from those formed in the twentieth century. Like most works from this early period, Cimabue's altarpiece was meant for a church. The figures he drew were not meant to represent the human beings that surrounded the artist. Rather the artist was evoking a spiritual reality through simplifying and idealizing of the human form. Nor were the relative sizes of the figures meant to be descriptive of the historical personages. Size is one aspect of a well-understood, hierarchical, and universal symbolic language. The Madonna is the largest figure in the painting, not because the historic Mary was a big woman, but because in the painting, she is the most important personage. As such, Mary with the Child on her lap is in the center of a symmetrical image carefully organized around them. Her gesture toward the infant Christ is a traditional presentation that appears in many depictions of the Madonna and Child. She sits above a structure that houses the Old Testament Hebrew prophets because the new faith supersedes, yet rests on the older faith. Indeed, the artist and the members of his workshop believed that the validity of their work derived from close adherence to the conventions of such images.

The artists who made altarpieces during medieval period avoided the visual reality of earthly experience, a reality that was filled with backbreaking work, crude living arrangements, and early death. People at that time knew all too much about the reality of earthly experience. They went to church for another, more ideal and beautiful reality. Medieval altarpieces transmitted spiritual Truth. In this context the artistic consciousness was the talent to communicate the precise combination of spiritual connectedness to God, awareness of tradition, and membership in a community. It was important for the artist to accurately transmit images from the past (during which the Truth was revealed) to the present. This was not the Truth we find in a photo-graph, but rather the pure and abstract Truth from God.

In the traditional setting, like that of the thirteenth-century Italian altarpieces, talent resided neither in the ability to make photographic depictions of visual reality—even had the people at the time understood such a concept—nor in the originality of the rendering, but rather in fitting the work into the religious and symbolic life of the community. Cimabue and his fellow artists reinforced social values and hierarchies. The modern concept of "artistic talent" would not have been under-stood. Appropriateness of ideas and images was far more important than originality. Unlike our contemporary definition of artistic con-sciousness, in the past, originality would have been disapproved. Shocking to us who value the "touch" of the artist, master artists like Cimabue usually did not paint the works themselves, but rather saw to the larger issues of planning and working with the patrons in order to meet their requirements. The lesser work of realizing the conception was left to assistants, apprentices and journeymen. Planning and crafts-manship were expected—as we today expect planning and careful execution in building a house or installing new kitchen cabinets. Neither the artist nor his public thought that the artist's job was to "create"; indeed, only God could "create."

If traditional artists regarded themselves as craftsmen whose job it was to effectively communicate accepted religious concepts, modern artists have a very different persona. This persona is characterized by the conception of art as an individualistic pursuit. In this characteriza-tion the intuitive, non-rational nature of artistic talent makes the artist more capable than the average person of delving deeply into emotional states. Art is based on emotional spontaneity, rather than on rational choices or planning. Talent is related to—if not derived from—various unhealthy mental states. The career of Vincent van Gogh, who com-mitted suicide just before the beginning of the twentieth century, is a good example of the popular conception of the modern artist. The brushy, curving, restless lines in his work are seen as symptoms of his mental instability. Even the medication that he supposedly took has been said to have affected the appearance of his paintings. (The blurred purple and gold rings around the stars in such paintings as *Starry Night*[2] were thought to be the result of his taking digitalis for his mental illness.) In such interpretations, genius is seen as deriving from—or at least related to—the unhealthy physical state of the brain; madness equals creativity. The peculiar mental state of artistic genius could be the result of injury, madness, or damage caused by chemicals such as medications or narcotics. Such conditions have been documented in countless articles in both medical journals and popular science maga-zines. Thus our conception of the artistic mind is based on a roman-ticized conception of scientific research into the nature of the mind, especially the deviant mind.

A cartoon in the "Bizarro" series reproduced in the *Wisconsin Journal*, 4 April 1997, underscores this common perception. In the cartoon we see the figure of an optometrist distorted as in a cubist painting. He is holding out a pair of glasses and bending down toward us. We, the viewers, are in the position of the patient, to whom the optometrist says, "Here, try these." The caption identifies the patient, "Well-meaning optometrist nearly ruins a young Picasso's career." We, the viewer, see what the artist sees. Picasso sees in a distorted way. Thus, he paints a distorted image. This cartoon from a daily newspaper indicates how widespread the popular conception of the artist is: The modern audience believes that art is the product of a mind with an abnormal physical or mental condition, especially a malady in the way of seeing, rather than believing that art is the product of an artist making considered choices as to what he or she wants to represent.

The Persistence of Memory,[3] the famous painting of 1931 by the surrealist artist Salvador Dali, demonstrates another commonly held belief concerning twentieth-century artists; that more than other people, artists are tuned into the deeper mental states that researchers such as Sigmund Freud described. Dali's painting shows giant pocket watches that appear to be melting, slumped over various features in an eery landscape. Dali and other members of the surrealist movement were familiar with the writings of Freud, which described the importance of childhood experience in forming adult behavior. Freud also discussed, in some detail, the symbolic visual language of dreams in which any number of objects could take metaphorical meaning, especially sexual meaning for people living in an age when frank discussion of sexual matters was taboo. Dali openly discussed the sexual meaning of the symbolism of the work. According to the artist, his parents suppressed his sexuality when he was a child, causing him to be impotent as an adult. Thus the drooping pocket watches are in an open infertile space, rather than tucked into a warm pocket. The title of the painting, *The Persistence of Memory*, is another key to Dali's idea of the indelible nature of early experience. While the stark landscape in *The Persistence of Memory* suggests a dream space, the landscape is also derived from Dali's memories of the area in Spain in which he grew up and experienced his parents' influence.

Dali depicted a mental state through the interaction of visual symbols. The model of consciousness to which he subscribed was based on a structure or set of feelings that can be distorted by unhealthy experiences. He called his artistic exploration, "paranoiac-critical method." His form of surrealism was realized through meticulous depiction of things that appear only in dreams, fantasies, and free associations. Dali's highly personal art was derived from his own memories, but based on the theories Freud had outlined.

Another stereotypical conception of art is that it is the product of the irrational mind in the grip of violent emotions. One of the most extreme forms of art of this type is called expressionism. This style is characterized by strong, even harsh, color, crude drawing, and slashing brush strokes. Such works appear to have been painted hurriedly, as if to catch violent feelings, such as anger and fear. Artists like Emil Nolde, Oskar Kokoschka, Ernst Ludwig Kirchner, and Erich Heckel, among others, created paintings that seem to be both personal and violent. The modern viewer often assumes that such paintings demonstrate the perceptions of an artist who is out of control, if not mad. Expressionistic works are often shown in popular films as being by insane or highly eccentric artists. Paradoxically, the art of those truly insane is controlled and repetitive; that is, the art of the paranoiac seems to be an antidote to the out-of-control mental state or the attempt to impose order on mental chaos. The intent of expressionist artists is quite different and demonstrates an important aspect of the modern conception of the artistic consciousness and the nature of the creative act.

Many artists—not all of whom are expressionists—have promoted the concept that art is based on an unbroken and coherent sequence of events that result in the creative act, the making of a work of art. First, the artist experiences an extreme emotion, usually concerning a religious, social, personal or political issue. According to this view of the consciousness, artists are more capable than the average person of contacting their more authentic emotional selves, not only for the subject (as did Dali), but also for the method of creation. Through their nature as artists, they contact these inner truths that society had wiped away or, at least, concealed from the rest of us. Then the artist embraces a subject related to that emotion-laden issue, or perhaps the artist begins to paint, letting the subject just come to her or him. The artist works through the subject very directly on the canvas without apparent planning and control. The image so produced is crude. Paint appears to be splashed on the canvas and the drawing is not photographic. The rough surface and spontaneous drawing do no permit the viewer to forget that the image was made by a human hand. Further the final image should at some level communicate and induce the feelings in the viewer that the artist felt during the process.

The expressionist artist Nolde was deeply religious, almost mystical, in his beliefs. In some works he dealt with the tragic nature of Christ's life. In others he was concerned with the combat of good and evil. For example, in *The Golden Calf*[4] the spinning and gesticulating dancers convey the artist's apprehension over the abandonment of true religious belief. Even the freely painted surfaces contribute to the sense that the artist was so in the grip of deep feeling that he was unable to control his technique as he executed the painting. The painting he produced in this emotional state was to evoke the same emotion in the viewer. Thus, the process unfolds from the artist's emotion, to the choice of the subject, to the blunt, spontaneous technique, to the brushy nature of the image, to the feelings of the viewer.

Picasso's well-known *Guernica,*[5] painted in 1937, is also derived from the artist's passionate beliefs, but in Picasso's case political rather than religious beliefs. Further, the style of *Guernica* is built on the intellectual base of cubism, rather than the emotional base of expressionism. In *Guernica* Picasso intentionally fragmented forms and dismembered bodies as a sign of political protest. In this painting the artistic temperament is associated not only with artistic rebellions, but also political rebellions, especially rebellions in support of leftist causes. This picture was a protest against the Fascist government of Franco. Indeed, the artist specified that the work would not return to Spain during Franco's regime. Like any characterization or stereotype, there are exceptions. While many artists are political rebels, others are not. Such paintings as Grant Wood's *The Ride of Paul Revere*, painted during the same era, is in extreme contrast to Picasso's image and indicative of the diverse manifestations of artistic consciousness in our century. It is almost a dollhouse idealization of the American countryside with Paul Revere and the landmarks of the story from

American history. It is an image of a heroic event from the United States history set in an idealistic American countryside. Hardly revolutionary in intent, it sings the praises of a way of life that was under assault during the Depression. In contrast to Picasso's treatment of nationalistic themes, there is no fragmentation. Rather the image is seamless. Its very smoothness makes it appear to be an idyllic dream derived from the personal vision of the artist and his contemporaries, who valued this idealized vision over the reality of bread lines and dust bowls. Such discrepancies between the stereotypical rebellious artist and the reality of individual artists makes clear that our conception of the artist is often one sided.

Our view that artists are highly individualistic and somewhat shocking people is derived from expressionist and surrealist conceptions. It is the belief that art is based on the personal preferences of the artist that makes it very difficult for us to understand the traditional art of our culture or the traditional art of cultures in which art was part of a common social fabric. The expressionists' subjects, methods, and the final appearance of their works feed our perception of art as highly individualistic and incomprehensible. Further, it is regularly assumed that works of art that are hard to understand are intended to be an affront to moral or political standards.

While we acknowledge the physical nature of the brain that forms the modern artistic consciousness, we also hold in high esteem the concept of the unique "creative" talent. The artist's very uniqueness makes his or her works valuable. No artist represents this cult of the personality better than Picasso. There is almost a mystic belief, born out by the prices at auction, that works by the artist's hand are special. Recall that at the time of Cimabue's *Madonna*, the master artist was the leader of a team and not usually the individual who actually painted the image.

Both in the artistic community and the popular culture, paintings by Picasso, Nolde, or Dali are considered imprints of the twentieth-century artistic consciousness. This conception of the artistic consciousness includes the physical nature of the mind, the extreme individuality of the artist, the link between emotional instability and talent, the sensitivity of artists to deep psychological truths, and the politically radical, if not revolutionary, nature of the artist.

While the forgoing are assumptions concerning the artistic consciousness commonly held by artists and the general public, there are other conceptions of art and artists that are not so well known or so widely understood or accepted. One of the most important of these is the ability of the artistic consciousness to engage in a complex relationship with the art of the past, with the art of other cultures, and with innumerable types of popular images. Artists have been in the forefront of a general appreciation of art of other cultures, photography and folk art. They have enlarged the general conception of what was to be considered art. In the past, artists like Cimabue looked only to their own traditions for models to emulate; the art of their present was a continuation of the art of their past. Artists, who are our contemporaries, hold in their consciousness a wide variety of forms drawn not only from their own traditions, but from other contemporary artists, from modern popular culture, and from other civilizations. The ability to accept the wealth and variety of visual modes of thinking puts the modern artistic consciousness back into a continuum—albeit, quite a different and broader one—than that in which Cimabue and his colleagues resided.

In 1907 Picasso painted a number of works with African themes. Works like *African Dancer* contain angular figures. The African Kota carved reliquary figures are likely, but not provable, sources for such works. Picasso considered African sculpture beautiful in form and powerful in its ability to elicit the mystic response. He admired the strong geometric shapes that the African artist used to describe the human figure. Whatever their relationship to specific works of African sculpture, paintings like *African Dancer* demonstrate Picasso's well-known interest in African art. African art is only one of the many types of art from other cultures that have engaged artists during our century. They have also looked to the arts of the pre-Columbian New World, Oceania, and all areas of Asia. Indeed, there is no art tradition that is unknown or unmined by modern artists.

Whatever their relationship to the arts of other cultures, twentieth-century artists also engaged in an active debate with the art of their own past. Picasso quoted from or reinterpreted the work of such artists as Manet and Delicroix, among many others of the historic cannon. Picasso was intent on placing himself into the continuum of great masters in western art, especially those works that took him back to his own Spanish roots. Picasso's *Las Meninas* was an interpretation of *Las Meninas* by the great Spanish Baroque painter Diago Velázques. Such modern works are statements of alliance, and of rivalry.

Assertions of association and continuation are also found in the work of such abstract expressionists, as in Jackson Pollock, William de Kooning, and Hans Hofmann. They look back to the freely brushed late paintings by Claude Monet of water lilies. The historic relationship between the abstract works of mid-twentieth-century American painters and the late works of the Impressionist who painted his water garden is at once enigmatic and obvious. We may assume that the non-representational paintings by abstract expressionists have no precedents. Certainly, in these painting the subject matter appears to be the hand-painted surface itself. But when we look at the late Impressionist work of Monet, painted during the first two decades of the twentieth century, we see that it is only one short step from observation to free abstraction. Monet was engrossed by the color harmonies he found in his gardens. Monet was also concerned with the decorative or abstract possibilities of two views–horizontal (the surface of the water delineated by the floating water lily pads) and the vertical (the upright trees and their reflections in the water). More to the point, he was attuned to how the combination of these two views result in a two-dimensional, highly decorative or abstract image. Both the abstract expressionists and Monet demonstrated their concern with personal touch conveyed by a style of brush work that is unique to each artist.

Whatever the complex engagement of contemporary artists with the traditions of western high art, many twentieth-century artists have confronted and used images from advertising and popular culture. Publicity photographs of the stars in movie magazines are only one form of popular imagery that became the subject of Warhol's work. He saw, not only the glamour of these images, but also the nature of modern communication and marketing that takes place on an enormous scale. Each of Warhol's many images of Marilyn Monroe from early in the 1960's is a translation of such mass-produced imagery into art. Even the vast number of Warhol's images of Marilyn Monroe themselves replicate the millions of images of the star reproduced in the mass media. Singly or as an aggregate, the silk-screened images of the star carry the implication that the person is the product which has been reproduced in millions of copies. In this action Warhol becomes the visionary, attuned to the nuances of his twentieth-century environment. In Warhol we see an artist who took one of the roles of the modern artist; that is, the seer, who is able to penetrate into the basic structures and weaknesses of modern life. The artist sees what others do not and points out those aspects of modern life that we should examine for insights into the condition of our lives and even for the beauty of the objects themselves. Andy Warhol not only took his subject from popular culture, but also replicated the process of its making by making multiple versions.

Dali was known for his startling depictions of mental states, but the methods he used for creating the works are traditional painting techniques. Many other modern artists drew on past traditions, but used new and unusual formats. One such tradition was that of still life. For centuries artists have painted still lifes that range from visual examinations of the simplest of everyday objects to complex, symbol laden images of every imaginable natural and manmade object. The still life offered artists a focused way of exploring the abstract forms and associations of objects. The still lifes of the past are given a compelling psychological cast in Meret Oppenheim's 1936 *Object (The fur-lined Teacup)*,[6] which is an ordinary tea cup, saucer and spoon that have been covered in fur. *Object* suggests a fetish or an odd bit of female craftsmanship. It refers to the elegant afternoon gatherings of women, at which tea is consumed and furs are shown off. As a woman, the artist is certainly referring to her own experience and her interpretations of the female role. But *Object* is most disturbing because it confuses the senses. We recall the smooth sensation of a wet china cup on our lips and touch of fur—whether it is that of a live animal or the coat made from the hide of a dead one. The confusion between these sensations is disquieting on the most sensuous level. For all its twentieth-century psychological associations, it is also a witty comment on the thousands of still lifes of the past. *Object* illuminates important aspects of the artistic consciousness of our own era because it is multifaceted. While it is takes from many types of experiences and traditions, its form is completely different from traditional high art techniques of making sculpture.

Oppenheim took real objects, slightly modified and combined them, and then isolated them in an "art" context. This process is very different from traditional art making. In this new process philosophic significance takes precedence over craftsmanship. The artistic consciousness in the twentieth century is no longer necessarily tied to the skill of the hand. Artists are not defined by what they *make*, but rather by what they *choose* out of the real world. It is the artistic thinking or philosophical stance that defines an artist. Artists no longer think of their ability to replicate, but rather their ability to select objects, modify them or leave them as is, and place them in provocative contexts. *Object (Fur-lined Teacup)* represents this new type of artistic consciousness.

Art in the modern context is a complex activity. To some degree, much of it is autobiographical, referring to the artists' experiences and beliefs. It makes use of traditional forms from the artists' own culture, cultures from around the world, and any image or object outside the usual definition of art. Some modern art protests social conditions or war. Some challenges the basis of rational thought as it is manifest in scientific proofs. Seeing the world in terms of a ruined past, some artists put together fragments of commercial art, scientific notation, tribal art and western high art. Everything is fragmented or disjointed and nothing is new. The conscious mind of the artist can be the organizer of the greater, but chaotic, meaning found in the unconscious. Still others continue to use the oldest traditional techniques and themes. Whether the average viewer is aware of the interaction of the present and the past in a work of modern art, the artist is generally aware of those traditions and their interaction with contemporary influences. However, whatever can be said of the work of one artist, cannot be said of all modern artists.

In traditional cultures, artists shared the same purpose for their art with each other and society as a whole. They looked to their own past for meaning, forms, and justification. We could think of their concept of consciousness as being a shared telescope narrowly focused on the traditions of the community and religion. Artists in the twentieth century look out in many different directions from a vantage point high on a mountain of information. The task of the modern artist is not to adapt traditional images, but rather to bring order to the variety of images brought to them in such abundance through television, print media, museum exhibitions, and seen while walking down any street. In a single day an artist can see high art in a museum, mass-produced advertising, objects from other cultures, folk art, and photographs that serve any number of purposes. It is only through the force of their own personalities and talent that artists achieve a sense of order, albeit a very personal, even unique, sense of order.

Notes

[1] http://keptar.demasz.hu/arthp/art/c/cimabue/madonna/madonna.jpg

[2] http://www.nelsonworks.interspeed.net/vangogh%20hypoth.html

[3] http://www.daliweb.com/clocksx.html1

[4] http://satie.arts.usf.edu/art/arhtest/lec3b.html

[5] http://grunt.space.swri.edu/picasso.html

[6] http://artnet.com/magazine/features/boettger/boettger4.html

Chapter 10

Consciousness, Communities and the Brain: Toward an Ontology of Being

Bruce K. Kirchoff

When we consider the question of consciousness we must, first of all, take ourselves and our own consciousness into consideration. We cannot consider the subject of consciousness apart for the fact that we ourselves are conscious. To do so is to ignore the impact of our own consciousness on our conclusions. If we ignore our own consciousness it may seem that we are drawing objective conclusions about consciousness, but we may merely be caught in our own pre-conceptions. The features of the world that we take as given may be conditioned by our state of consciousness. The only way that we can know if this is so is to begin to take our own consciousness into account. As we do so we will begin to recognize connections between what we take to be reality, the communities to which we belong, and our state of consciousness. A reality/community/consciousness system will emerge. A system that I will refer to as a being.

This paper considers how our participation in communities of human beings can influence our state of consciousness and our perception of what is real in the world. In this sense, I am seeking an inter-personal theory of consciousness.[1]

Theories of Consciousness

Many contemporary theories of consciousness place consciousness on, in, or associated with some external aspect of the world (some object or process) that is taken as the given bearer (or correlate) of consciousness (see Chalmers, 1997). This aspect of the world is then, a priori, taken as the basis for the phenomena of consciousness that the author is trying to explain. Often this aspect of the world is the physical brain, or some aspect or state(s) of the brain. In these cases, the question of consciousness becomes a question of how, or if, the brain forms the basis for consciousness. In either case, the brain is taken as a potent physical object whose manifestation is, or might be, consciousness. What remains unexamined in these theories is the role of the investigator's consciousness in creating what he takes to be the physical brain. In this sense, most investigations of consciousness are incomplete. They deal with consciousness as caused by or correlated with some other object (or process) without dealing with the role that consciousness plays in the creation of these objects (or process) (Churchland, 1985; Newman, 1997a, 1997b). Thus, the foundation upon which most theories of consciousness are based is unsound. These theories assume that consciousness plays no significant role in the creation of the conditions that they take as determinative of consciousness. This is not an assumption that should go unchallenged.

Taking Consciousness Seriously

How can we take our own consciousness into account when we consider the nature of consciousness? At first it seems impossible. Can we take our own consciousness into account in our theories? Can consciousness explain itself? Let me approach these questions obliquely, beginning with a consideration of our experience of ourselves in our normal waking state of consciousness.

When, in our waking state of consciousness, we turn our attention inward we see not just our self, but what we have come to know as the objective world as it is reflected in this self. When we look into our self introspectively we always become aware of a specific content which, at that moment, constitutes our experience of our self. Our direct experience of our consciousness is always as consciousness of something (Husserl, 1962).

If I pause in my writing, close my eyes and turn my thoughts inwards, I am aware of not just a sense of myself but of a specific content that is unified with (and by) that self. I am aware of pressure from the chair on which I sit; of a patterned darkness that I have learned to associate with closed eyes; of the pressure of my muscles and the dull pain in my stomach; of images of trees and people and objects that flit through my consciousness; of feelings of fatigue and worry and contentment that somehow all exist together; of myriad remembered sensations, feelings, experiences that form the content of my momentary consciousness and are unified through my memory and sense of self. Through experiences such as these we become aware of our self as someone who is in constant intercourse with the world. We are not unitary monads who bear our own essential being in ourselves and who stand apart from the world. Rather, when we consider ourselves, we immediately come into contact and relationship with the things, events and people that surround us. We experience ourselves as intentional beings. We are never without an object of our consciousness, though the attainment of this state is the goal of some forms of meditative training. In this light, to take our consciousness seriously seems to mean to take these other aspects of the world seriously too. We can not take consciousness seriously if we do not also take the content of consciousness seriously. Our normal assumption is that this content is a reflection of a preexisting physical world. Does this not lead us back to reconsidering the objects of our world to be a priori given? Are we not back to the problem that I suggest plagues most theories of consciousness?

As long as we theorize about consciousness as if it were a unitary state we will be faced with questions of the a priori reality of the world. From a perspective of a unitary consciousness, the evidence points toward the existence of the world prior to my conscious awareness of it. This world seems to be communicated to my consciousness as a given that shapes my experience.

But our consciousness is not unitary; it is legion. The perspective that takes the physical world as preexisting and prior to our experience, is just one of many possible perspectives on our relationship to the world. It is a perspective based on a hypothesized unitary state of consciousness. If we begin to question this hypothesis, the world begins to look less like an a priori given and more like a multiplicity of potentialities that we instantiate into perceptions through our activity in various states of consciousness.

Daily States of Consciousness

During the span of 24 hours we are subject to a great range of conscious states. During the night we alternate between the states of dreamless and dreaming sleep (Farthing, 1992). As we wake up we pass though, or even linger in, states of consciousness between sleeping and waking (hypnopompic period; Tart, 1969, p. 75). We are aware of some but not all of the perceptions that we have when fully awake. In these states we may have dream-like sensations in which environmental stimuli are incorporated into our half-dream, half-waking consciousness. At some point we become fully awake and experience our surroundings in what we consider to be our waking mode of consciousness.

Once awake we experience many different states of consciousness during the course of a day. Our awareness of ourselves is different while we are writing, speaking in front of an audience, eating, and sitting quietly and thinking. In all of these experiences we retain a core sense of ourselves, but we come into relationship with this core in quite different ways.

The fact that our consciousness varies in these ways can be illustrated by a very simple experiment. Sit quietly with your eyes open in a place where you will not be disturbed for a minute or two. During this time pay attention to your experiences as you inhale and exhale. You should notice a subtle increase in your sense of self on inhalation and a subtle increase in your sense of your surroundings on exhalation. Inhale - self; exhale - world. We live in this rhythm of consciousness but are seldom aware of it. It is a simple example of the complexity of the changes in our consciousness that take place throughout the day. Neither our sense of self, nor our consciousness is unitary. We pass through many different conscious states, yet somehow retain a connection with this abiding memory/perception/thought that we call our self. We retain this connection while our conscious states come and go. This connection allows us to talk and act as if we had a single state of consciousness when in fact we have many.

Non-Self-Conscious States

Up to now I have been writing as if all of our conscious states were self-conscious. In reality, many of them are semi-conscious or unconscious. We interact with the world in a variety of ways in which we do not come to consciousness of ourselves. Although they are unconscious, these interactions may often be more immediate, authentic, and valuable to our survival than our conscious states. Despite this we tend to ignore our unconscious or semi-conscious states when we conceptualize our day-to-day activities. We also tend to ignore them in developing theories of consciousness. Here I will explore only one or two aspects of our unconscious experience to make my point.

If we restrict our discussion to our immediate experience of our everyday lives, we see only a limited number of examples that we can call semi-conscious or unconscious. These examples have to do with our reactions to the events that take place around us.

More dramatic examples of unconscious processing come from the study of hypnotism (Braude, 1991). Although hypnotic states are not parts of our normal waking consciousness, their existence illustrates a potentiality of our consciousness. We have the potential to enter states where we perform seemingly normal actions but are unconscious of them, both while carrying them out and in retrospect. Some of the most striking examples of this come from the field that Binet (1896) calls systematized anaesthesia, or unconscious perception. In unconscious perception a hypnotized subject is directed to ignore some phenomenon in her environment (for a more current review of unconscious perception see Merikle & Daneman, 1998). Upon being woken from the hypnotic state the subject fails to see the object that has been "suggested away." The lack of perception is so acute that, if a person has been suggested away, the subject becomes almost completely insensible to the actions that this person performs. These actions can include sticking the subject with needles to a depth at which they adhere to the skin (Binet, 1896). Although the subjects are seemingly awake and aware during this process, they perceive neither the sensation of the pricking nor the person who performed it. However, if another person whose presence has not been suggested away performs the same action, the subject immediately feels the pin prick and often cries out. In systematized anesthesia something happens to change the subject's perception of, and response to, stimuli. Portions of the external world cease to exist for them.

A second set of examples concerns the perception of colored figures and afterimages while under hypnosis. To understand these experiments first recall the well known example of colored afterimages (Hurvich, 1981). To experience a colored afterimage first stare at a brightly colored shape on white paper, say a red triangle in the center of an otherwise blank page. After staring at this image for several minutes look away at a completely blank, white page. Most people will see a complementary colored triangle on, or floating above, the page. If you began with a red triangle, the triangle in your afterimage will be cyan.[2]

Binet's (1896) experiments with afterimages were conducted by first hypnotizing a subject and suggesting away a red square drawn on a piece of paper (Binet, 1896, p. 300). The subject was then woken and asked to stare, for some minutes, at a paper with a red square on it. Of course they did not see the red square. They saw only a blank piece of paper. Their hypnotic suggestion prevented them from seeing the square. For the first minute or so their vision of the blank piece of paper persisted unchanged. They saw only a blank piece of paper. After a few minutes a cyan square gradually appeared on the piece of paper. The sensation of this complementary square persisted as long as the subject looked at the "invisible" red square.

I will quote Binet (1896) for one final example of unconscious perception and for a brief interpretation of these surprising results.

From ten cards that were exactly alike I selected one and showed it to the somnambulist,[3] and suggested to her that she would not see it when she awoke, but that she should see and recognize all the others. When she awoke I gave her the ten cards; she took them all, except the one that we had shown her during the somnambulistic state—the one I had made invisible by suggestion. How, we may ask, is it possible for the subject to carry out so complicated a suggestion? How does it come about that he does not confuse the invisible card with the others? It must be that he recognized it. If he did not recognize it he would not refuse to see it. Whence this apparently paradoxical conclusion—that the subject must recognize the invisible object in order not to see it! (p. 301)

Binet (1896) goes on to cite other evidence to support his hypothesis of unconscious perception, including work performed along the same lines by William James (1896).

States of Consciousness and Theories of Consciousness

The varied modes of conscious and unconscious perception are significant for our current project because they provide examples of various states from which we interact with the so called external (physical) world. What we normally think of as our unitary waking state of consciousness is really a succession, or perhaps even a superimposition, of conscious and unconscious states through which we define the world and regulate our interactions with it (Ludwig, 1969). The examples from hypnotism are particularly striking because they lead us to question the objective quality of the external world. Binet's (1896) interpretation of his experiments as demonstrating unconscious perception is predicated on the fact that there were others in the room who perceived what the subject could not. The existence of the red square could be attested to by Binet and by the other non-hypnotized subjects. If no one had seen the red square, Binet's conclusions would have been quite different!

One question that arises from these considerations is the question of which state(s) we take as definitive of our relationship to the world. Our relationship to the world changes with each change in our consciousness, so we must choose one state as primary if we are to assign any fixed characteristics to the world. That is, we must learn to interpret the world based on what we agree is the most important state of consciousness for our interactions with that world.

It is clear that our culture has decided to take our so-called daytime consciousness as primary. Still, we are forced to ask, Which state of day-time consciousness? In the previous sections I have spoken of a "normal" daytime consciousness as if we knew what that was. I now put the word normal in quotation marks as an indication that the meaning of this word is ambiguous (see Tart, 1969 p. 1). Since we have no objective way of defining which of our many consciousnesses is "normal," we must accept as "normal" that consciousness which is tacitly accepted as "normal" by most of the people who we meet and interact with in the course of our daily lives. In our culture this is the consciousness through which we create, accept, and interact with the world that we take to be "there" in some physical sense. To say that we take our "normal" daytime consciousness as determinative of the physical world is just to say that most of the people in our culture accept the existence of the physical reality that is determined by this consciousness. It does not mean that the world is "really" the way we take it to be in this state of consciousness. Our state of consciousness and our taking of the world to be a certain way are in a mutually supportive/creative relationship. The world is the way we take it to be because we invest that world with reality by crediting a specific state of consciousness, which has that world as its content.

Any characteristic that is putatively put in the external world exists only as such relative to the state of consciousness in which we see this characteristic. When we change states of consciousness, we change our relationship to the world and, in doing so, we change what we take to be in the world. Changes in consciousness due to hypnosis (or various dissociative disorders such as multiple personality disorder) are striking examples of the effects of changes in consciousness on our creation and experience of an external world (Braude, 1991). In these states we do not experience the objects of the world in the same enduring way that we do when we are in our "normal" consciousness. Objects can disappear from our consciousness and reappear later (or perhaps not at all).

The process of selecting one of our multiple consciousnesses as determinative is inherently social. It involves the formation of, and communication among, a group of individuals who cooperate in selecting and defining a mode of consciousness. This community[4] then takes this mode of consciousness as definitive of what the world is like.

Science as Social Knowledge

Perhaps the most well studied example of social influences on knowledge is the study of the social creation of scientific knowledge. Latour and Woolgar (1979), Latour (1987) and Longino (1990) provide excellent analyzes of how scientific communities influence the practice of science. Their analyzes focus both on how values are incorporated into science and how criticism transforms individual into scientific (i.e., community) knowledge. According to these authors, new scientific knowledge is always produced and evaluated in a specific context, by specific people. For Longino (1990), this context is expressed through the background assumptions that infuse the discipline in which the scientist works. These background assumptions establish acceptable methodologies and express theoretical concerns which the researcher must accept. They may specify the types of experimental procedures to be used, such as requiring clinical research to follow a double-blind protocol, or they may specify theoretical positions to which research must adhere. Examples of the latter type of assumptions are "consciousness is an emergent phenomenon" or "all human disease is genetic in origin" (Berg quoted in Olson, 1989, p. 7). These assumptions provide the vehicle for the incorporation of values and ideology in science. They are part of the context of scientific discoveries.

Not only do scientific results[5] bear the stamp of their context, they also bear the stamp of the scientist(s) who made them. In the initial stages following publication, this stamp may be idiosyncratic. It may embody the scientist's subjective preferences for certain methods, theories, modes of presentation, or what she sees as the relevance of her data to social or spiritual concerns. As the results are assimilated into the body of science they are subjected to the scrutiny, support, and criticism of other members of the scientific community. This scrutiny is the process by which the community removes individual idiosyncratic elements from the discovery and converts the individual's results into scientific knowledge (Longino, 1990). The result is objective scientific knowledge: knowledge that is accepted by the community as being true of the world.

The propensity of scientific communities to turn an individual's results into certain knowledge gives science a Janus face (Latour, 1987). One face is "scientific knowledge," the other is "science in the making." The face that is "scientific knowledge" sees science as based on enduring facts of Nature. Science, as expressed by this face, is about the world of Nature as it exists apart from any investigation of it (figure 1). This is the mature face of science, the face that is often taught to students in introductory classes. The face that is "science in the making" creates what the mature face takes to be Nature through the social process of discovery of results and community scrutiny (figure 1). This face creates Nature. Any of the qualities that the mature face of science takes as existing in Nature were put there by the youthful face of "science in the making." The following example will help make this clear.

Fig. 1. The Janus face of science (after Latour, 1987). Science both creates Nature (young face) and sees its results as based on Nature (mature face).

Among other cases, Latour (1987) analyzes the purported discovery of the structure of Growth Hormone Releasing Hormone by Schally, Baba, Nair and Bennett (1971). In a partly fictional account based on Wade's (1981) description of Schally's work, Latour (1987) evaluates the social process by which scientists marshal support for their results. Whether the discovery is accepted or not depends not only on the original results (Schally et al., 1971), but on many social factors such as the status of the investigator, his institutional affiliation, his relationships with other scientists in the field, which of these scientists accept his results as valid, the status and institutional affiliation of his supporters and critics, etc. These and similar considerations show us that a seemingly simple discovery is, in fact, not simple at all. For Schally's result (a published amino acid sequence) to be regarded as a valid scientific discovery it must be accepted as such by a community of qualified scientists. Once his result is acknowledged by this community, it becomes useful to others. The result begins to fade from view and a discovery takes its place. At this stage, his result can then be accepted as worthy of further attention on the basis of the credentials of the community that endorses it. The result can now be used in other experiments. If these experiments are successful (as judged by the scientific community) the discovery becomes a fact of science whose existence is seen as dependent only on external Nature. The social process that transforms the result into a fact of Nature is ignored. This process of science is not seen as playing a significant role in the discovery, which is viewed as inevitable given the facts of Nature.

This Janus view of science is quite different from the conventional view that sees only the mature face of science, not "science in the making." As we learn to see and credit the face that is "science in the making" we learn that it is not only scientific results, but also scientific communities that create science as a system of discoveries about Nature. In this sense we can say that the properties of Nature are created by community practices. Without a community of scientists to critique, support and utilize a result, the result would remain the province of a single scientist (or laboratory). It would not become a discovery that was accessible to all working scientists.

Although community criticism transforms individual results into discoveries and incorporates these discoveries into the canon of science, it does not remove all values from science. Rather, it brings the investigator's assumptions and idiosyncrasies in line with those of the community. In other words, it incorporates the discovery into the context of the larger scientific community as expressed through the background assumptions of that community (Longino, 1990). The new results are imbued with the values embedded in this larger community.

The transformation of a result and its incorporation into the mature face of science need not transform just the result, it can also change the community. New discoveries (now considered broadly to include new theories) always have the potential to transform the preexisting values and assumptions of the larger scientific community. This transformation may be subtle or radical depending on how the discovery is received and how it fits with other work currently occurring in the field. The fate of a new discovery also depends on the strength of the supporting evidence, the number of unresolved problems in the field, and, not least, on the standing of the scientists who support and instantiate the discovery.

Can we use this knowledge of social processes in science to understand what happens when we select one of our multiple consciousnesses as determinative of our relationship with the world?

Social Influences on Consciousness

In our "normal" waking consciousness the world appears to us as composed of preexisting objects and relationships. At some basic level, I see a tree and know that it is really there. I have an immediate and seemingly unmitigated understanding that the tree is not created by my consciousness but exists outside of me as an independent entity. This understanding is reinforced both by the predictability of events and by my ability to manipulate my environment. Events do not seem to happen at random. My days are patterned with repeated occurrences. Through years of experience I come to know myself as an active agent in a preexisting world.

Although the existence of a preexisting world often seems indisputable, we can begin to question the validity of this experience through the study of other cultures. Certain cultures experience the world in quite different ways. For instance, the Aranda people of Australia use the term altjiranga mitjina to refer to the time-outside-time that exists in dreams and which, to the Aranda, is also the time in which their ancestors live (Rheingold, 1988). To the Aranda there is no difference between the time of their ancestors and the time during which they themselves dream. The term altjiranga mitjina, and the culture that surrounds it, implies a very different relationship to the world than we experience based on our Western objectifying consciousness. To credit the concept of altjiranga mitjina with power and reality the Aranda must approach the world from a different consciousness than we do. Our normal daytime consciousness allows us to form theories about dreams and dreaming consciousness (e.g., Freud, 1942) but we do not, as a rule, experience our ancestors as present among us in a kind of time-outside-time. We may even take persistent experiences of this sort as indicators of serious psychological problems. To the Aranda, however, altjiranga mitjina is real. It is part of what they call the preexisting world.

The view of knowledge that sees the nature of the preexisting world as dependent on our state of consciousness is uncommon in the sciences. Sir Arthur Eddington (1930) explains the more common view in the following manner.

> But consider how our supposed acquaintance with a lump of matter is attained. Some influence emanating from it plays on the extremity of a

nerve, starting a series of physical and chemical changes which are propagated along the nerve to a brain cell; there a mystery happens, and an image or sensation arises in the mind which cannot purport to resemble the stimulus which excites it. Everything known about the material world must in one way or another have been inferred from these stimuli transmitted along the nerves. It is an astonishing feat of deciphering that we should have been able to infer an orderly scheme of natural knowledge from such indirect communication. But clearly there is one kind of knowledge which cannot pass through such channels, namely knowledge of the intrinsic nature of that which lies at the far end of the line of communication ... The mind as a central receiving station reads the dots and dashes of the incoming nerve signals ... But a broadcasting station is not like its call-signal; there is no commensurability in their natures. So too, the chairs and tables around us which broadcast to us incessantly those signals which affect our sight and touch cannot in their nature be like unto the signals or to the sensations which the signals awake at the end of their journey. (Eddington, 1930, pp. 34-36)

While Eddington recognizes that our images of the world are shaped by our senses, he accepts the existence of a preexisting world of objects apart from our experience of them. To see the problem with this view, we need only ask ourselves how Eddington knows that there is a world of chairs and tables that "broadcasts" to us. If, as he claims, his only evidence is our reception of these "broadcasts," how does he know that there is a world of objects standing behind these experiences? Either he is claiming access to privileged knowledge that allows him to know the world apart from the way it appears to his senses, or he has created that world by projecting his representations into the world. Since Eddington never explicitly claimed access to privileged knowledge I will only deal with the later case, the projection of sense experience into a pre-experiential world. In doing this, Eddington is making an assumption about the legitimate types of things that can be in the world. But this is not a mere intellectual assumption. It seems unlikely that Eddington holds the theory that there is a world of objects that "broadcast" to us. He more likely, like most of us, sees chairs and tables as really existing in the world. He creates these objects from his sense experiences. As he does this he selects a state of consciousness out of which it is possible to create objects. In other states of consciousness he could not take this creative step. For instance, dream consciousness does not lend itself to the creation of enduring objects. Dream objects appear and disappear from the dream world in a way that is not possible for objects in the world of our normal daytime consciousness. The objects and the state of consciousness that engender them exist as components of a self-supporting system. Physical objects only have their characteristic externality because they take their genesis from a state of consciousness that creates externality.

Although this externality-creating consciousness is necessary for the creation of the world of our everyday experience, it is not sufficient for this task. Eddington creates the external world out of this consciousness but he does not do so alone. He does not think or act in a vacuum. He is part of a community of individuals who hold similar views and who modify their views based on interactions with the world, and among community members. These communities are similar to, though often less coherent than, scientific communities. The creation and shaping of consciousness that takes place in communities does so through social processes that reinforce certain parts of our experience at the expense of others. Those experiences that are reinforced are emphasized, while those that find little or no reinforcement are down played.

To see that community processes select and reinforce specific states of consciousness, and not just the content of consciousness, recall that all consciousness is inherently intentional (Husserl, 1962). Consciousness is always consciousness of. Thus, as we change consciousness we change the "of-ness" of which we are conscious.[6] Dream consciousness is the state in which we are conscious of dreams. Daytime object consciousness is the state in which we are conscious of the objects of our everyday world. Consciousness, and the of-ness of which we are conscious, exist in a mutually supportive, interdependent relationship. Each is dependent on the other for the creation of the content of our experience.

As community processes shape the of-ness of our experience, they change our consciousness. A community that accepts the reality of the time-outside-time of altjiranga mitjina engenders a state of consciousness that allows the experience of altjiranga mitjina. Altjiranga mitjina can thus be seen both as an experience held by the members of a certain community and as the consciousness out of which this experience occurs. In the same way, a physical object is both an element of our experience and the consciousness out of which the object is created. Consciousness and the reality engendered by that consciousness exist in a mutually supportive system that is maintained by social processes.

The relationship between these elements changes with each change in consciousness so that it becomes difficult to determine any fixed characteristics that exist in the world.

Another way of seeing the relationship between consciousness and its content comes with the recognition that no state of consciousness is self-determinative. A certain state does not arise in us as an inevitable consequence of being alive. At the grossest level, the ability to sustain any form of consciousness is dependent on receiving sufficient nutrition. This, in turn, is dependent on a stable social and political situation that allows the production and distribution of food. At a more subtle level, states of consciousness are elicited and trained through social institutions. College is as much about learning to think as it is about learning facts (Erickson & Strommer, 1991; Meyers, 1986). As any college teacher knows, learning to think is no easy matter. It demands a specific, focused, state of consciousness that can only be evoked through practice. The fact that we are familiar with the transitions that take place during college should not diminish their importance for us. All states of consciousness are substantially deter- mined by social interactions: the culture we inhabit, the times we live in, the institutions we attend, the company we keep, etc. Barfield (1965) makes a similar point in his elegant book on appearance and reality: *Saving the Appearances*. He marshals evidence to show that the medieval world was not our world. The inhabitants of different his- torical periods took different kinds of experiences to be about the real world. In this sense, history is a record of changes in consciousness and the concomitant changes in the nature of the world.

Consciousness and Beings

The picture that has emerged in the preceding discussion is one of an interdependence between social groups, consciousness and the con- structed reality that is taken for granted by a community. None of these components exist in isolation. They form a system in which the indi- vidual elements are linked into a larger whole (figure 2). The existence of this whole makes it difficult to speak about the individual elements in isolation. When we do so, we tend to emphasize a specific element at the expense of the others. To say that a specific state of consciousness engenders specific characteristics of reality emphasizes the creative power of consciousness and down plays the role of the community and the World,[7] which cooperate in the process of interpersonal validation of the contents of experience. Interpersonal validations are built out of community interactions with the constructed reality that the community takes to be real. In trying to make one of the three parts of the system clear we inevitably downplay the role of the other two.

The following phrases are attempts to find an adequate way of expressing the relationships diagramed in figure 2. The first three sentence pairs each describes one link in the system. The numbers are keyed to the links in figure 2.

1. Communities construct reality.
2. Reality shapes communities.

3. Reality contents[8] consciousness.
4. Consciousness creates reality.

5. Shared consciousness creates community.
6. Community engenders and strengthens consciousness.

Each of the following aphorisms takes one of the points of the circle as its starting point and moves around the circle of causality in one direction (figure 2, dotted arrow). All of the aphorisms are equally true.

Reality defines and gives meaning to a community that maintains consciousness in a way that allows that reality to manifest itself.

A community selects a state of consciousness that allows reality to manifest itself in a way that the community finds to be true.

Consciousness engenders a reality in a way that the community that sustains that consciousness finds to be true.

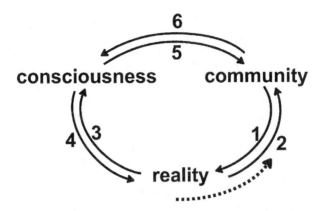

Fig. 2. Reality/community/consciousness system. The numbers and dashed arrow are keyed to the text.

I want to introduce a term for individual instances (instantiations) of this tripartite system of reality/community/consciousness. I call these specific instances, beings. Though constituted differently, they share many characteristics with other types of beings. They have their own qualities, tendencies, temporal extent, and can be resistant to change. Just as different species have different characteristics, different reality/community/consciousness beings have different characters. We feel these characters through our experiences as members of different communities. We experience the world differently when we are with different people.

There are two main, and interrelated, problems we face in trying to describe these beings: language and unfamiliarity. Despite some excellent work on systems theory (Bertalanffy, 1969; Forrester, 1971; Wiener, 1961) we still do not have a way of talking about and understanding systems as wholes that does full justice to their reality.[9] We can point to some general characteristics of systems, but have great difficulty in speaking about these characteristics when they are instantiated in a real system. For instance, according to systems theory causality is contextual not linear (Bateson, 1967). For any effect there is more than one cause. General descriptions like these work fine as long as we stay at this level of description. Problems arise when we begin analyzing specific cases. When we look at a specific system we are tempted to revert to the language of causality, to select one of the elements as primary and to relate the others, as effects, to the actions of this cause. As we begin to speak of reality/community/consciousness systems as beings, one natural tendency is to see the community of individuals as the being. But this does not do justice to the nature of the system. The group is no more the being than is the state of consciousness that is selected and maintained by the group, or the reality that is intended by this state. The being is the system of reality/ community/consciousness that both transcends and is immanent in the elements that compose the system. Reality is constructed both by communities and by states of consciousness. None of these factors can be meaningfully isolated from the others. From a systems perspective, reality is constructed out of the context that is the system (figure 2). The context is the cause of the reality.[10]

One way of understanding these beings is to think of them as analogous to individual organisms. I want to stress that this is a crude analogy. We would be mistaken to draw too much from it. Still, it may be helpful to think about what it means to be a being/system in terms of organisms with which we are more familiar.

From a non-systems point of view organisms are composed of various parts that function harmoniously together to make the organism. This point of view sees the organism as extrinsically membered into a number of parts that compose the organism. I say extrinsically membered because, from this point of view, the parts do not have any inherent (intrinsic) connection with each other. The parts are externally connected through the fact that they happen to belong to an organism.

From a systems viewpoint the organism is a whole that is intrinsically membered into parts. The parts do not happen to belong to the organism. Rather they are parts because they belong to the organism. When we take this holistic view we see the parts as intrinsically connected to the organism as a whole. Part and whole stand in a different and more intimately connected relationship than we are normally accustomed to. From a holistic point of view it would be more correct to say part/whole than part and whole. The relationship is one where the part and the whole are so intimately connected that they take their meanings from each other (Bortoft, 1996). There is no whole without the parts that comprise it, but the parts are only parts because they are "of the whole." Abstract definitions of "part" and "whole" miss this relationship.

The reality/community/consciousness beings that I am describing have this part/whole character. The "parts" of the being are the (1) community members; (2) state of consciousness out of which the members of this community participate in the community; (3) constructed reality sustained by and sustaining (1) and (2). None of these "parts" exists in isolation. The do not happen to belong together. They are not extrinsic parts. They are intrinsic participants in the part/whole that is the being. They are parts because they belong to the being. If I have emphasized their part-ness it is because we, from our academically trained analytic consciousness, see parts more easily than we do wholes. I could, for a different audience, have begun with the whole (the being) and membered it into its parts.

Another way to understand that these beings are more than just theoretical constructs is to recall that it "feels like something" to be with a specific group of people. Our consciousness shifts as we come into contact with different groups of people. Snow (1959) refers to some of these experiences in his description of scientific and literary cultures in England after World War II. Although we all have these impressions, they are very difficult to describe. Instead of attempting inadequate descriptions, let me draw your attention to your own experience by asking you to reflect on questions like the following. What does it feel like to be at home with your family? How is this different from what you feel in your place of employment? What does it feel like to be at a conference in your discipline? How is this different from what you feel when you go to a football game? What does it feel like to have a friendly audience for a talk? How is this different from a hostile audience? We all experience these differences, but seldom pay much attention to them. I suggest that they are the result of subtle differences in the nature of the reality/community/consciousness beings that create the atmosphere in each of these places or situations.

The examples given above represent minor changes in reality/community/consciousness that occur within a culture. It is between cultures that more striking differences occur. Different cultures can be based on radically different reality/community/consciousness beings/systems. It feels different to be in them. This is true even within Europe. It feels different to be in England than on the continent; different to be in France than Germany; different to be in the Italian speaking part of Switzerland than in the French speaking part. The differences are real and immediate. They illustrate that reality/community/consciousness beings/systems are not merely theoretical. As theory, they are systems. As experience, they are beings.

What is The Brain?

From the perspective introduced here the brain[11] is an extrinsic part of an external physical reality that is constructed by the activity of a reality/community/consciousness being. It is a consciousness/social construct of this being. We, the participants in this being, imbue the brain with a number of characteristics that we then take to be determinative of the consciousness through which we create external reality. As such, the brain cannot be accorded any more (or less) credence as an effective agent than can any other part of constructed reality. For those who are members of the community, the brain will always seem real, given. It will be indisputable that the brain has a role in consciousness. The exact role may be the subject of vigorous debate, but, within this being, the fact that the brain must be the cause (or correlate) of consciousness will be indisputable. As Chalmers (1996) notes (though in different terms), it is difficult to convince those who participate in this being that there is a Hard Problem to consciousness. The being that participates them does not see it.

Consciousness and Communities

What about consciousness? Is consciousness the cause of the brain? Do we create physical reality and thus the brain through consciousness. Is consciousness more primary than physical reality? Although these are natural questions, the form in which they are put unintentionally leads away from understanding the relationship between consciousness and reality suggested here. I see neither consciousness nor physical reality as primary. Rather they exist as intrinsic parts of a system with a community of people who credit the type of consciousness that is sustained by the physical reality that this consciousness creates. To say that consciousness creates physical reality is to see only one part of the system. It is equally true to say that physical reality contents consciousness. Looking from this direction it appears that physical reality is primary. It is active in the process of "contenting" consciousness.

Are the systems I am speaking of identical with concrete communities of human beings? Again the question misses the point. Communities are the vehicles for the expression of a given state of consciousness that is embodied in the individual human beings that comprise the community. These individuals comprise the community precisely because they embody this consciousness. In instantiating this state of consciousness the community becomes a vehicle for a specific reality that is the content of this consciousness. The whole system (reality/community/consciousness) is the being, not the community.

Conscious and the Theoretician

In closing, let us return to my original objection that theories of consciousness do not take the consciousness of the theoretician into account. I believe that the theory of reality/community/consciousness beings elaborated here answers this criticism. The state of consciousness out of which I wrote this paper was engendered through readings and discussions with other people who share similar ideas. While no one shared exactly my ideas, there were enough similarities to make discussion possible. My views were shaped by these readings and discussions. The more I think about, discuss, and write about these ideas, the more clear they become both to me and to those with whom I interact. We begin to form a community that shares a specific state of consciousness with a specific content. The reality/community/consciousness beings of which I write are this content. They are as real as any community/consciousness created reality. My state of consciousness is an intrinsic part of this being whose content is the existence of reality/community/consciousness beings.

Acknowledgements: I thank Michelle Gibson for drawing figure 1, and Andrea Shapiro, Ken Caneva and J. Scott Jordan for comments and discussions that improved the manuscript. This paper was prepared with support from the Fetzer Foundation and is based on ideas that were developed with support from the Future Value Fund of the Anthroposophical Society in America and the Institute of Noetic Sciences. The ideas elaborated herein were presented as a poster at Toward a Science of Consciousness, Tucson III, April 27 - May 2, 1998.

Notes

[1]Burns and Engdahl (1998) undertake a similar project.

[2]Binet (1896) refers to this complementary color as "greenish." However, if it were really complementary to red it would be cyan.

[3]The subject who had been hypnotized.

[4]I use the word community in a very broad sense to mean a group of individuals who feel themselves united by common views or in search for a common goal. In this sense, a community can be as small as two people or as large as a culture. All that is needed to create a community is (1) some type of interpersonal communication, and (2) the willingness of one or both of the parties to modify their ideas or practices based on that communication. As communication increases, the chance for social interactions to effect theories and perceptions also increases but I do not see the amount of social interaction as being of primary importance. The willingness of an individual to modify his ideas is of equal or greater importance. In this I differ from Daston (1992) who restricts the ability of scientific communication to substantially influence scientific theories (i.e., to lead to socially constructed objectivity) to the period beginning with the middle decades of the last century when communication between scientist greatly increased.

[5]In the following I distinguish between a scientific result and a discovery. A result is a published account of some item of scientific interest by a specific individual or laboratory. A discovery is a result that has been accepted by the larger scientific community as being true. The transformation of a result into a discovery is a social process.

[6]I avoid saying that we are conscious of "something" or of "objects" because these words imply that the of-ness of which we are conscious are things or objects having the type of externality that is created by only one kind of consciousness.

[7]It is difficult to explain, in a short space, what I mean by the word "World." Barfield (1965) approaches my meaning with his concept of the unrepresented. For Barfield, the unrepresented is the ground of existence as

described by contemporary physics. He is struck by the discrepancy between our experiences and this underlying ground of reality. Faced with this discrepancy he concludes that the multitude of perceptions that we call reality are really representations (or figurations, to use his term) of this underlying ground.

I want to go one step farther. To me, the theories of physics are also constructions of reality. We cannot rely on these theories for a direct description of the ground of the world (the World). The World is what reality is like before it is figured into perceptions by our sense apparatus and thinking. We become aware of its existence only through our experience of agreement/disagreement with other people. It is the basis for all agreements and disagreements. I am tempted to say that the World is that which underlies the of-ness that is the content of consciousness: the of-ness on which communities agree. However, this formulation tends to objectify the World, to give it thing-like qualities. The word "underlies" implies that there is some physical thing that lies under the characteristic "of-ness." The World cannot have thing-like characteristics because the quality of thingness is a community creation as much as any physical object. The World is no-thing with no-characteristics. At the same time it is expressed in and through all things and all characteristics. It is the no-thing expressed in all things. It is no-consciousness expressed in all consciousness.

[8]I am led to unusual word constructions because I want to avoid two related problems in talking about reality. The first concerns the use of the passive voice for the relation between consciousness, reality and community. The passive voice implies that a passive subject receives the action specified by the verb. Saying that reality is reflected in consciousness implies that consciousness is active and reality is passive. This is an artifact of our language that is not implied in the system diagrammed in figure 2. The second problem occurs when we speak of reality as taking an active role in creating consciousness. Our colloquial understanding of reality as primary and consciousness as secondary makes it difficult to speak of reality as creative. Doing so encourages the reader to loose sight of the reality/community/consciousness system that creates/ sustains reality and consciousness. I use the word "contents" in an attempt to get around these problems. By "contents" I mean an active process in which reality participates in and sustains a specific state of consciousness.

[9]The reality to which I refer here is a constructed reality just like any other. I am not suggesting that system theorists have access to privileged knowledge about the true nature of reality.

[10]Note that the (constructed) reality is part of its own context. This seems to be a general characteristic of complex adaptive systems (Gell-Mann, 1994). The inputs to a complex adaptive system include the states of the system itself.

[11]By "brain" I mean that human anatomical object that is taken as to be a nexus of structures or processes that are (or that produce) consciousness.

References

Barfield, O. 1965. *Saving the appearances*. New York: Harcourt, Brace & World.

Bateson, G. 1967. Cybernetic explanation. *American Behavioral Scientist* 10:29-32.

Bertalanffy, L. von. 1969. *General system theory; Foundations, development, applications*. New York: G. Braziller.

Binet, A. 1896. *Alternations of personality*. London: Chapman and Hall.

Bortoft, H. 1996. *The wholeness of nature*. Hudson, NY: Lindisfarne Press.

Braude, S. E. 1991. *First person plural*. London: Routledge.

Burns, T. R., and Engdahl, E. 1998. The social construction of consciousness. Part 1: Collective consciousness and its socio-cultural foundations. *Journal of Consciousness Studies* 5:67-85.

Chalmers, D. J. 1996. *The conscious mind*. New York: Oxford University Press.

———. 1997. Moving forward on the problem of consciousness. *Journal of Consciousness Studies* 4:3-46.

Churchland, P. M. 1985. Reduction, qualia and the direct introspection of brain states. *Journal of Philosophy* 82:8-28.

Daston, L. 1992. Objectivity and the escape from perspective. *Social Studies of Science* 22:597-618.

Eddington, A. S. 1930. *Science and the unseen world*. New York: Macmillan.

Erickson, B. L., and Strommer, D. W. 1991. *Teaching college freshman*. San Francisco, CA: Jossey-Bass.

Farthing, W. G. 1992. *The psychology of consciousness*. Englewood Cliffs, NJ: Prentice Hall.

Forrester, J. W. 1971. *Principles of systems*. Cambridge, MA: Wright-Allen Press.

Freud, S. [1899] 1942. *The Interpretation of dreams*. London: Allen and Unwin.

Gell-Mann, M. 1994. Complex adaptive systems. In *Complexity: Metaphores, models, and reality*, edited by G. Cowan, D. Pines and D. Meltzer. Santa Fe Institute Studies in the Sciences of Complexity, Proceedings Vol. XIX. Reading, MA: Addison-Wesley.

Hurvich, L. M. 1981. *Color vision.* Sunderland, MA: Sinauer Associates.

Husserl, E. [1913] 1962. *Ideas: General introduction to pure phenomenology.* Reprint, New York: Collier Books.

James, W. 1896. *The principles of psychology.* New York: Henry Holt & Co.

Latour, B. 1987. *Science in action.* Cambridge, MA: Harvard University Press.

Latour, B., and Woolgar, S. 1979. *Laboratory life: The social construction of scientific facts.* Beverly Hills, CA: Sage Publications.

Longino, H. E. 1990. *Science as social knowledge: Values and objectivity in scientific inquiry.* Princeton, NJ: Princeton University Press.

Ludwig, A. M. 1969. Altered states of consciousness. In *Altered states of consciousness,* edited by C. T. Tart. New York: John Wiley & Sons.

Merikle, P. M., and Daneman, M. 1998. Psychological investigations of unconscious perception. *Journal of Consciousness Studies* 5:5-18.

Meyers, C. 1986. *Teaching students to think critically.* San Francisco, CA: Jossey-Bass.

Newman, J. 1997a. Putting the puzzle together. Part I: Towards a general theory of the neural correlates of consciousness. *Journal of Consciousness Studies* 4:47-66.

————. 1997b. Putting the puzzle together. Part II: Towards a general theory of the neural correlates of consciousness. *Journal of Consciousness Studies* 4:100-121.

Olson, S. 1989. *Shaping the future: Biology and human values.* Washington, D.C.: National Academy Press.

Rheingold, H. 1988. *They have a word for it.* Los Angeles, CA: Jeremy P. Tarcher, Inc.

Schally, A. V., Baba, Y., Nair, R. M. G., and Bennett, C. D. 1971. The amino acid sequence of a peptide with growth hormone releasing activity isolated from porcine hypothalamus. *Journal of Biological Chemistry* 246:6647-6650.

Snow, C. P. 1959. *The two cultures and the scientific revolution.* New York: Cambridge University Press.

Tart, C. T. 1969. *Altered states of consciousness.* New York: John Wiley & Sons.

Wade, N. 1981. *The nobel duel.* Garden City, NY: Anchor Press.

Wiener, N. 1961. *Cybernetics; or, Control and communication in the animal and the machine* (2nd ed.). New York: M.I.T. Press.

Chapter 11

"Not-Self" Consciousness and the Aniconic in Early Buddhism

Michael D. Rabe

According to the calendar observed in Theravada Buddhist countries like Thailand and Sri Lanka, a South Asian prince named Siddhartha achieved Enlightenment 2,584 years ago,[1] while meditating beneath this tree (plate 1). While the Bodhi tree itself may be a replanted off-shoot of the original, it is reasonably certain that that epochal event occurred at this very spot, at Bodh Gaya, in Bihar State, north India, for it has been designated as such since at least the mid-3rd century B.C.E. by the beautiful throne-like slab of sandstone, installed there by the emperor Ashoka, the first Imperial sponsor of Buddhist monuments.[2]

Of equal significance to our inquiry into the nature of that Enlightenment, and the many subsequent attempts that have been made to extrapolate its ramifications for our understanding of consciousness and "Self", is the early Buddhist aversion toward the making of anthropomorphic icons—an aversion that persisted without any known violation for an additional two centuries after Ashoka's reign. What explains, in other words, the half millennium gap between the Buddha's "Awakening" and the earliest figural depictions of him as such, seated in the lotus position with the mudra/hand gesture known as "Bhumisparsha: Calling the Earth to Witness [that Awakening]" by which he touches the ground with the outstretched fingers of his right hand?[3]

After a full century of scholarly inquiry, this question still rankles. It remains unsatisfactorily answered, in part because the vast canons of Buddhist scripture and commentarial literature are conspicuously silent on the issue. Presumably, this textual reticence reflects the fact that even the earliest among them were not redacted in their present written forms until after the practice of making Buddhist icons became commonplace, starting in the first century B.C.E.[4] Earlier iconophobic proscriptions, should they have existed, were necessarily vitiated or "lost" altogether once figural icons gained official sanction.[5]

Though still not widely known or cited in the art historical literature on these twinned problems of the so-called "aniconic period" and the subsequent "origins of the Buddha image" there is one telling exception to the otherwise blanket-silence in Buddhist texts on the presumptive five-century prohibition against Buddha icons. In the Vinaya or monastic handbook of the Sarvastivadin sect,[6] there is a long passage which deals with the decoration of monasteries. A monk named Anahapindika is said to have addressed the Buddha as follows: 'World-honoured one, if images of yours are not allowed to be made, pray may we not at least make images of Bodhisattvas[7] in attendance upon you!' Buddha then grants permission.

This fine distinction—between the prohibited Buddha icons, but sanctioned Bodhisattvas[8]—accords perfectly with the epigraphic evidence for the first securely dated buddha images, dedicated in the late First century of the Common Era, with dates in regnal years of the Kushan Emperor Kanishka.[9] Engraved on this frequently published masterpiece known as the Katra Buddha (plate 2), for example, is the claim by its donor, a woman called "Amoha-asi, mother of Buddharakhita," to have installed this "Bodhisattva" image in her own convent for the happiness of her parents and all other sentient beings."[10]

Why, one wonders, are the earliest dated images, including this one, identified insistently by inscription as "bodhisattva" images when clearly they bear all the marks and monastic dress of what soon thereafter came to be known as actual "Buddha" icons—by contrast to "bodhisattvas" properly so-called (plate 3) i.e., "potential buddhas," still possessing the jeweled accouterments of a prince, as if not yet having taken final vows of renunciation and entry into full-Buddhahood. Particularly, since one of that first set of seemingly conflationary

Buddhas-called-bodhisattvas bears an inscription dedicating it to teachers of the Sarvastivadin sect[11]—the same order whose monastic handbook contains that sole textual prohibition against Buddha images with the concessionary option to make Bodhisattvas—it appears that the inscriptions constitute cautious euphemisms, as if reflective of a still conscious taboo against Buddha icons per se.[12] Buddha images they certainly appear to be, in every way but name only. Significantly, this technical discrimination between proscribed buddha images and sanctioned bodhisattvas is anticipated by a vitally important group of narrative relief panels that pre-date the first free-standing buddha icons by two centuries or more.

Because they also predate any extant written texts, they constitute the very oldest documentary records of the historical Buddha's bio-graphy and teachings. Carved in the sandstone railings, cross-beams and gateways of reliquary stupas at places like Bharhut and Sanchi, these earliest surviving Buddhist documents consistently avoid depic-tion of the Buddha in human form—even in narrative episodes such as that depicted in plate 4, where his presence is unmistakably called for by contextualizing clues of setting or the activities of other characters—in this case the monkey who danced for joy when the meditating Buddha (his presence implied by the platform beneath a bodhi-tree) accepted his offering of a bowl of honey. No such scruple prevented the Bharhut artist from showing the bodily form of the buddha in an earlier incarnation, however, when as a leader of a troop of monkeys (plate 5) he, the "bodhisattva"/not yet the buddha, enabled his followers to escape from hunters by crossing a river on his back.

The rule held true for all the Buddha-to-be's human incarnations as well, as in depictions of his life as the unicorned yogi (plate 6) or, in his penultimate life as Prince Vessantara, the Paragon of Generosity, as depicted in a long continuous narrative on the lowest architrave of the north gate at Sanchi,[13] where he is shown in fully human form giving away by turn from the right, his sacred White elephant, then horses and chariot, to be followed on the other side of the architrave (plate 7) by gifts of his children and even his wife (lower scene below, from the right)—to the disguised god Indra who subsequently reunited the family and prophesied Vessantara's imminent Enlightenment in his very next life.

Significantly, it is that very event, prince Siddhartha's achievement of Enlightenment beneath the bodhi tree, that is depicted on the gateway's middle architrave (plate 7), immediately above, but in strictly aniconic form. While a great but comic band of demons are gathered to the right in a futile attempt to prevent Siddhartha's transformation from bodhisattva status to full-fledged Buddhahood, the prince himself is not visible—his presence only implied by the vacant seat beneath the Bodhi tree to the left, with a royal parasol hovering tellingly above.

So why the double-standard? When it was perfectly acceptable to depict the Buddha's earlier, bodhisattva incarnations, why were such elaborate circumventions devised for depicting events in his final life without including the central character in human form? Again, in the absence of surviving textual proscriptions, scholars have sought to infer explanations from core doctrines of the Buddhism tradition as it subsequently developed.

Could the reason be, some have wondered, that the Buddha's defining experience was so ineffable as to defy any means of visual or verbal characterization? Certainly, the Buddha refused to define the state of consciousness he called nirvana, only hinting obliquely that "anyone who achieves it will be no more seen by men or gods."[14] Others have cited a text which states that "He who is passionless regarding all desires, resorts to nothingness."[15] ... As flame ... blown by the force of wind goes out and is no longer reckoned ... Even so the sage, [released from the constructs of individual existence, vanishes from perception].[16] Accordingly, the absence of Buddha images in the early art reflects his "true Nirvana essence [which is] inconceivable in visual form and human shape."[17]

As logical as these inferences may seem, one must admit that vociferous objection to the very existence of aniconic conventions in early Buddhist art has been made by some. Consider, for example, Susan Huntington's alternative reading of the panel that ostensibly represents the Buddha's enlightenment as depicted at Bharhut (plate 8). Dating from approximately one century before the Sanchi gateway we have just been looking at, and as if reflective of its relative novelty at the time of its creation in the mid-Second century B.C.E., this oldest known depiction of the Enlightenment bears an explanatory label inscription: "Bhagavato Sakamunino Bodho." About the first two words there is no dispute. Unmistakably they refer to the historical Buddha as "the Venerable Sage of the Shakyas", the aristocratic family into which Siddhartha had been born. But does the third word, "Bodho" for Enlightenment signify the Enlightenment event itself or might it be intended adjectivally, as Huntington has argued,[18] to identify the place, Bodh Gaya, or more narrowly the Bodhi tree shown growing from the admittedly anachronistic hypaethral shrine that could only have been built around it at a much later time? Restating the question with reference to the worshipful attendant figures, do they represent divine witnesses present at the very moment when Bodhisattva Siddhartha became the Buddha, or do they represent later human visitors to the site of Bodh Gaya—in which case the need for inferring the Buddha's own presence from aniconic symbols does not arise?

Fortunately, this question need not detain us long, for collateral inscriptions on two lower panels are compatible only with the traditional aniconic reading of the narrative as referring aniconically to the Buddha's own attainment of Enlightenment (plate 9). Clearly assembled as witnessing hosts for precisely that occasion are several classes of named terrestrial deities. Seated, most tellingly to the far left, is the defeated god of death, Mara, dejectedly scrapping in the dirt with a stick, as reported in subsequent texts. The pillar's lowest panel (of three) is engraved with the names of heavenly dancers who seem to be celebrating the Buddha's triumph by performing a biographical pageant in his honor.[19]

Read accordingly, the smallest figure may represent the new-born babe, Siddhartha, standing to make his solemn declaration of eminent Buddhahood, immediately after issuing painlessly from his mother Maya's side in the Lumbini garden. Then, fast forwarding to the moment at hand in the two upper panels, might not the other Apsaras be reenacting the futile wiles of Mara's daughters? If so, they are the earliest surviving depictions of the threesome that came to be known in later Buddhist texts as Tanha ("Thirst"), Arati ("Dissatisfaction"), and Raga ("Passion"). What an exquisite visual conceit was thus created by the unknown master of the Bharhut vedika (stupa railing): goddesses celebrating the Buddha's triumph by reenacting the frustrated dances of Death's daughters, to the accompaniment of harps, drums and a flute! An early Buddhist passion play, indeed.

So the aniconic reading of such scenes survives the Huntington challenge. We are supposed to recognize the invisible signs of the Buddha's presence there at Bodh Gaya on the occasion of his Enlightenment (plate 8)—but still the question lingers—why not just show him, unambiguously seated here beneath the Bodhi tree in human form? For the sake of clearing conceptual space upon which to erect an alternative explication, I must also point out that there are problems with the conventional wisdom of scholars Susan Huntington has argued against. How can it be, as Richard Gombrich has stated, for example, that the Buddha was not shown to symbolize the fact that he was nibbuta ('extinguished'),[20] when clearly that was not the case until 40 years later, at the moment of his death known as the Parinirvana? During the intervening years, the Buddha remained fully active in the flesh, recruiting adherents to his Dharma and fellow members of a monastic Sangha.

Thus, I presume there is ample justification for developing the alternative hypothesis to which I have alluded in the title of this paper: "'Not-Self' Consciousness and the Aniconic in Early Buddhism." In a future paper I propose to construct discrete equations between several teachings of the Buddha and correspondingly specific aniconic symbols. By the doctrine of "not-Self," for example, one may be relieved to learn, the Buddha did not intend to deny our common sense awareness of individual existence. To the contrary, he fully accepted and moreover reinforced the pan-Indian notion of karmic laws that bind past moral actions with future consequences, even across multiple rebirths.[21]

Rather, his intent was pragmatic, one might even say therapeutic,[22] aimed at enabling his followers to rise above overly literal identification with body or cognitive or emotive phenomena that trigger attachment and lead inevitably to dukha—i.e., the sorrow or frustration that accompanies every reminder of human inadequacy. It is true that he faulted Brahmanical definitions of the Atma, or Self/capitalized, as overly reified—and thus denied the existence of an eternal, unchanging Soul-like ghost in the human machine. Emphasis is required on the word "unchanging" in the teachings of one who wished to stress processes of becoming over declarations of immutable Being.

How appropriate, therefore, it was for early Buddhist artists to visualize the subject of a series of "not-self" meditations as an invisible entity, his presence indicated, nevertheless, by the venerating gestures of a receptive audience, together, more often than not, with a pair of footprints.[23] The intent was not to claim (falsely) that he wasn't physically or psychologically present, nor to allude to his eventual freedom from the vicious cycle of karmically conditioned rebirths in Samsara, but merely to assert consciousness of being other than body or ego or any of the other so-called five aggregates[24] or the 12 bases (*ayatana*) of consciousness[25] or the 18 elements (*dhatu*) of empirical experience.[26]

Not that any of them are non-existent phenomena—but merely that the meditator is fostering the cessation of desire via detachment. (This, after all, is the ultimate goal of Buddhism: according to the Third Noble Truth, the cessation of suffering via the cessation of desire, and thus the attainment of Nirvana.)[27]

Likewise, the stream of consciousness characterized by the Buddha as a process of dependent origination, his denial of an eternally unchanging Soul-Essence, and assertion of causality patterns among phenomena can be graphically illustrated by a spinning wheel (plate 10), the so-called Dharma-cakra that came to be the standard aniconic symbol for the Buddha as teacher. Imagine the illusion that would be produced by one flickering light source if affixed to a spinning wheel's rim.[28] Whether or not Picasso had heard of this ancient Indian metaphor I cannot say but Gjon Mili's famous 1949 time-lapse portrait of him drawing a light-minotaur perfectly illustrates the point.[29] Strictly speaking, at any given instant, the minotaur does not exist, but the illusion of one is produced by the perception of a series of instantaneous but momentary points of light as a continuously flowing line. Likewise, "a succession of thoughts does not a Thinker make," one might characterize the Buddhist tradition as saying, at least not an eternally unchanging One.

Finally, I close with a rare match between Buddhist text and visual image, one associated with the aniconic symbol of expanded lotus blossoms. As illustrated on an inside panel of the second terrace at Borobudur,[30] and according to a Buddhist "Pilgrim's Progress" known as the *Gandhavyuha*, on one occasion at the Jetavahana ashram, neither the assembled senior monks, nor the world-guardian deities, nor bodhisattvas were able to comprehend the great power of the Buddha, his all-prevading wisdom, his miraculous virtues, etc. They hoped that the Buddha would manifest to them some of these miraculous powers, and the Buddha, having understood their wish lowered his level of consciousness to a meditative state known as the "lion's yawn samadhi" whereupon they all rejoiced to be able to see him visibly again.

Here, I believe, we see clear visual evidence, together with an accompanying proof text no less, of the instructive intentions latent in early Buddhist aniconism.[31] Many centuries after the properly designated "aniconic period" was superseded by the practice of making anthropomorphic icons, we find as part of the vast microcosm of Vajrayana Buddhism at Borobudur, a rare surviving instance in stone of doctrinally-specific meaning. Apparently, conventions established by the earliest Buddhist iconographers for creating visualizations of the ineffable did not die out entirely for at least a good millennium. Whatever else it was that the Buddha experienced upon Awakening to a new level of consciousness at Bodh Gaya, of at least this we can be sure: beyond our consciousness of mundane reality there are many additional levels awaiting exploration.

Notes

[1]The Theravada era is reckoned from the year of the Buddha's final passing, 40 years after his enlightenment: thus the year 2000 is the 2,543rd year since the Buddha's Parinirvana.

[2]If one accepts the shorter chronology of Richard Gombrich the gap between event and its surviving commemorative marker is a century and a half less, between the Buddha's most probable life dates (481-401 BCE) and those of Ashoka's reign (272-231): Richard Gombrich "Dating the Buddha: a Red Herring Revealed," *The Dating of the Historical Buddha. Die Datierung des historischen Buddha, edited by Heinz Bechert*, Part 2, Symposien zur Buddhismusforschung, 4/2 (Gottingen: Vandenhoeck & Ruprecht, 1991), pp. 237-259.

[3]For a color photograph of a much later example see the following: http://www.sxu.edu/~rabe/asia/bodhgaya/aniconic2.html. This supreme example of the Sukhodaya-period style is currently installed in the Wat-Traimitr temple, central Bangkok, Thailand, a ten foot image weighing approximately four tons that was cast in pure gold in the Thirteenth Century.

[4]I accept A.K. Narain's judicious appraisal of the evidence in favor of dating the Bimaran reliquary, with a standing Buddha image, to the reign of Azes II (c. 35-0 B.C.E.) which together with a coin of this same king bearing a seated meditator constitute the earliest datable images of the Buddha in human form. A.K. Narain, "First Images of the Buddha and Bodhisattvas: Ideology and Chronology," A.K. Narain ed., *Studies in Buddhist Art of South Asia* (New Delhi: Kanak Publications, 1985): 1-21; For contrary arguments (albeit less compelling to this writer), see: Rowland on the Roman arcade motif being late (Benjamin Rowland, "The Vine-Scroll in Gandhara," *Artibus Asiae* XIX (1956): 353-361; see also Étienne Lamotte, *History of Indian Buddhism: from the Origins to the Saka Era* (trans. by Sara Webb-Boin (Louvain-la Neuv: University Catholique de Louvain 1988) ; David L. Snellgrove, ed.,*The Image*

of the Buddha (Paris: UNESCO, 1978); on the dating of the Pali canon, Peter
(Brian Peter Harvey, *The Selfless Mind: Personality, Consciousness and
Nirvana in Early Buddhism* (Surrey : Curzon Press, 1995); Richard Gombrich,
How Buddhism Began (London, Athlone, 1996) and Lemotte.

[5]It is no longer possible to attribute the first impetus to messianic
tendencies in Mahayana (cf. Huntington's straw man, namely Foucher's theory
of Hellenistic influences centered in Gandhara. John C. Huntington, "The
origin of the Buddha image: Early image traditions and the concept of
Buddhadarsanapunya," A.K. Narain ed., *Studies in Buddhist Art of South Asia*
New Delhi: Kanak Publications, 1985: 23-58). Epigraphic evidence points
clearly to the Theravada sect of the Sarvastivadins as the first proven sponsors
of anthropomorphic icons: See A.L. Basham, "The Evolution of the Concept of
the Bodhisattva," also in A.K. Narain ed., *Studies in Buddhist Art of South
Asia*; Lewis R.Lancaster, "An Early Mahayana Sermon About the Body of the
Buddha and the Making of Images," *Artibus Asiae* 36 (1974): 287-291. Narian,
p.6; Gregory Schopen, "The Inscription on the Kushan Image of Amitabha and
the Character of the Early Mahayana in India," *Journal of the International
Association of Buddhist Studies*, 10-2 (1987).

[6]First cited by Arthur Waley ["Did Buddha die of eating pork? with a note
on Buddha's image," *Mélanges Chinois et bouddhiques*, 1 (1931-32): 343-
254], it survives only in a Chinese translation made in 404 CE. In Chapter 48
of the *Shih Sung Lu, Taisho Tripitaka*, xxiii, 352. Later I intend to explicate
possible significance from the role played by the Sarvastivadins, per se, in the
inauguration of Buddha icons.

[7]Waley, n. 4 "Though in later Buddhism new ideas centred round the term
Bodhisattva, its occurrence does not necessarily imply a late date. Possibly
some of the figures identified as Nagas in early Buddhist sculpture would have
been regarded by the writer of this passage as Bodhisattvas."

[8]namely future Buddha not yet withdrawn into final Nirvana.

[9]His reign began in 78 A.D., namely year 1 of the still-widely observed
Shaky era. While some scholars still favor dates 40 or 80 years later, arguments
in favor of coinciding Kanishka's accession with Shaky year 1 seem stronger in
the following comprehensive review of the problem: A. L. Basham, ed.,
Conference on the Date of Kaniska (1960 : London) Papers on the date of
Kaniska. Submitted to the Conference on the Date of Kaniska. London, 20-22
April, 1960. Australian National University. Centre of Oriental Studies.
Oriental monograph series, v.4 (Leiden: E. J. Brill, 1968).

[10]"Budharakhita's mother, Amoha-asi, in her own convent, for the welfare and happiness of her parents and all sentient beings has erected this Bodhisattva." Similarly on the Kosambi: "In the year 2, of Maharaja Kanishka, on the ... day in the 2nd month of Hemanta, the nun Buddhamitra, who is well versed in the Tripitika set up this image of Bodhisattva at the promenade of the Lord Buddha."

[11]At Sravasti [now Allahabad] "... on the 19th (day, [the year is missing], [this] Bodhisattva (together with) an umbrella and a shaft [to support it], (being) a gift of Bala, a teacher of the Tripitika ("3 baskets") (and) fellow-wanderer of the monk Pusya (-mitra) (has been set up) in Sravasti at the place where the Blessed One used to walk, in the Kosambakuti, for the acceptance of the teachers belonging to the Sarvastivada school."

[12]Contra: Basham's rejection of this line of reasoning; and Verardi on the Sarnath image.

[13]See: http://www.sxu.edu/~rabe/asia/bodhgaya/aniconic9.html the Vessantara Jataka, part I, wherein the perfectly generous prince gives away in turn (from the right), his white elephant, chariot and team of horses. Lowest architrave, exterior face, of the north gate of the Great Stupa at Sanchi, c. 50 BCE.

[14]A.B. Griswold, *What is a Buddha Image?* (Thai Culture, New Series, no. 19, 1990, p. 9. "The passage that you are looking for is given in *ditthijala* section of *Dighanikaya* 1. 7. 147-148," emailed Gautama Vajracharya on Saturday, 22 Feb 1997 in reply to my query on the Indology listserv.

[15]David L. Snellgrove, ed., *The Image of the Buddha* (Paris: UNESCO, 1978), 23. *Suttanipata* v.1074.

[16]my paraphrase for the statement, which continues: "Released from names and form, goes out and is no longer reckoned. For him who gains the goal there is no measurement, By means of which one tells of him; for him this just is not. When all the elements are removed, all terms of reference are likewise non-existent." Snellgrove's translation (p. 23), quoting the Pali *Suttanipata*. Also, Susan Huntington, Early Buddhist Art and the Theory of Aniconism," *Art Journal* vol. 49:4 (Winter, 1990), p. 401, n.4 quotes Richard F. Gombrich, "the Buddha was not shown at all, to symbolize the fact that he was *nibbuta* ('extinguished'): *Precept and Practice: Traditional Buddhism in the Rural Highlands of Ceylon* (Oxford: Clarendon Press, 1971), 112.

[17]Snellgrove, p. 24.

[18]Susan Huntington, p. 403.

[19]At http://www.sxu.edu/~rabe/asia/bodhgaya/aniconic14.html one can find an enlarged view of this image. The dancers are identified as Mishrakeshi, Sambhadra, Padmavati and Alambusha, together with this gloss: "The music of the gods accompanied by a mimic dance." Above them, in the middle register, attendant inscriptions translate as follows: "In the eastern quarter the Suddhavasa gods; in the northern quarter the 3 (classes of) gods whose kindness extends to all beings; in the southern quarter the 6,000 Kamavacharas"; plus an abraded reference to Mara, nagas and winged gods (like Garuda) of the West.

[20]Richard F. Gombrich (1971), p.112, as cited by S.Huntington (1990), p. 401, n.4.

[21]Richard Gombrich, *How Buddhism Began* (London: Athlone, 1996), esp. chapt 2, "How, not What: Kamma as a Reaction to Brahmanism" .

[22]Peter (Brian) Harvey, *The Selfless Mind: Personality, Consciousness and Nirvana in Early Buddhism* (Surrey: Curzon Press, 1995).

[23]E.g., http://www.sxu.edu/~rabe/asia/bodhgaya/aniconic16.html, showing veneration of the enthroned Buddha (his presence indicated only by footprints) on the Ajatasatru pillar, from Bharhut, mid 2nd c BC; India Museum, Calcutta.

[24]*skandhas*: i.e, corporeality, feelings, perceptions, volitions, consciousness; Étienne Lamotte, History of Indian Buddhism: from the Origins to the Saka Era (trans. by Sara Webb-Boin (Louvain-la Neuv: Université Catholique de Louvain 1988) p. 28.

[25]The twelve *ayatana* or bases of consciousness are said to be two-fold: 6 internal sensory organs (eye, ear, nose, tongue, body and mind); and their corresponding external objects, namely the visible (*rupa*), sound (*shabda*), odor (*gandha*), taste *(rasa)*, touchability (*sparshtavya*) and the object of thought (*dharma*): Lamotte, p. 29.

[26]The eighteen *dhatus* constitute an augmentation of the two sets of *ayatana*, with a third and corresponding set of consciousness states, viz, cakshur-vijnana (consciousness of sight) etc.; Lamotte, p. 31.

[27]Lamotte, p. 40 ff.

[28]as I have cited elsewhere ["The Interaction of Dance and Sculpture in South India," George Kliger, ed., *Bharata Natyam in Cultural Perspective*

(Delhi: American Institute of Indian Studies and Manohar, 1993), pp. 110-143], the twirling fire-brand metaphor appears in *the Mandukyopanisad with Gaudapada's Karika and Sankara's Commentary*, trans. by Swami Nikilananda (Mysore, 1974), pp. 260, 261; and the Sixth c. buddhist Mahavairocana Sutra, trans. from Chinese by Minoru Kiyota, *in Tantric Concept of Bodhicitta: A Buddhist Experiential Philosophy* (Madison: South Asia Center, University of Wisconsin, 1982), p. 79.

[29]See: http://www.sxu.edu/~rabe/asia/bodhgaya/aniconic18.html for the 1949 photograph of Picasso drawing a minotaur seemingly in midair; Gjon Mili, *Picasso's Third Dimension.* (New York: Triton Press; distributed by Tudor Pub. Co., 1970)

[30] For an aerial view of the labyrinthian Diamond World Mandala built in Central Java, Indonesia, by the Sailendra Dynasty in c. 800, see http://www.sxu.edu/~rabe/asia/bodhgaya/aniconic19.html; and http://www.sxu.edu/~rabe/asia/bodhgaya/aniconic20.html. Approximate dimensions of Borobudur: 408 feet square and 105 feet high.

[31]According to Lokesh Chandra, *Sudhana's Way to Enlightenment,* Sata-Pitaka Series, Indo-Asian Literature, vol. 224, (Delhi: Jayyed Press, 1975), the Gandhavyuha, constituting the final portion of the Mahavaipulya Buddha Avatamsaka Sutra, was first translated into Chinese by the Yueh-Chih monk Lokakshema (AD 166-188).

Plate 1. Mauryan period platform (3rd c. B.C.), marking the spot where the Buddha achieved Enlightenment, Bodh Gaya. Photo Credit: ACSAA. Reprinted with permission.

Plate 2. The "Bodhisattva" attended by Yakshas and flying devas, beneath the Bodhi tree; from the Katra Mound; Mathura Museum, late 1st c. Unless stated otherwise, this and all subsequent photographs are by the author.

Plate 3. The Bodhisattva Maitreya (Buddha of the Future), from ancient
Gandhara (present-day Pakistan/Afghanistan), c. 2nd c. CE; Boston Museum of
Fine Arts.

Plate 4. The Monkey's Offering of Honey (to the Buddha—not shown, upon the platform beneath the tree); Panel carved on the North gate, Sanchi, c. 50 BCE.

Plate 5. The "Kapi Jataka," depiction of the future buddha as compassionate leader of a troop of monkeys who escape across a river on his back; carved on a stupa railing pillar at Bharhut, c. 150 BCE; India Museum, Calcutta.

Plate 6. The Bodhisattva Rishishringa, the Unicorn-boy, shown twice with his father (and mother-deer), on the lower architrave, exterior face of the north gate of the Great Stupa at Sanchi, c. 50 BCE.

Plate 7. The Vessantara Jataka, concluded; lowest architrave, and the Great Temptation of the buddha by the [comic] demon-host of Mara, above. Interior face of the north gate of the Great Stupa at Sanchi, c. 50 BCE.

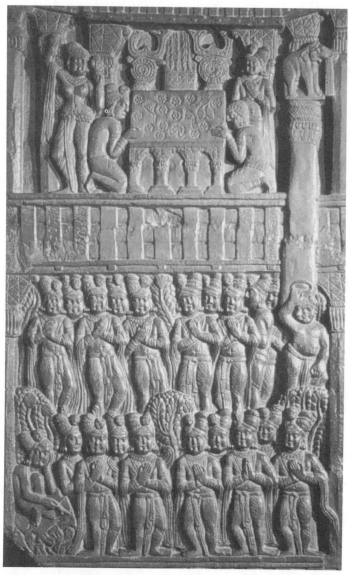

Plate 8. Veneration of the Buddha's Enlightenment at Bodh Gaya, as depicted on a stupa railing pillar from Bharhut, mid 2nd c BC; India Museum, Calcutta. Photo credit: ACSAA. Reprinted with permission.

Plate 9. Composite photograph of the entire "Prasenajit" pillar (of which Figure 8 is a detail), from Bharhut, mid 2nd c BC; India Museum, Calcutta: Photograph taken from Alexander Cunningham, The Stupa of Bharhut: a Buddhist Monument Ornameted with Numerous Sculptures Illustrated of Buddhist Legend and History in the 3rd Century B.C. (London: W.H. Allan & Co., 1879).

Plate 10. King Vidudabha coming and receiving instruction from the Buddha; from Bharhut, mid 2nd c BC; Freer Gallery, Smithsonian Institution, Washington,D.C.

Chapter 12

Many Realisms

Harald Atmanspacher
Frederick Kronz

Realists, Realisms, and Realities

A *realist*, in one philosophical sense of this term, is someone who holds that the entities posed by a well-established theory exist (and may be contrasted with an anti-realist who regards such terms merely as convenient fictions). The corresponding notion of realism thus characterizes a descriptive concept (a theory), the referents of which can be conceived as elements of *reality*. Every scientist is a realist in a minimal sense insofar as the standard methodology of science requires that models and theories are empirically checked by such elements of reality. This check can confirm or disprove a given hypothesis. It always rests on empirical tools (e.g., measuring instruments) which are presupposed in an unsophisticated, common sense manner. For this reason and in this sense, the concepts of realism and reality are to be understood as *relative* to such tools. In spite of the option to use empirical facts and data for checking models and theories, it is, however, everything else than clear how these two domains are related to each other. There are levels of discussion at which it seems unnecessary to consider any such relationship at all, and there are other levels of discussion which require such a relationship to be explicitly taken into account.

The question of relationships between the material world with its facts or data and its apparently non-material counterpart or complement, the domain of models and theories, respectively, belongs to the oldest, most puzzling, and most controversial questions in the long history of philosophy and the history of science. One of the main reasons for its controversial nature is that the question itself is understood in different ways depending on basic assumptions concerning our conceptions of reality. What makes all approaches toward this question as well as the discussions about those approaches so difficult is the fact that those assumptions are most often implicit rather than explicitly clarified.

For many good reasons, any related inquiry has to take into account the corpus of knowledge we have acquired so far. The contemporary status of the sciences is the result of centuries of history, built upon various lines of empiricist tradition and upon the Cartesian distinction of res cogitans and res extensa. At present, there are quite a number of scientific topics touching this distinction itself. More and more aspects of mind-matter research become timely and sensible research topics, and it may be hoped that the knowledge we have acquired so far provides a sound basis for substantial progress in this field. Of course, this requires detailed work rather than mere verbal assertions or ungrounded speculations.

From the viewpoint of a philosophically informed contemporary physicist (who typically disregards any kind of "mind-over-matter" idealism), there are two general frameworks within which reality can be conceived. (For more details about these topics the reader is referred to the relevant literature, e.g., Chalmers [1996].) One of them is typically denoted as *physicalism* (or *materialism*) and expresses the idea that the basis of reality consists of the material world alone; anything like qualia, consciousness, psyche, mind, or spirit is based on the material elements and fundamental laws of physics. For physicalists, the way in which these apparently non-material higher-level properties can be explained is a follow-up question, again answered differently within different ways of thinking, using conceptual schemes such as, for example, emergence, supervenience, or reduction. These concepts are tightly related to each other.

In general, it is helpful to keep in mind that emergence is an extremely colorful, often not well-defined concept that has to be discussed together with supervenience and reduction. Some useful sources are Silberstein (1998), Scheibe (1997), Chalmers (1996), Crutchfield (1994), Eisenhardt and Kurth (1993), and Kim (1984). All these topics have to do with instabilities (of different kinds) and have been addressed in various fields such as morphogenetics, synergetics, complex systems, non-equilibrium thermodynamics, catastrophe theory, and others. It seems to be a good guess that emergence or supervenience are connected with a weak type of reduction insofar as emergent properties must not contradict fundamental laws at a basic level of description, but also neither are uniquely determined nor can be uniquely derived from that level without further (contextual or contingent) conditions. For instance, physical processes in the human brain must not violate any applicable physical laws, but by no means are these laws sufficient to understand any of the higher-level properties and functions the brain has and performs. Nevertheless, the fundamental laws of physics can be assumed to be exhaustive at the basic level, and the existence of higher-level properties does not necessarily require us to add further "fundamental laws".

The other general framework is characterized as *dualism*, ranging from ontological to epistemological and methodological versions. Briefly speaking, ontological dualism maintains that the world *consists* of mind and matter (or other, corresponding concepts) as ultimately separate "substances". Epistemological dualism refers to mind and matter as fundamentally different domains with respect to our modes of gathering and processing knowledge of the world, irrespective of what this world "as such" ("in itself") may or may not be. Methodological dualism reflects an attitude that is neutral to the claims made by the other two variants. It utilizes the mind-matter distinction as a basic, but maybe not the only possible methodological tool to inquire into the structure of the world.

In its weakest (methodological) form, dualism is a prerequisite of any physicalist approach insofar as the latter presupposes a distinction between matter and something that appears to be non-material and—in one way or another—has to be related to, explained by, or even derived from the elements and laws of the material world. Within such a kind of minimal dualism, which is hard to avoid, we may use distinctions such as that of models and data, theories and facts, and so forth (compare

Atmanspacher, 1994a). In the present article, any dualistic kind of argument is meant at this methodological level.

For a physicalist approach, the concepts of emergence, supervenience, or reduction seem to refer explicitly to the world of material facts; they refer to a reality addressed by a certain type of realism. However, keeping in mind that this reference presupposes the (possibly nonunique) selection of a viewpoint, we may also argue that emergence, supervenience, or reduction primarily refer to our (non-material) descriptions of the material world rather than to elements of that world itself. Depending on the logical structure of those descriptions, they populate the entire spectrum between a naive *realism*, an unreflected belief in an external reality, and a radical *relativism*, hardly found attractive by working scientists who are used to dealing with or relying on the regulative power of events that do "really" happen in the material world.

Emergence, supervenience, and reduction are concepts which have been applied to facts ascribing properties to systems in the material world (i.e., in an assumed material *reality*) or in the sense of our descriptions of those properties (i.e., different kinds of *realism*). In a rough terminology, there are emergent facts and emergent theories. Mixing both of them up, inevitably leads to category mistakes and misunderstandings. The methodological dualism that helps us to avoid this must, however, not at all be understood as a predecision concerning the structure of the world and our knowledge of this world. As mentioned above, it should be understood as a tool to inquire into this structure. It may be a preliminary tool that can, for instance, lead to a precise description of its own limits.

The present contribution deals primarily with realisms (conceptions of reality). It will be argued that neither a naive realism, addressing the material world as a collection of facts that are ready for observation in a theory neutral way, nor a radical relativism with a collection of models posing facts in a theory dependent, more or less arbitrary way, is the right tool to deal with those issues properly. A specific conceptual scheme will be sketched that allows us to combine a certain kind of relativism with the belief that the material world cannot be described arbitrarily. In other words: although facts are certainly model-dependent, they are more than just illusions. There are many (contextually) correct descriptions with well-defined relationships among each other rather than just one (universally) correct description of the world—and there certainly are incorrect descriptions.

Ontic and Epistemic Descriptions

Assuming the methodological distinction between a material world with events, facts, or data and a mental world with concepts, models, or theories, it is possible to describe elements of the material world by elements of the mental world. The question then is how to distinguish different elements within the two domains. Modern physics, in particular quantum physics has developed tools to address this question with respect to the material world. A most important distinction in this context is that of systems (objects) and their environment. This distinction is sometimes metaphorically called the *Heisenberg cut* (Heisenberg, 1936).

Together with the fact that descriptions of isolated systems are radically different from descriptions of open systems, the Heisenberg cut and the corresponding formal tools play a major role in modern quantum theory. It turns out that a proper understanding of these issues can be achieved using two different descriptions of reality; namely, the ontic and the epistemic, respectively.[1] Primas has developed this distinction in the formal framework of algebraic quantum theory (Primas, 1990; see also Atmanspacher, 1994b for some indications of possible limitations of this distinction). The basic structure of the ontic/epistemic distinction as it will be used subsequently can be understood according to the following rough characterization (for more details, the reader is referred to Primas, 1990,1994a).

Ontic states describe all properties of a physical system exhaustively. ("Exhaustive" in this context means that an ontic state is "precisely the way it is", without any reference to epistemic knowledge or ignorance.) Ontic states are the referents of individual descriptions, the properties of the system are formalized by *intrinsic observables*.[2] Their temporal evolution (dynamics) follows *universal, deterministic laws* given by a Hamiltonian one-parameter group. As a rule, ontic states in this sense are empirically inaccessible. *Epistemic states* describe our (usually inexhaustive) knowledge of the properties of a physical system (i.e., based on a finite partition of the relevant state space). The referents of statistical descriptions are epistemic states, the properties of the system are formalized by *contextual observables*. Their temporal evolution (dynamics) follows *phenomenological, irreversible* laws which can be given by a dynamical one-parameter semigroup if the state space is properly chosen. Epistemic states are empirically accessible by definition.

Although the formalism of algebraic quantum theory is often hard to handle for specific physical applications, it offers significant clarifications concerning the basic structure and the philosophical implications of quantum theory. For instance, the modern achievements of algebraic quantum theory make clear in what sense pioneer quantum mechanics (which von Neumann [1932] implicitly formulated epistemically) as well as classical and statistical mechanics can be considered as limiting cases of a more general theory. Compared to the framework of von Neumann's monograph (1932), important extensions are obtained by giving up the irreducibility of the algebra of observables (not admitting observables which commute with every observable in the same algebra) and the restriction to locally compact state spaces (admitting only finitely many degrees of freedom). As a consequence, modern quantum physics is able to deal with open systems in addition to isolated ones, it can involve infinitely many degrees of freedom such as the modes of a radiation field, it can properly consider interactions with the environment of a system, superselection rules, classical observables, and phase transitions can be formulated which would be impossible in an irreducible algebra of observables, there are in general infinitely many representations inequivalent to the Fock representation, and non-automorphic, irreversible (hence non-unitary) dynamical evolutions can be successfully incorporated.

In addition to this remarkable progress, the mathematical rigor of algebraic quantum theory in combination with the ontic/epistemic distinction allows us to address quite a number of unresolved conceptual and interpretational problems of pioneer quantum mechanics from a new perspective. First of all, the distinction between different concepts of states as well as observables provides a much better understanding of many confusing issues in earlier conceptions, including alleged paradoxes such as those of Einstein, Podolsky, and Rosen (EPR; 1935) or Schrödinger's cat (Schrödinger, 1935). Second, a clear-cut characterization of these concepts is a necessary precondition to explore new approaches, beyond von Neumann's projection postulate, toward the central problem that pervades all quantum theory since its very beginning: the measurement problem. Third, a number of much-discussed interpretations of quantum theory and their variants can be appreciated more properly if they are considered from the perspective of an algebraic formulation.

This applies in particular to the deep (though notoriously vague) deliberations of Bohr, to Einstein's and Schrödinger's contributions, to Bohm's ideas on explicate and implicate orders, to Heisenberg's distinction of actuality and potentiality, or to d'Espagnat's scheme of an empirical, weakly objective reality and an observer-independent, objective (veiled) reality.[3] An important example: the core of the well-known Bohr-Einstein discussions in the 1920s and 1930s (see Jammer, 1974) can be traced back to the belief that only one of the mentioned concepts of reality can be (primarily) relevant. While Bohr clearly emphasized an epistemic, contextual realism referring to the results of measurements, Einstein was deeply convinced of an ontically determined realism to which he attached a common-sense type local realism that—as we would say today—applies to an epistemic viewpoint. In the framework of algebraic quantum theory, both kinds of realism play significant roles, and even some of the formal relations between them have been clarified successfully. More details about this issue have been discussed by Howard (1985, 1997).

One of the most striking differences between the concepts of ontic and epistemic states is their difference concerning operational access (i.e., observability and measurability). At first sight it might appear pointless to keep a level of description which is not related to what can be verified empirically. However, a most appealing feature at this ontic level is the existence of first principles and universal laws that cannot be obtained at the epistemic level. Furthermore, it is possible to rigorously deduce (to "GNS-construct"; cf. Primas, 1994a) a proper epistemic description from the ontic description if enough details about the empirically given situation are known. This is particularly important and useful for the treatment of open and macroscopic (quantum) systems.

The distinction of ontic and epistemic states provides an important clue to understand the distinction between holistic and local realisms (i.e., concepts of reality). Ontic states and intrinsic observables refer to a holistic concept of reality and are operationally inaccessible, whereas epistemic states and contextual observables refer to a local concept of reality and are operationally accessible. It is exactly the process of observation, essentially one or another kind of pattern recognition, which represents the bridge between the two. Observation suppresses (or minimizes, respectively) the EPR correlations constituting a holistic reality and provides a level of description to which one can associate a local concept of reality with locally separate (or "approximately" separate, respectively) objects. In this sense it is justified to say that observation generates objects by introducing a Heisenberg cut as a metaphor for the suppression of EPR correlations.

Another way to look at the distinction of ontic and epistemic states and the associated algebras of observables is the following. The ontic holistic realism of quantum theory is related to all sorts of inquiries into a context-, mind-, or observer-independent reality of the outside world. Focusing on an epistemic local realism expresses a change of perspective to the effect that the question "*What is* this independent reality?" is replaced by "*What can we know* about such a reality?" Philosophically the distinction between these two questions is very much in the spirit of Kant's distinction of transcendental idealism and empirical realism, and in this sense one may consider an ontic description as a kind of "idealization" of an epistemic description. As an empirical science, physics addresses only questions of the second kind. But on the other hand, the mathematical formalism that constitutes the formal basis of physics often leads into a way of thinking very much in accordance with the first kind of question. An instructive discussion along these lines, emphasizing those topics as non-standard realism, is due to d'Espagnat (1999).

One of the basic conceptual implications of the distinction of ontic and epistemic descriptions of reality is the fact that it is inadmissible to speak of objects and environments or their observation at the ontic level. Here is the domain of nonlocal, holistic correlations between those properties that are, technically speaking, described by non-commuting operators. Local objects and their environment are generated by a change of perspective from the ontic to the epistemic level, which generally involves the breaking of a symmetry, introduces new contexts (e.g., abstractions that are deliberately made to distinguish between "irrelevant" and "relevant" features), and is intimately related to the distinctions necessary for any kind of observation. This makes it easy to understand why ontic states are non-empirical by definition.

Empirical access requires the separation of objects which are not a priori (i.e., ontically, given).

A widespread category mistake resulting from a lack of proper ontic/epistemic distinctions and the associated distinction of holistic/local realism is reflected by the assertion that EPR correlations can be interpreted such that the parts of a holistic system communicate superluminously (i.e., with signal velocities greater than the velocity of light). The state of the system as a whole is an ontic state. If a system as a whole is to be described ontically, then it is in general inadmissible to speak of parts within this same description, and consequently there is no way to talk about communication between such parts.[4] Only if the ontic state of a system is decomposed in order to describe subsystems or parts, the result is a description in terms of epistemic states of those subsystems. They can communicate, but of course not superluminously.

Another consequence of the same category mistake is the misleading interpretation that due to EPR correlations "everything is correlated with everything else". Ontically, there is only "one thing", a system as a whole. Epistemically, where it is admissible to speak of "many things" and consequently of "everything", there are no holistic correlations. Any empirically accessible aspect of those correlations relies on the condition that parts of the environment (e.g., detection instruments) are *not* correlated.[5] All empirical evidence we have for quantum holism is obtained by "destroying" that same holism. Ironically, nonlocality can only indirectly be demonstrated in a local way, conceptually using counterfactual reasoning.

As Primas has discussed extensively (Primas, 1998), the transition from an ontic to an epistemic level of description often goes hand in hand with the emergence of properties that are not defined ontically. Almost all known classical properties (in the sense of commuting observables) of objects emerge due to contexts that are not given by the intrinsic properties of an ontic description, but have to be selected properly, adapted to the given situation. Some of the examples that are formally well-understood refer to properties such as chirality, temperature, or chemical potential. Another example is the emergence of irreversibility; the time evolution of ontic states is given by a one-parameter group describing a reversible dynamics.[6] The notion of emergence is also used (in a physicalist sense) for much more complicated and fairly little understood properties such as life or consciousness. A common tenet shared by most physicists (not every physicist is a physicalist) is the restriction of the problem of measurement to the material world alone. Consequently, observers are considered as observing apparatuses, and any consciousness of living observers remains disregarded (cf. Atmanspacher, 1997; Primas, 1993).

Relative Onticity

What is a suitable way to address situations which confront us with holistic *and* local features at the same level of description? In such situations, mixtures of ontic and epistemic elements are required at the same level of description, thus forbidding a unique assignment of ontic/epistemic descriptions and holistic/local realisms. (As indicated above, such a mixture is unavoidable from the very beginning since every epistemic description presupposes an ontic description of measuring tools.) This difficulty can be resolved if it is realized that two levels of description are not enough to cover the entire hierarchy leading from fundamental particles in basic physics up to living systems in biology and psychology. It is then suggestive to consider ontic and epistemic descriptions as *relative to* two successive levels in the hierarchy. Concerning material reality, this is particularly relevant to the study of hierarchical complex systems, and some ideas toward a corresponding formal approach have been specified elsewhere (Primas, 1994b).

Let us start with an example for such a *relative onticity*[7] in the material domain of reality. From a fundamental viewpoint of quantum theory as sketched above, atoms and molecules are highly contextual objects whose properties can be described by interactions of electrons, nuclei, and their environments. However, from the viewpoint of chemistry one may not be interested in these complicated interactions, but in the shape and other features of molecules, for which it is reasonable to consider the concept of an atomic nucleus ontically as a whole rather than composed of protons, neutrons, or even "more basic" constituents. This leads to the description of a molecule as a contextual object resulting from the interaction of nuclei, electrons, and their environments. The ontic/epistemic distinction can then be shifted from the levels of electrons and nuclei to that of molecules. While molecules are epistemically described within the first realm, they acquire an ontic description within the second. In this manner, the result of a composition of ontic nuclei and electrons (the epistemic molecule) at a certain level can be considered ontically as a basic entity (the ontic molecule) if it is viewed from a successively higher level in the hierarchy.

In a more detailed version of this example one can even address specific relationships between different levels of description. Let us discuss the concept of water as an example. At a rather basic physical level, one might think of water in terms of hydrogen and oxygen nuclei and electrons. Leaving the nuclear level of description (protons, neutrons, etc.) involves a change of perspective which, roughly speaking, abstracts from any nuclear forces due to strong interactions, and focuses on electromagnetic (Coulomb) forces. In a general sense, this abstraction leads from a description in terms of ontic states of nuclei and electrons and their properties to the epistemic concept of a water molecule, H_2O.

One of the most important further abstractions in this context leads to the so-called Born-Oppenheimer picture, disregarding the electron mass as compared to the masses of the nuclei. In a corresponding description, the water molecule has properties which H and O nuclei did not have (e.g., the property of a nuclear frame). A special feature of nuclear frames is the chirality (handedness, see Amann, 1993) of molecules. Molecular chirality is a property that emerges at an epistemic molecular level of description and is absent at any lower level. However, this is not to say that this property is just a matter of description and has no *real* impact. For instance, thalidomide is a chiral molecule. Today it is well-known that the disastrous consequences of thalidomide-based remedies in the 1960s are caused by only one of the two different chiral species. The remedies were produced as mixtures of both species.

In a thermodynamic description, other properties emerge due to consideration of *many* ($N \to \infty$) entities such as molecules. It is intuitively obvious that one single water molecule H_2O is not wet. The property of liquidity is an emergent property for which the level of a description in terms of individual molecules has to be left and replaced by a statistical or thermodynamical description. The same applies to other properties such as chemical potential or temperature, for which rigorous mathematical derivations are available (Müller-Herold, 1980; Takesaki, 1970). Again a remark concerning the factual "reality" of a property such as temperature: whoever has burned one's fingers once will have serious doubts that temperature might be nothing else than a descriptive tool that has nothing to do with reality.

For a molecular chemist or biologist, molecules are the building blocks of his mode of description. In this sense, their states and properties are considered ontically. A molecular biologist is not at all concerned with the justification of a molecular (Born-Oppenheimer) picture. He may, however, be interested in the way in which different phosphates (adenine, thymine, guanine, cytosine), so-called nucleotides, can be combined to different DNA sequences. For such a point of view, the phosphate molecules are entities to be described by ontic states and their properties, the different ways they are organized in DNA give rise to an epistemic description with emergent properties (genetic information, e.g., the faculty of self-reproduction) at the level of the DNA. At this conceptual level, there is an analogy between the ontic/epistemic distinction and the distinction of genotypes and phenotypes which deserves further study.

The systems and objects the "man on the street" usually deals with in everyday life are the trees, tables, bricks, icecubes, and so forth of common sense realism. It would be entirely unreasonable not to include this kind of realism in the framework suggested here. Although for a scientist a tree has to be described as a highly complicated composition of material subsystems with emergent properties of different types (solidity, texture, etc.), common sense realism holds that a tree *is* simply a tree, an object in an ontic state *having* those properties. Many trees together can form a forest, and there certainly are issues for which the forest as a whole is the right object to be addressed rather than many trees. If it is addressed in terms of many trees, the forest is the referent of an epistemic description. If it is addressed in terms of an ecosystem as a whole (e.g., for purposes of its reliable utilization; see Hauhs, Dörwald, Kastner-Maresch & Lange, 1998), the forest becomes relevant as the referent of an ontic description.

The central issue of the general concept of relative onticity is that states and properties of a system, which are treated epistemically at a given level of description, can be considered as ontic from the perspective of a higher level. Objects can be epistemically described to be composed of lower level objects, but alternatively they can be ontically described as wholes, giving rise to "building blocks" of higher level objects. Emergent properties at successively higher levels of description can be *formally* addressed by a change of perspective which is not uniquely given but depends on contexts and conceptual schemes that must be selected properly.

However, this does not imply that *any arbitrary* description is proper. An interesting example for an improper conceptual scheme is given by a supposed "atomic" level of description between nuclear and molecular levels. Since we do not know the interaction between atoms as entities in themselves, molecules must not be conceived as composed of atoms but of nuclei and electrons. Taking atoms seriously in an ontic sense leads to problems and inconsistencies if one wants to use them for the construction of an epistemic molecular picture. Although "atomic physics" doubtlessly was a very important field of research early in the 20th century, a modern point of view suggests that it is more appropriate to consider atoms as a special chapter of molecular physics.

The entire approach discussed so far essentially looks at different levels of description in the sense of increasing diversity. Generally speaking, moving from one level to the next higher level corresponds to a symmetry breaking; in one way or another, a holistic system is considered to be broken up into parts. Such a kind of so-called "bottom-up" approach is usually assumed as a proper way to reflect the evolution of more and more complex systems in the material world. In this framework, it is, however, a natural question whether all conceivable symmetry breakings are to be regarded as feasible, or whether there are some of them which are more feasible than others. For instance, it seems plausible that the symmetry breaking of the ontic state of a *photon pair* in an EPR type situation *before* measurement generically leads to the epistemic states of *two single photons* rather than arbitrary other subsystems *after* measurement.

Teller (1989) has proposed the concept of "relational holism" in very much the same spirit. In Teller's parlance, a local realist tries to interpret EPR-type correlations in terms of nonrelational properties of the relata which underlie any such correlations. On the basis of those (subvenient) properties it should be possible to explain the correlations as supervenient. By contrast, Teller asserts that any EPR-type "correlation—as an objective property of the pair of objects taken together—is simply a fact about the pair. This fact will arise from and give rise to other facts. But it need not itself be decomposable in terms of or supervenient upon some more basic, nonrelational facts" (Teller,

1989, p. 222). On the other hand, there are, of course, decompositions of a system as a whole into subsystems, such as the decomposition of a photon pair into two photons with their individual (emergent or supervenient) properties.

Clearly, it would be desirable to have a way of explaining that certain decompositions of a system as a whole are more natural than others. Slight variations of the context should not in general (but can in exceptional cases) result in different epistemic states. This is a requirement that can typically be taken into account by stability considerations. What we want is that certain decompositions of a holistic system are more stable, more robust than others. A first attempt into this direction has been indicated by Amann and Atmanspacher (1998). This means that any ontic, holistic level of description does already carry some inherent tendencies for more or less stable decompositions. A forest is more likely to be decomposed into individual trees rather than into strange mixtures of them. In this sense, holistic systems are *not* totally void of internal distinctions. It is an unresolved problem how such "preformed tendencies" for the stability of certain decompositions can be taken into account formally. It may be speculated that elements of "top-down" thinking could play a role in this regard, thus closing a self-referential loop between any pair of ontic and epistemic frameworks at any level of description. Such a scheme would imply that ontic and epistemic elements of a description mutually depend on each other, thus rendering any ultimate "primacy" of one over the other as ill-posed.

Ontological Relativity

The formal concept of "relative onticity" resembles to some extent the (less formal) discussion of "ontological relativity" as introduced by Quine (1969). In this essay, Quine argues that if there is one ontology that fulfills a given theory, then there is more than one. This claim is the crux of his doctrine of ontological relativity, claiming that it makes no sense to say what the objects of a theory are, beyond saying how to interpret or reinterpret that theory in another. Moreover (Quine, 1969),

Ontological relativity is not to be clarified by any distinction between kinds of universal predication—unfactual and factual, external and internal. It is not a question of universal predication. When questions regarding the ontology of a theory are meaningless absolutely, and become meaningful relative to a background theory, this is not in general because the background theory has a wider universe. One is tempted ... to suppose that it is; but one is then wrong. What makes ontological questions meaningless when taken absolutely is not universality but circularity. A question of the form 'What is an F?' can be answered only by recourse to a further term: 'An F is a G'. The answer makes only relative sense: sense relative to the uncritical acceptance of 'G'.[8] (p. 53)

For Quine, any question as to the "quiddity" (the "whatness") of a thing is meaningless unless a conceptual scheme is specified relative to which it is discussed. It is not the uniqueness of such a scheme (e.g., any "theory of everything" with universally given referents) but the faculty of reinterpretation of one scheme in another which belongs to the important features of scientific work. Nevertheless, Quine encourages "ontological commitment" in the sense that a most proper conceptual frame should be preferred for the interpretation of a theory. The circularity which he mentions as the crucial point of ontological relativity expresses itself in an inscrutability of reference. This stresses his conviction that the issue of reference causes the problems necessitating ontological relativity, not the unique assignment of referents as objects in the external world of a realist (cf. Gibson, 1995).

After his farewell to functionalism (cf. Chalmers 1996), Putnam (1981, 1987) has developed a related kind of ontological relativity within an approach rejecting both naive (spectator) realism and relativism. His approach rather attempts to reconcile the two and was first called "internal realism", later sometimes modified to "pragmatic realism". Ontological (sometimes conceptual) relativity is a central feature of Putnam's internal realism, but it differs from Quine's usage of the term in an important detail. In an interview with Burri (1994),[9] Putnam characterized Quine's ontological relativity as due to the impossibility of a uniquely fixed relationship of our concepts to the totality of objects which those concepts refer to. Putnam's own position is more radical insofar as he questions that we know what we mean when we speak of a totality of objects:

If we start with the notion of a totality of objects it becomes entirely untransparent how our terms—maybe except those referring to sense data—can refer in a fixed way. But from this I have not concluded that

no term other than sense data terms refer in a fixed way; rather I have
concluded that the premises leading to such a conclusion must be
wrong. In this context I basically think of the assumption that we know
what we mean when we speak of a totality of all objects. (Burri, 1994,
p. 185)

Considering the perspective of quantum holism, this position is
highly sensible. If an object can only be reasonably defined within the
framework of some preselected conceptual scheme, as Putnam's internal realism holds, then it is evident that any definition of an object is
only relevant within a given context (i.e., objects are "ontologically
relative" entities). But Putnam's point of departure is *not* quantum holism; it is our common sense realism, referring to "a usage of the word
'object' which we cannot change without loss of its meaning. The
notion of an object roots in speaking of tables, chairs, and bricks.
Tables, chairs, and bricks are objects in a fundamental sense of the
word" (Burri, 1994, p. 182). "The actual problem is to work out the difference between our common sense realism on one side and a
transcendental or physical, respectively, realism on the other. Currently
I try to criticize physical realism from the viewpoint of common sense
realism." (Burri, 1994, p. 177)

Concerning the main features of this position, Putnam admits that
his

ideas keep being subject to change. At present I see the crucial points
other than immediately after the turn. The publications which I wrote
by the end of 1976 ... finished a period of my thinking in which I
began to see more and more clearly that the semantics underlying
classical realism are hopelessly metaphysical. In particular, I became
convinced that numerous concepts of metaphysical realism are
untenable, for example the idea that one can reasonably talk about 'all
entities'—as if the terms 'entity' or 'object' had a unique, fixed
meaning—as well as the illusion that there is an answer to the question
of which objects the world consists. Later I called this conviction
'internal realism' or 'conceptual relativity'. It rests upon the idea that
there is a real world, but it does not dictate its own descriptions to us.
Internal realism does not imply 'anything goes' but rather accounts for
the fact that there are many descriptions of the world, depending on our
interests and questions, and on what we intend to do with the answers
to those questions. The assumption that certain descriptions cover the
world as it is in itself seems to be pointless to me. (Burri, 1994, p.
177f)

In his version of ontological relativity, Putnam wants to maintain a meaningful concept of reference and gives up the concept of a totality of uniquely defined objects as a precondition for any attempt to fix references once and for ever. Objects cannot be uniquely defined, but they can be defined with respect to conceptual frames. Within a pre-selected frame, it is then possible to establish reference without inscrutability. Putnam's discussion of water on a twin earth is illuminating in this context. If inhabitants of a "twin earth" use the term water to refer to a chemical substance other than H_2O (say XYZ), then Putnam holds that due to the best of our knowledge ("expert knowledge") the *proper* referent of "water"—at the level of a molecular description—is H_2O in the external world; H_2O is the extensional referent of "water". Putnam's example can only roughly be sketched here, for more details see Putnam (1975), Putnam (1981, Sect.II). It seems to be related to what Quine calls ontological commitment, but other than Quine's, Putnam's ontological commitment explicitly takes extensions into account. Quine's ontological relativity relates to inscrutability of reference, Putnam's relates to non-uniqueness of objects. (For other viewpoints in this discussion, see Searle, 1983, Sec.8, and Chalmers, 1996, Sec.I.2.4.)

In Putnam's thinking, conceptual schemes serve a purpose very similar to contextual representations in the framework of quantum theory. In this regard, relative onticity and ontological relativity are tightly related to each other. They both refer to the domain of empirical (local) realism where objects have to be described relative to a context. Both Putnam's internal realism and the realism of quantum theory agree with regard to a basic assertion according to which there is a "real world as such". The starting point for Putnam, however, differs from the starting point of a quantum theoretical perspective. For Putnam, objects in a fundamental sense are common sense objects such as "tables, bricks, icecubes". From the viewpoint of quantum theory, a universe of discourse in a fundamental sense does simply not consist of objects (although every quantum theoretical statement presupposes such objects, e.g., observational tools). Objects at each level of description are generated by symmetry breakings within a holistic universe of discourse, addressed by a holistic realism. The concept of relative onticity entails a recursive application of formal transformation principles (some classes of which are well-known, see Primas, 1998), translating between successive levels of description. Such principles or even rules of transformation are called for (at least by Quine), but not given in the framework of Putnam's or Quine's ontological relativity. In the scheme of relative onticity, common sense objects are objects just in a very special contextual framework, high up in the hierarchy of descriptions. But nevertheless they are considered as "real" objects in an external reality.

In his more recent writings, Putnam often refers to Kant and his distinction between (empirical) realism and (transcendental) idealism. It seems that the philosophy of Kant had an important impact on Putnam's way of thinking: "Only after I rejected metaphysical realism I began to understand what is correct in Kant's philosophy. Nevertheless, I am not a Kantian idealist. But he was the first philosopher who saw that we do not simply represent the world. To describe the world does not mean to represent it. It seems to me that this is an important insight." (Burri, 1994, p.178)

> [Kant] does not doubt that there is some mind-independent reality; for him this is virtually a postulate of reason. He refers to the elements of this mind-independent reality in various terms: thing-in-itself (Ding an sich); the noumenal objects or noumena; collectively, the noumenal world. But we can form no real conception of these noumenal things; even the notion of a noumenal world is a kind of limit of thought (Grenzbegriff) rather than a clear concept. Today the notion of a noumenal world is perceived to be an unnecessary metaphysical element in Kant's thought. (But perhaps Kant is right: perhaps we can't help thinking that there is somehow a mind-independent ground for our experience even if attempts to talk about it lead at once to nonsense.) At the same time, talk of ordinary empirical objects is not talk of things-in-themselves but only talk of things-for-us. (Putnam, 1981, p. 61)

> Internal realism says that the notion of a 'thing in itself' makes no sense; and *not* because 'we cannot know the things in themselves'. This was Kant's reason, but Kant, although admitting that the notion of a thing in itself *might* be 'empty', still allowed it to possess a formal kind of sense. Internal realism says that we don't know what we are talking about when we talk about 'things in themselves'. And that means that the dichotomy between 'intrinsic' properties and properties which are not intrinsic also collapses—collapses because the 'intrinsic' properties were supposed to be just the properties things have in 'themselves'. The thing in itself and the property the thing has 'in itself' belong to

the same circle of ideas, and it is time to admit that what the circle encloses is worthless territory. (Putnam, 1987, p. 36)

According to these selected quotations, it is Putnam's view that we can only reasonably talk about the empirically accessible world of ontologically relative objects. Their relativity is due to different conceptual schemes with extensional referents in a real world. The concept of things-in-themselves has to be rejected not only as empirically empty but primarily because they do not make sense. It has to be added that for Putnam "making sense" means more precisely: making sense in the sense of common sense. In other words, it is the absurdity of things-in-themselves that causes Putnam to reject them—although he admits that the concept of a (noumenal) world independent of empirical access may be an unavoidable idea.

The perspective of modern quantum theory offers an interesting alternative to Putnam's viewpoint. Putnam's (and Kant's) empirical realism is the local realism of any working scientist. Objects as the referents of local realism are always contextual, they are relevant with respect to a conceptual scheme corresponding to a preselected level of description. The states of those objects are epistemic at this level. On the other hand, it is also possible that there are ontic states at the same level (e.g., molecules described as wholes rather than described as consisting of nuclei and electrons). These ontic states refer to a holistic realism which—from the perspective of an empirical (local) realism— seems as "absurd" as Putnam claims. However, it does so for other reasons and with other implications.

Quantum holism invalidates the concept of objects at any level to which it is applied in terms of an ontic description. In this regard, things-in-themselves are not relevant as empirically accessible entities and it does indeed not even make sense to address them as separable entities. (As discussed in the preceding section, one might nevertheless think of some kind of tendency that objects with emergent properties can be obtained by moving to another, higher level of description.) However, quantum holism indicates that this has to be understood as an encouragement to question an unrestricted application of common sense realism beyond its significance as a necessary precondition for gaining empirical access to quantum holism by classical, uncorrelated measuring tools.

This is a decisive difference from Putnam's viewpoint. He interprets absurdity in the sense of common sense as an argument for rejecting conceptual schemes that are absurd in this sense. Quantum holism interprets such absurdity as an argument for questioning common sense if it is applied beyond its proper domain.[10] Of course, arguments of this latter type have to be investigated extremely carefully before they can be accepted. The present state of discussions in the foundations of quantum theory with its necessarily indirect, but overwhelming empirical evidence for holism provides strong evidence that its apparent "absurdity" must be taken seriously. Quantum holism might give us the right hint to understand Kant's transcendental idealism more properly than in terms of things-in-themselves.

Speculative Remarks on Mind and Matter

There is a considerable non-mainstream tradition of physicists who have suggested that quantum measurement has to do with consciousness. One of the pioneers of this conception is Wigner, among its more recent advocates are—with different arguments—Penrose and Stapp. Quite a number of publications addressing the relationship between the philosophy of quantum theory and the philosophy of mind over the last decade (cf. the overview by Butterfield, 1995) shows that there is a steadily growing interest in this idea. Already in the mid 1940s, and presumably as an offspring from his extensive discussions with Pauli, Jung has discussed a distinction similar in spirit to that of epistemic and ontic states with respect to conscious and unconscious levels in the mental world.[11] In an afterword to his essay *On the Nature of the Psyche* (Jung, 1971), Jung quotes Pauli with the statement that

> the epistemological situation with regard to the concepts 'conscious' and 'unconscious' seems to offer a pretty close analogy to the ... situation in physics ... From the standpoint of the psychologist, the 'observed system' would consist not of physical objects only, but would also include the unconscious, while consciousness would be assigned the role of 'observing medium'. (p. 261)

In other words, mental objects and their mental environments are conceived to be generated by the transformation of elements of the unconscious into consciously and empirically accessible categories.

Analogous to the material world, it might be appropriate to consider the possibility of different levels of descriptions, regarded as elements of a mental world, providing a whole spectrum between the most fundamental and the most contextual ones. One end of this spectrum would refer to a "most ontic" level of description, serving as a limiting case, meaning that it has no broken symmetry at all. At the other end, we would find a "most epistemic" level of elements of a cultural environment, manifesting themselves in individual human psyches. A nice example is given by national or regional versions of cultural key ideas by contrast with more general versions. A certain element of a cultural environment may have ontic meaning with respect to a local environment whereas it is regarded as epistemic in a larger scope. Cartesian dualism is epistemic from the viewpoint of a worldwide cultural perspective, from which it can be regarded as a regional version of the more general principle of duality. However, it represents a concept that has implicitly acquired almost ontic (collective and unconscious) features within the narrower scope of traditional Western science and technology. An additional appealing feature of such a multilayered scheme is the fact that there are many ways to draw distinctions (break symmetries) at every level. Each distinction is con-textual relative to the preceding level and generates its own specific features.

Applying the idea of relative onticity, it is conceivable that under suitable conditions epistemic elements at a certain level of description can be transformed into ontic elements when considered from the perspective of the next higher level. In other words: explicit elements of the sociocultural environment at a certain epoch can become implicitly ontic elements in a later epoch, thus leading to additional (archetypal) features in the collective unconscious in Jung's parlance. In addition to the Cartesian distinction, other basic concepts of traditional science such as determinism, causality, and locality may serve to provide further examples. What was once explicitly "invented", has later to be "discovered" as an implicit assumption underlying a new epistemic level. Such processes can be expected whenever a new epistemic level in the hierarchy of descriptions *emerges*, rendering the preceding one as its own ontic basis. More details of this picture, particularly with respect to the concept of archetypes, have been addressed by Nunn (1998) and Atmanspacher (1998).

Jung and Pauli (and others) have speculated that at a level which is "ontic enough" the symmetry breaking according to the Cartesian distinction of matter and mind dissolves, providing an "unus mundus" in which fundamental physics and depth psychology refer to the same unbroken reality (see Atmanspacher & Primas, 1996). Such a scenario points toward an interesting alternative to the idea that consciousness (mind) emerges as a higher level property of the brain (matter) just as, roughly speaking, liquidity emerges as a higher level property of water (see, e.g., Searle, 1984). The Pauli-Jung approach considers the mind-matter distinction as a fundamental symmetry breaking at a very primordial level of description. In this scheme, *both* mind and matter are emergent domains of description (not only mind emerges from matter), used to describe the world in terms of the corresponding distinction. The holistic features of modern quantum theory might induce and even support speculations of this kind. At present, however, the available knowledge about these extremely difficult issues is far from sufficient to flesh out the corresponding ideas. It remains mandatory to distinguish sound results from wishful thinking.

Reprinted with permission from *Acta Polytechnica Scandinavica* (May 1998) 91:31-43.

We are grateful to Hans Primas for numerous inspiring discussions and for his substantial comments on an earlier version of this article.

Notes

[1]These terms are due to Scheibe (1973) and must not be mixed up with the distinction between "ontological" and "epistemological". The distinction between ontic and epistemic descriptions can, for instance, itself be discussed as an ontological or epistemological topic, according to whether its observer-independent *existence* or its observer-dependent status as a *descriptive tool* is addressed. Moreover, Fetzer and Almeder (1993) emphasize that "an ontic answer to an epistemic question (or vice versa) normally commits a category mistake". The literature on mind-matter questions is full of such category mistakes. Numerous examples can also be found in the context of quantum physics.

[2]Note that the term "observable" was historically developed as a technical term for a property of a system. Prima facie it has nothing to do with the actual observability of that property.

[3]Since detailed discussions of these issues would be far beyond the scope of this contribution, they are omitted here. Some corresponding indications can be found as scattered remarks in recent papers by Primas (1990, 1994a, and others). Among the approaches listed above, d'Espagnat (1995) gives some hints in a non-algebraic terminology but does not substitute a yet-to-be-written systematic algebraic presentation.

[4]Other terminologies such as "uncontrollable influence" (Bohr, 1935) or "passion-at-a-distance" (Shimony, 1984) rather than communication or signaling are less suggestive of a direct conflict with the special theory of relativity. They indicate something like an "internal structure" of a system even when it is considered as a whole, an issue that will be taken up in the following section.

[5]Technically speaking, for every quantum system in a given pure state ϕ there is a factorization such that ϕ is a product state. This is to say that there are always (perhaps fictitious) subsystems which are *not* correlated with each other.

[6]A long-standing misunderstanding in many discussions about the approach to irreversibility as advocated by the Brussels-Austin-group of Prigogine and collaborators can be boiled down to the question whether an ontic or an epistemic description is "primary"—an issue very similar to the Bohr-Einstein-controversies addressed above. The assignment of reversibility and irreversibility to ontic and epistemic levels, respectively, is not controversial: "irreversibility is an emergent property" (Petrosky & Prigogine, 1997).

[7]This term has been coined in discussions with Chris Nunn in the context of an attempt to understand archetypes as memes à la Dawkins (1976) and to develop a corresponding hierarchical structure (Atmanspacher, 1998; Nunn, 1998).

[8]In this spirit, the concept of quantum holism does only make sense relative to the uncritical acceptance of measuring tools that are *not* EPR-correlated.

[9]To our knowledge, this interview of January 14, 1994 (given at Cambridge, Massachusetts) is the most recent source directly addressing the issues of interest for the present discussion.

[10]In the early days of quantum theory, in 1922, Heisenberg once asked Bohr: "If the interior structure of the atoms is so inaccessible to any illustrative description as you say, if we actually don't have any language to talk about this structure, will we ever be able then to understand the atoms?" Bohr hesitated for a moment, then he said: "We will. But at the same time we will understand the proper meaning of 'understanding'." (Heisenberg, 1969, p. 64)

[11]Pauli's position in this regard was ambivalent: though he always stressed the fact that quantum theory refers to the material world alone, there are letters by Pauli in which he expressed his uneasiness with that state of affairs (see Atmanspacher & Primas, 1996).

References

Amann, A. 1993. The Gestalt problem in quantum theory—generation of molecular shape by the environment. *Synthese* 97:125-156.

Amann, A., and Atmanspacher, H. 1998. Fluctuations in the dynamics of single quantum systems. *Studies in the History and Philosophy of Modern Physics* 29:151-182

Atmanspacher, H. 1994a. Objectification as an endo-exo transition. In *Inside versus outside*, edited by H. Atmanspacher and G. J. Berlin: Springer.

———. 1994b. Is the ontic/epistemic distinction sufficient to describe quantum systems exhaustively? In *Symposium on the foundations of modern physics 1994*, edited by K. V. Laurikainen, C. Montonen, and K. Sunnarborg. Gif-sur-Yvette: Editions Frontières.

———. 1997. Cartesian cut, Heisenberg cut, and the concept of complexity. *World Futures* 49:333-355.

———. 1998. Commentary on Chris Nunn's 'Archetypes and Memes'. *Journal of Consciousness Studies* 5:355-361.

Atmanspacher, H., and Primas, H. 1996. The hidden side of Wolfgang Pauli. *Journal of Consciousness Studies* 3:112-126. Reprinted in *Journal of Scientific Exploration* 11:369-386. 1997.

Bohr, N. 1935. Can quantum-mechanical description of physical reality be considered complete? *Physical Review* 48:696-702.

Burri, A. 1994. Interview with Hilary Putnam, in *Hilary Putnam*. Frankfurt: Campus. Translation into English by H. Atmanspacher and F. Kronz.

Butterfield, J. 1995. Worlds, minds, and quanta. *Proceedings of the Aristotelian Society* 69:113-158.

Chalmers, D. 1996. *The conscious mind*. Oxford: University Press.

Crutchfield, J. 1994. Is anything ever new? Considering emergence. In *Complexity—Metaphors, models, and reality*, edited by G. A. Cowan, D. Pines, and D. Meltzner. Reading: Addison-Wesley.

Dawkins, R. 1976: *The selfish gene*. Oxford: Oxford University Press.

Einstein, A., Podolsky, B., and Rosen, N. 1935. Can quantum-mechanical description of physical reality be considered complete? *Physical Review* 47:777-780.

Eisenhardt, P., and Kurth, D. 1993. *Emergenz und dynamik*. Cuxhaven: Junghans.

d'Espagnat, B. 1995. *Veiled reality*. Reading: Addison-Wesley.

————. 1999. Concepts of reality. In *Quanta, mind, and matter*, edited by H. Atmanspacher, A. Amann, and V. Müller-Herold. Dordrecht: Kluver.

Fetzer, J. H., and Almeder, R. 1993. *Glossary of epistemology/philosophy of science*. New York: Paragon House.

Gibson, R. 1995. Quine, Willard Van Orman. In *A companion to metaphysics*, edited by J. Kim and E. Sosa. Oxford: Blackwell.

Hauhs, M., Dörwald, W., Kastner-Maresch, A., and Lange, H. 1998. The role of visualization in forest growth modeling. In *Proceedings of a Conference on "Empirical and Process-Based Models for Forest Tree and Stand Growth Simulation"*.

Heisenberg, W. 1936. Prinzipielle Fragen der modernen Physik. In *Neuere Fortschritte in den exakten Wissenschaften. Fünf Wiener Vorträge, fünfter Zyklus*. Leipzig: Franz Deuticke.

————. 1969. *Der Teil und das Ganze*. München: Piper. Translation into English by H. Atmanspacher and F. Kronz.

Howard, D. 1985. Einstein on locality and separability. *Studies in the History and Philosophy of Science* 16:171-201.

————. 1997. Space-time and separability: Problems of identity and individuation in fundamental physics. In *Potentiality, entanglement, and passion-at-a-distance*, edited by R. S. Cohen, M. Horne, and J .Stachel. Dordrecht: Kluwer.

Jammer, M. 1974. *The philosophy of quantum mechanics*. New York: Wiley.

Jung, C. G. 1971. Theoretische Überlegungen zum Wesen des Psychischen. In *Gesammelte Werke, Band 8*. Walter: Olten.

Kim, J. 1984. Concepts of supervenience. *Philosophy and Phenomenological Research* 45:153-176.

Müller-Herold, U. 1980. Disjointness of β-KMS states with different chemical potential. *Letters of Mathematical Physics* 4:45-48.

Nunn, C. 1998. Archetypes and memes. *Journal of Consciousness Studies* 5:344-354.

Petrosky, T., and Prigogine, I. 1997. The Liouville space extension of quantum mechanics. *Advances in Chemical Physics* XCIX:1-120.

Primas, H. 1990. Mathematical and philosophical questions in the theory of open and macroscopic quantum systems. In *Sixty-two years of uncertainty*, edited by A. I. Miller. New York: Plenum.

————. 1993. The Cartesian cut, the Heisenberg cut, and disentangled observers. In *Symposia on the foundations of modern physics*, edited by K. V. Laurikainen and C. Montonen. Singapore: World Scientific.

————. 1994a. Endo- and exotheories of matter. In *Inside versus outside*, edited by H. Atmanspacher and G. J. Dalenoort. Berlin: Springer.

————. 1994b. Hierarchic quantum descriptions and their associated ontologies. In *Symposium on the foundations of modern physics 1994*, edited by K. V. Laurikainen, C. Montonen, and K. Sunnarborg. Gif-sur-Yvette: Editions Frontières.

———. 1998. Emergence in exact natural sciences. *Acta Polytechnica Scandinavica* 91:83-98.

Putnam, H. 1975. The meaning of 'meaning'. In *Philosophical papers Vol. I: Mind, language, and reality.* Cambridge: Cambridge University Press.

———. 1981. *Reason, truth, and history.* Cambridge: Cambridge University Press

———. 1987. *The many faces of realism.* LaSalle, Ill.: Open Court.

Quine, W. 1969. *Ontological relativity and other essays.* New York: Columbia University Press.

Scheibe, E. 1973. *The logical analysis of quantum mechanics.* Oxford: Pergamon.

———. 1997. *Die Reduktion physikalischer Theorien. Teil I: Grundlagen und elementare Theorie.* Berlin: Springer.

Schrödinger, E. 1935. Die gegenwärtige Situation in der Quantenmechanik. *Naturwissenschaften* 23:807-812, 823-828, 844-849.

Searle, J. 1983. *Intentionality.* Cambridge: Cambridge University Press.

———. 1984. *Minds, brains, and science.* Cambridge: Harvard University Press.

Shimony, A. 1984. Controllable and uncontrollable non-locality. In *Proceedings of the international symposium 'Foundations of Quantum Mechanics in the Light of New Technology'*, edited by S. Kamefuchi et al. Tokyo: Physical Society of Japan.

Silberstein, M. 1998. Emergence and the mind-body problem. *Journal of Consciousness Studies* 5:464-482.

Takesaki, M. 1970. Disjointness of the KMS states of different temperatures. *Communications in Mathematical. Physics* 17:33-41.

Teller, P. 1989. Relativity, relational holism, and the Bell inequalities. In *Philosophical consequences of quantum theory*, edited by J. T. Cushing and E. McMullin. Notre Dame: University of Notre Dame Press.

von Neumann, J. 1932. *Mathematische Grundlagen der Quantenmechanik.* Berlin: Springer.

Chapter 13

Liberal Education as a Reflection of Our Assumptions Regarding Truth and Consciousness: Time for an Integrative Philosophy

J. Scott Jordan
Larry R. Vandervert

The Trouble with Liberal Education

The Assumed Problem

Since the 1970s, the higher-education community has witnessed a proliferation of reports and books condemning the state of higher education in the United States. *Missions of the College Curriculum* (1977), a report issued by the Carnegie Foundation for the Advancement of Teaching, described the undergraduate curriculum as "a disaster area." Reasons given for this state of affairs ranged from professionally-driven education goals on the part of students, to a loss of nerve and vision of the part of faculty. Similar sentiments were expressed in former Secretary of Education William Bennett's *To Reclaim A Legacy: A Report on the Humanities in Higher Education* (1984).

Bennett describes the problem as one of overspecialization and narrow departmentalism, and further claims the reduced number of students majoring in the humanities to be indicative of the deteriorating fabric of American higher education.

Perhaps the most well-known of the critiques to emerge during this time period was Allan Bloom's (1987) *The Closing of the American Mind: How Higher Education has Failed Democracy and Impoverished the Souls of Today's Students*. (It sat on the New York Times' non-fiction best-seller list during the Summer and Fall of 1987, and was described by Paul Zingg [1987] as being one of the loudest shrieks regarding the state of higher education.) In this book, Bloom makes assertions similar to those made by the previously mentioned critics, and ultimately claims higher education to be in a state of irreversible crisis. The root of this crisis is to be found in the School of Arts and Sciences, where nowadays departments go about the business of advancing their fields with an air of intellectual independence. Bloom believes such overspecialization and narrow departmentalism have radically altered the nature of universities, departments, and professors.

> They have been entirely emancipated from the old structure of the university, which at least helped to indicate that they are incomplete, only parts of an unexamined and undiscovered whole. (p. 339)

Bloom acknowledges that others are aware of this issue, and further admits that attempts have been made to promote this notion of an undiscovered whole. One such attempt is the bolstering of the core curriculum. The purpose of this strategy is to ensure each student experiences a sample of all that is available within the arts and sciences. To this approach he responds,

> But this is not a liberal education ... It just teaches that there is no high-level generalism, and that what they are doing is preliminary to the real stuff. Without recognition of important questions of common concern, there cannot be serious liberal education, and attempts to establish it will be but failed gestures. (p. 343)

Another approach Bloom discusses is the development of *composite* courses, what are today, perhaps better known as *multidisciplinary* courses. To this approach he responds,

Unless the course has the specific intention to lead to the permanent questions, to make the student aware of them and give him some competence in the important works that treat of them, it tends to be a pleasant diversion and a dead end. (p. 343)

Given his negative evaluation of these strategies, Bloom then reveals what he believes to be a potential solution; namely, the utilization of Great Books. In them, he believes, we find documentation of our best efforts at grappling with the eternal issues. This opinion is shared by others (Weigert, 1984; Zingg, 1987).

An Alternative Description

If the assignment of Great Books truly constitutes a solution to the lack of integration in liberal education, then (1) there should be some degree of consensus regarding which books qualify as Great, and (2) such books should actually serve to integrate the various disciplines. Research indicates neither of these conditions to be the case. Tomcho, Norcross, and Correia (1994) recently conducted a survey of colleges and universities utilizing a Great Books (GB) curriculum. Of the 77 institutions they identified as offering such a program, 69 responded to the survey, and only 39 of these were later judged to actually offer a GB program. Of the 1,604 books identified by these 39 programs as being Great, only three were identified as being utilized in at least half of the programs. And further, of the 43 books being utilized by at least 20% of the programs, not a one was written by a twentieth-century scientist!

How does a curriculum that uses Great Books to teach the humanities and text books to teach the sciences, pass on to students the notion of an undiscovered whole? Most likely, it does not. Rather, what it does is reveal what some might consider to be the real problem in liberal education; namely, the perpetuation of the notion that the arts and the sciences represent different enterprises. Such division is, arguably, a hindrance to liberal education, for even though the liberation of one's mind from dogma requires exposure to the various perspectives in the arts and sciences, these perspectives alone cannot complete the liberation. Left unintegrated, they come to be seen as disjointed, unrelated bits of information for which the student finds no immediate application in his or her life. Only through the attempt to integrate these bits of information do they attain the status of perspectives, the very meaning of which implies a common object of observation; a whole.

To be sure, concerns regarding integration versus specialization have a long history in the liberal arts. Bruce Kimball (1996) made the following observation:

> historians have come to attribute the origins of the ancients/moderns debate to fourteenth-century Italy, where budding humanism began to challenge the regnant scholasticism of the universities. Even this attribution, however, overlooks the debate that took place during the Middle Ages between *antiqui* and *moderni* who advocated conserving and speculative interpretations, respectively, of the *artes liberales*. (p. 12)

Despite such concerns, the gap between integration and specialization continues to grow. Adrift without a map as to the nature of the whole, we either call for a retreat to a "Golden Age" of liberal education, or bounce our students back and forth between the disciplines, all the while hoping that somewhere along the way they come to develop a map of their own. This sentiment was expressed over forty years ago by the prominent Harvard professor Kirtley F. Mather:

> One of the criticisms of general [liberal] education is based upon the fact that it may easily degenerate into the mere presentation of information picked up in as many fields of inquiry as there is time to severe during a semester or year ... If you were to overhear several senior [graduating] students talking, you might hear one of them say, "our professors have stuffed us full, but what does it all mean?"... More important is the search for basic concepts and underlying principles that may be valid throughout the entire body of knowledge. (1951)

As we continue to develop our disciplines and lose site of the need for basic concepts and underlying principles, we become less capable of serving those students who come to the university with a raw, unsophisticated sense of "ought." As we fail to satisfy their quest for unity, the confidence with which they pursue a liberal education dissipates. The lure of material gain, embedded within a context of increasing financial constraints, serves to further erode such confidence, and ultimately places liberal arts students on the defensive. Zingg (1980) touches on this issue in his article, *The Liberal Arts Student—A Sphinx in the Land of Academe?*;

> Racked with self-doubt, confronted with critics, and apparent witness
> to the material rewards of the pre-professionals, the liberal arts student
> may retreat behind a wall of idealism and tradition, and hurl assertions
> of curricular superiority at all within earshot. (p. 324)

Does this lack of integration influence only our students? Apparently not, for most of the critiques of liberal education to appear since the 1970s seem to *retreat behind a wall of idealism and tradition, and hurl assertions of curricular superiority at all within earshot!* Such pleas indicate our awareness of the problem, but they do not indicate an understanding of its nature. Specialization is not the problem. Rather, specialization is an inevitable consequence of the evolution of knowledge.[1] Specialization without integration is the problem. And this lack of integration will not be overcome by enhancing the core, offering multidisciplinary courses, or assigning Great Books, for a curriculum is nothing more than a manifestation of our collective ideals about what students should learn. This idea is shared by Zingg;

mb

> whatever curriculum is in place at a given moment is, in effect, the
> statement an institution makes about what it considers useful, appro-
> priate, important and relevant to the lives of the men and women it
> strives to educate. (1987, p. 182)

What needs to be acknowledged by those administrating and administering liberal education, is that what we consider useful, appropriate, important and relevant to the lives of our students is a direct reflection of our underlying assumptions regarding truth and consciousness. For example, while the goal of a GB curriculum is to make students aware of the better treatments that have been given to the eternal questions, the list of Great Books indicates a lack of consensus among GB programs as to whether or not such questions are being addressed within the sciences. Implicit in this treatment of the eternal questions is a dualistic philosophy in which what we call the *phenomenological* properties of the world (i.e., the human condition) are believed to be of a different nature (be it epistemically, ontologically, or both) than what we call the *physical* properties of the world (i.e., the material world in which the human condition plays itself out).

This philosophy, which manifests itself in the curriculum, is not one that integrates the arts on the one hand and the sciences on the other. Rather, it servers to keep them separate. Interestingly enough, this dualism used to be the topic of a great debate that included such names as Plato, Aristotle, Descartes, Berkeley, Locke, Hume, and Kant. But as the sciences have come to produce better and better descriptions of what we refer to as the "physical world", acceptance of the physical/ phenomenological distinction has waxed, while the debate regarding the validity of this distinction has waned. This waxing and waning has produced a state of affairs in which the liberal arts community accepts such dualism as given. As the sciences have come to "explain" more and more of the world, the humanities have been forced to lay claim on an ever-decreasing portion of that which can be known. It appears as though the dualists have won, and the arts and sciences are free to go their separate ways.

It is our unwavering adherence to this mental/material dualism, resulting from our inability to develop a world view that integrates the arts and sciences, that serves to erode the search for common, trans-disciplinary principles within the liberal arts community. Our curricula are simply manifestations of this adherence. And an examination of how this adherence came to be and how it is perpetuated may serve to reveal how it might, in fact, be overcome.

Epistemology in the Arts and Sciences

Historical Roots

The debate over the origins and limits of knowledge (i.e., epis-temology) has been one of the staple issues in higher education since the dawn of western culture. And until the advent of the scientific method during the Renaissance, the debate was carried out predo-minantly in a philosophical manner. Due to the success of the scientific method within the natural sciences during the eighteenth- and nine-teenth-centuries however, it was to some extent inevitable this methodology would eventually be applied to knowledge itself. This application was made in the late nineteenth-century, and its result is perhaps best known as experimental psychology. In its attempt to investigate the nature of knowledge scientifically, experimental psychology modeled itself after nineteenth-century physics and adopted, lock-stock-and barrel, the philosophy of the Vienna Circle.

The purpose of the group [the Vienna Circle] was the replacement of philosophy by a systematic investigation of the logic of science. In that manner there began a movement which Feigl later named *logical positivism*, because it reduced all scientific language to the communal language of physics, and which in psychology became *behavioristics* because the psychological operations are all observation of behavior. Even the mentalistic entities, when they are reduced to the physical operations by which they are observed, reduce to behavior. That is the *reductio ad actionem* of behavioristics. (Boring, 1950, p. 655)

As pointed-out by Boring, the adoption of logical positivism demanded that phenomena be reduced to, described as, and defined by the operations utilized in their construction. As also pointed-out by Boring, this resulted in the behaviorist movement in psychology. This was not, however, how experimental psychology began. Rather, psychology's earliest attempt to become a science involved the investigation of consciousness. Most often awarded the credit for initiating this endeavor is Wilhelm Wundt, who, in 1875, founded a laboratory for the study of consciousness at the University of Leipzig. Wundt's method for measuring the basic elements of consciousness was introspection. In this methodology, subjects were trained to introspect, or think about, and then report, the basic qualities of their immediate experience. However, due to the methodology's inability to produce replicable "elements" of experience, it fell into disfavor. Still wanting to apply the scientific method to the human condition, but now certain that consciousness could not be studied scientifically, American psychologists turned to a methodology capable of producing replicable data; namely, behaviorism.

This logical-positivistically driven turn of psychology from the investigation of experience to the investigation of behavior, carried with it certain implicit assumptions that came to have profound effects on psychology's relationship with the humanities. The most important of these, perhaps, is what Menicas and Secord (1983) refer to as the *foundationist epistemology* that is inherent in any science driven by logical positivism:

A foundationist epistemology, although made relative in practice, sees scientific propositions founded on "data." The test of the truth of propositions is "correspondence" between theory and data ... In other words, while perhaps no one any longer supposes that there is a preinterpreted "given" or even some transhistorical, theory-neutral data base, it is generally held that some propositions at least, are basic in that they constitute the test sentences for scientific theory. More roughly stated, hypotheses are to be tested against the "facts." (p. 400)

It is this notion of "facts" that came to be problematic for psychology's relationship with the humanities. For even though the word "facts," in and of itself, is psychophysically neutral (i.e., it does not necessarily beg a physical/phenomenological distinction) its connotation of "real" (i.e., those things that are "facts" are those things that are "real") is in no way neutral. "What is real?" is an ontological question. "What are facts?" is an epistemological question. Confusing the two by equating those things we call "facts" with what is "real," is troublesome, for once we assume that the "facts" of psychology are to be found in what we refer to as "behavior," and then further assume that these "facts" constitute what is "real" about individuals, those things referred to by words such as "experience," "consciousness," "purpose," and "desire," all of which tend to constitute the playing field of the humanities, lose their status as "real." Rather, they come to be seen as "inferences" we make about people, based upon our observation of what is "real" about them—namely, their behavior.

Without a model of the world that could satisfy the ontological and epistemological questions without confusing the two, the descriptions of the human condition given by the humanities and sciences were bound to become polarized. This polarization can be described as *Academic Dualism*. And in what follows, it will be argued that it was the acceptance of this dualism, *in both the arts and the sciences*, that led to, and continues to underlie the erosion of integration in the arts and sciences.

Academic Dualism

The term Dualism, as it is used here, refers to Rene Descartes' distinction between res cogitans and res extensa—between mind and body.[2] The addition of the adjective *Academic* is meant to imply that such a *mind-body* dualism exists within the arts and sciences, where experts in the area of *body* or *material* are to be found in the sciences, and those knowing the *mind* or the *spirit* are to be found in the humanities. On the surface, such an arrangement appears appropriate; the sciences describe one aspect of the world, while the humanities describe another. Daniel Boorstin (1994) discusses these different manners of describing the world in his essay, *The Cultures of Pride and Awe*.

Specifically, the Scientist (the Discoverer) and the Humanist (the Creator) take different paths in their attempt to understand the world. The Discoverer takes the path of convergence, and the Creator, the path of divergence.

> People competing and collaborating in the search for knowledge are inevitably converging. Discovery is what men everywhere have found on our same earth. But creation is what men have added to this world. Its hallmark is autonomy, the freedom to make the new. (p. 24)

This description of the different paths taken by the sciences and the humanities seems appropriate and non-controversial. As the amount of information to be mastered in the various disciplines continues to increase however, we must spend more time and effort in the mastering of our own discipline. Notions of integration becomes secondary, and we come to see our different methodologies as ends unto themselves. As our certainty in this perspective increases, we come to see these methodologies as incompatible; the sciences refuse to tolerate the non-empirical nature of the humanities, while the humanities, likewise, see no promise in the empiricism of the sciences. Both then go their own way, and the lack of integration increases. This is the essence of Academic Dualism.

Does this impact liberal education? It most certainly does. For in this age of ever-advancing technology, students come to believe that *real knowledge* can only be obtained through the empiricism of the sciences. Knowledge gained through the humanities, if it qualifies as knowledge at all, is, at best, an expression of faith, a non-empirically founded curiosity which some day, more than likely, will fall under the microscope of the sciences and be exposed for what it truly is, once and for all. Conversely, the humanities come to see the sciences as having nothing to say about the human condition. This became clear during a conversation with a group of humanities majors. It was odd how sure these students were that they had nothing to learn from the sciences. At one point during the conversation, a graduate-student of religious history pronounced with extreme conviction, "The sciences will never have anything meaningful to say about the human condition!" This comment was truly disturbing, for it smacked of *retreating behind a wall of idealism and tradition, and hurling assertions of curricular superiority at all within earshot.*

But how do we overcome Academic Dualism? When every depart-ment in both the sciences and the humanities has its own methodology and accompanying language, how do we conduct a search for under-lying, unifying principles? A possible first step is to acknowledge our common role as describers.

Our Common Role: Description

Each of us is attempting to describe some aspect of our world. Further, we all believe ourselves to be describing something real. When the historian describes the development of western culture; the philo-sopher, the development of nihilism, and the biologist, the development of the seed into a plant, they do not believe their descriptions to be fantasies having no basis in reality. Rather, they believe such descrip-tions describe something which truly has happened, is happening, or will happen. Further, they believe themselves to be generating descrip-tions which anyone with the proper training would be capable of under-standing. This is why we write papers and make presentations. We do not believe our endeavors to be isolated, trivial, personal opinions. If we deny the existence of some reality which we are attempting to des-cribe, we, by definition, equate our endeavors with the cataloging of noise. No, we believe in reality, and we believe that our work culminates in new perspectives on reality. And even though we know our descriptions to be tentative, we still believe they represent attempts to describe something real.

Radical Skepticism

Most would probably agree that the sciences and the humanities share the common role of describing. Further, most of us would probably admit to a faith in the existence of some reality. But when we also hold to Academic Dualism, to the belief that the sciences and the humanities describe different substances, our simultaneous belief in reality forces us to claim that we are describing (1) different realities, or (2) different aspects of the same reality. Some may believe themselves to have purchased something by selecting the latter over the former option. But both positions beg the question of how it is that the material and the mental, be they separate realities or separate aspects of the same reality, interact. How is it that we come to know, in the mental realm, the nature of those things that exist in the material realm?

If we continue to maintain a distinction between the mental and the physical, the most plausible characterization of this interaction is the one utilized by the British empiricists as they responded to Rene Descartes' dualistic distinction between mind and body. Specifically, they claimed that the material reality reveals itself to us (i.e., gives rise to those things mental; our ideas, emotions, and perceptions) via the *senses*. That is, the material world produces representations of itself in our sensory systems, and it is from these sensory representations that experience arises.

However, if we believe that our knowledge of the world comes to us via the senses, we should immediately become skeptical of the existence of a material reality beyond our senses. For if all we know of the material world is the representation of itself it produces in our senses, how can we be sure of what it is that is causing our sensations? What we know is the representation in the senses, not the thing in and of itself. How can something beyond our ability to experience reveal itself through experience? It cannot, for all we can know are the sensations. The world beyond sensations is beyond our ability to know. Thus, if this material reality exists, we will never be able to know it.

This radical skepticism, which was experienced by David Hume[3] (1977) as he attempted to further the epistemology of the British empiricists, is unavoidable when we claim that the material gives rise to the mental. Yet such skepticism, for both the layman and the scholar, is utterly intolerable. Everyone one of us believes that when we see, hear, touch, taste, or smell something, there is something real about the experience.

A means of overcoming such skepticism might be to examine why it is we believe in "real" experiences. In addition, such an analysis may provide a means of overcoming Academic Dualism.

Theories of Truth and What is Real

This brand of epistemology, in which the material gives rise to the mental, reflects a *Correspondence Theory of Truth*. That is, reality, or that which is real, exists in the material realm, beyond our experience. The experience of that reality *corresponds* to that reality. Again, unexamined, this position appears acceptable; one's experiences are brought about by the objects in the world to which those experiences correspond. But as soon as we scratch the surface and ask, "But how do we know what it is to which our experiences correspond if all we know are experiences?" we are forced to accept the possibility, as pointed out by Daniel Dennett (1991), that we are nothing more than *brains in a vat* having our experiences fed to our senses by some evil scientist we can never directly experience. As absurd and contrary to immediate experience as this statement might appear, it nonetheless serves as a description, just as viable as any other, of the material reality beyond our senses that we cannot know.

Not a one of us believes ourselves to be a *brain in a vat*! Rather, we believe our experiences to be real. And within this belief in *real experiences* lies our escape from radical skepticism. For if a *Correspondence Theory of Truth* can lead us to nowhere but the intolerable doubt of radical skepticism, it must be abandoned.

In its place, one might propose a theory of reality in which the distinction between mental and physical is not based upon the side of the senses to which things belong, but rather, upon the degree to which a given experience is *replicable*. Those experiences that can be replicated across observers, such as the whiteness of this paper or the blackness of the ink, are referred to as *objective*, and are believed to reveal something real about the world that does not depend upon the particular observer—the world of *objects*. Those phenomena that cannot be replicated across observers, such as the degree to which one agrees with the arguments presented in this paper, are referred to as *subjective*, and are believed to reveal something real, not about the world of objects, but rather, about the particular observer (i.e., subject).

This distinction between objective and subjective is not based upon two different interacting substances, thus requiring us to posit the existence of a material reality we cannot know. Rather, it is based on that which we can know; our experiences, what Kant (1929) referred to as *phenomena*.

Within such an epistemology, truth is not found in the degree to which a phenomenon corresponds to some material *it* we cannot know. Rather, truth refers to the degree to which our phenomena and our descriptions of those phenomena are coherent. For example, suppose four laymen leaf through the score of Mozart's *Requiem Mass*. While observing the first page, one of the observers states, "The ink is black and the page is white". If all agree, the observers then believe that the descriptions, *white*, *black*, *ink*, and *page* serve to describe experiences that are common to all of them. The common phenomena are thus believed to be real, and the descriptions, objective. This is *between-observer coherence*. If, however, one of the observers states, "No, the ink is actually red!" the observers now have between-observer coherence on three of the four descriptions (i.e., *white*, *ink*, and *page*), but lack it on the fourth (i.e., *black*). How do they get beyond this lack of coherence? They leaf to the second page. If the three that are in agreement, again use the description black, while the dissenter now states, "No, the ink is green!" the first three tell the fourth that his description is not "true." This is because the fourth has demonstrated neither *between-instance coherence*, nor *between-observer coherence*. If, however, the dissenter had stated, "No, the ink on the second page is, like that on the first, red!" the agreeing three would assume his *between-instance coherence* to be indicative of a real phenomenon, but would interpret his lack of between-observer coherence as indicative of a real *subjective*, versus *objective*, phenomenon.[4]

These tests of the realness of our phenomena and the truth-status of their descriptions, *between-instance* and *between-observer coherence*, respectively, constitute our meaning of the word *Truth*. If we deny this and claim the existence of an absolute truth, an absolute reality to which our experiences correspond, we are inevitably led to radical skepticism, and are left with the intolerable assumption that our convictions regarding reality are unfounded. Such convictions are indeed founded, but not in *correspondence*. They are founded in *coherence*.

In such a *Coherence Theory of Truth* then, which was made explicit by William James (1970) in *The Meaning of Truth* (a book, by the way, that did not appear in any of the Great Books curricula reported by Tomcho, Norcross & Correia, 1994) the word *truth* loses its status as a noun; the absolute *it* to which our experiences correspond, and metamorphosises into an adjective; a modifier indicating the degree to which our experiences are replicable, and our descriptions of those experiences, coherent.[5]

A similar interpretation of James' philosophy, which is perhaps better known as pragmatism, was presented by the Berkeley Physicist Henry P. Stapp (1972) as he applied James' pragmatism to the Copenhagen interpretation of quantum mechanics.

> The contention that underlies James's whole position is, I believe, that a relationship between an idea [phenomenon] and something else can

be comprehended only if that something else is also an idea [phenomenon]. Ideas are eternally confined to the realm of ideas. They can "know" or "agree" only with other ideas. There is no way for a finite mind to comprehend or explain an agreement between an idea and something that lies outside the realm. So if we want to know what it means for an idea to agree with reality we must first accept that this reality lies in the realm of experience. (1972, p. 1104; for an in-depth analysis of how the principles of quantum physics are related to ontologies and epistemologies, see Atmanspacher & Kronz, 1999).

It is revealing that Stapp applies James' pragmatism to quantum mechanics in much the same way the present paper applies it to the nature of knowledge in general;

> the statistical predictions of quantum theory are definitely incompatible with the existence of an underlying reality whose spatially separated parts are independent realities linked only by causal dynamical relationships. The spatially separated parts of any underlying reality must be linked in ways that completely transcend the realm of causal dynamical connections. The spatially separated parts of any such underlying reality are not independent realities, in the ordinary sense. (p. 1103)

Stapp is making clear for quantum physicists, what the present paper is attempting to make clear for all disciplines: The corpus of knowledge in all disciplines is, in its most basic sense, description of what Kant referred to as phenomena, and what James referred to as ideas. They are what is 'given,' and any inference regarding an underlying 'material' reality that gives rise to, or corresponds with, such phenomena/ideas, is just that—*inference* (Jordan, 1997, 1998a, 1998b, 1999, in press).

Such an approach to 'truth and what is real' is conducive to integration in the arts and sciences because it allows one to remain neutral regarding the ontological issue. Such neutrality, in turn, allows one to recognize that the 'of-ness' of the arts and sciences resides within the coherency of the phenomenal. Freed from the scientifically non-testable notion that the material gives rise to the phenomenal, one is then prepared to see the products of the arts and sciences as descriptions of *phenomena*, and one is also prepared to entertain the notion that despite their supposed differences, the truth-status of such descriptions is determined by the same criteria; namely, coherency and parsimony.

Coherency and Parsimony in the Arts and Sciences

The descriptions we give of phenomena serve as a sort of map. The word *map* is used here in the same manner it was used by S. I. Hayakawa (1949) in his book, *Language in Thought and Action*. In this book, Hayakawa makes the distinction between *territories* and *maps*, where *territories* refers to phenomena, and *maps* refers to the word or words we use to refer symbolically to those phenomena. The true difference between the sciences and the humanities is to be found in the nature of the phenomena their maps describe, not in the manner by which they construct those maps.

As a matter of practice, the sciences restrict themselves to constructing maps that point to *objective* phenomena. And like the layman, the truth-status of these maps is found in the degree to which they work. In other words, they are truthful to the degree they pass tests of *between-observer-* and *between-instance-coherence*. However, unlike the maps of the layman, the maps of the scientist do not describe phenomena in the manner dictated by immediate experience (i.e., common sense). For example, Copernicus probably did not watch a sunset and think, "Oh, what a lovely earth rotation!" His experience of the sun and earth was probably very similar to ours. Further, at the time Copernicus developed his heliocentric system of the universe, there really was no practical need for it. Daniel Boorstin comments on this in his book, *The Discoverers* (1983).

> It *(the Ptolemaican system)* described the heavens precisely as they looked and fitted the observations and calculations made with the naked eye. The scheme's simplicity, symmetry, and common sense made it seem to confirm countless axioms of philosophy, theology, and religion. And it actually performed some functions of a scientific explanation. For it fitted the available facts, was a reasonably satisfactory device for prediction, and harmonized with the accepted view of the rest of nature. (p. 295)

Despite all of this, Copernicus nonetheless came to doubt his common sense, and proposed the heliocentric system. Why? Boorstin asks this very same question. Specifically,

> Why did Nicolaus Copernicus (1473-1543) go to so much trouble to displace a system that was amply supported by everyday experience, by tradition, and by authority. The more we become at home in the Age of

Copernicus, the more we can see that those who would remain
unpersuaded by Copernicus were simply being sensible. The available
evidence did not require a revision of the scheme. Decades would pass
before astronomers and mathematicians could gather new facts and find
new instruments, a century or more before laymen would be persuaded
against their common sense. (p. 296)

Copernicus proposed his heliocentric system of the universe because, while watching the sunset, he probably thought to himself,
'There must be a simpler way to describe the motions of heavenly
bodies; one that does not require us to postulate epicycles, deferents, or
concentric spheres of ether which carry such bodies through the
heavens.' This is consistent with Boorstin's claim that Copernicus'
neoplatonic viewpoint forced him to suspect that the structure of the
universe should be much simpler than that postulated in the geocentric
or Ptolemaican system. In other words, Copernicus, like all scientists,
was looking to describe as many phenomena as possible with the fewest
number of statements. He was looking for *parsimony*. This parsimony is
one of the major advantages the maps of the scientist have over those of
the layman. They can describe many more phenomena with a remar-
kably fewer number of statements.

To be sure, these parsimonious statements must be rooted in observation, in tests of *between-observer- and between-instance-coherence*
which anyone with the proper training (i.e., proper experiences) can
conduct. Such empirically-based descriptions make it possible for
others to use the very same map and, as pointed out by Boorstin, converge. However, such empirically moored maps simply represent our
best attempt at producing non-conflicting descriptions. If one discovers
a conflict in the description, the map will have to be redrawn. This is
the methodology of the sciences. It seeks parsimonious descriptions that
are rooted in our common ability to sense, and whose truth-status is
assessed by their ability to accomplish parsimony *coherently*.

What of the maps developed in the humanities? Are they rooted in
our common ability to sense? Is their truth-status assessed by their
ability to be parsimonious and coherent? The answers to both of these
questions must be "yes." For if we respond "no" to either, we reduce
the descriptions given by the humanities to nothing more than unsub-
stantiated personal opinion, nothing more than purely subjective
conjecture that says more about the describer than the phenomenon
being described. This is a characterization of one's work perhaps no

member of the humanities would accept. But how can descriptions of those things found in the humanities; art, music, philosophy, and literature, ever be objective?

To answer this, we return to our laymen friends whom we left leafing through Mozart's *Requiem Mass*. If two of our four observers are replaced by musicologists, all four may still participate in *between-observer-* and *between-instance-coherency* tests of the truth-status of descriptions such as *white, black, page,* and *ink.* But if the conversation turns to the historical context in which Mozart composed the piece, and the impact that context may have had upon the act of composing, the musicologists will come to dominate the conversation. For since the laymen do not find phenomena such as *historical context* and *composition* available within immediate experience, within common sense, they will find it difficult to participate in tests of coherency, and thus, may come to believe such statements to be descriptions of *subjective* phenomena which reveal nothing more than the perspective of the individual musicologist. For the musicologists, however, who have read the same books on *historical context* and *composition* and experienced a similar education (i.e., had similar experiences), tests of coherency are still possible. This possibility, brought about via common education, further makes it possible for statements about such things as *historical context* and *composition* to be based upon our common ability to sense, to be parsimonious, and to be coherent; in other words, to be more *objective.*

But this sounds like the scientific method. If both the sciences and the humanities strive to produce objective descriptions, what is it that is different between them? The answer, simply, is the nature of the phenomena they are attempting to objectively describe. In an admittedly rough sense, one might say that the sciences objectively describe objective phenomena, while the humanities objectively describe subjective phenomena.

The lawful manner in which Beethoven's *9th Symphony* moves us from a state of confusion to one of rapture is indicative of the lawful, territory-like nature of our confusion and rapture.[6] When we attempt to draw maps of such territories, their inherently more-subjective nature renders the resulting descriptions less-open to convergence. This is the methodology of the humanities. Though the maps produced therein are less convergent than those coming out of the sciences, they nonetheless point to real *phenomena*. And even though the nature of these phenomena is subjective, the common education of humanities scholars makes it possible for their descriptions of these phenomena to be submitted to tests of coherency, to be based in our common ability to sense, and to be parsimonious. In short, common education makes it possible for the descriptions given by the humanities, as well as the sciences, to attain the status of objectivity.

Time for an Integrative Philosophy

The objective and parsimonious description of phenomena is what the arts and sciences have in common. The basic data for both are steeped in phenomena, and need not be thought of as the *material* in the sciences and the *mental* in the humanities.

But does this notion that all data are inherently phenomenal truly satisfy? Can't one simply kick a rock to prove the existence of the material? What this question truly means is that any epistemology has to have some ontological *Macht*. It has to provide a theory of knowledge that accounts for what we *call* the phenomenal, and what we *call* the material. Dualism simply assumes the two to be different substances. But this is tantamount to confusing the map with the territory; the symbol with the thing being symbolized. Physical and mental are descriptions of experience, they are not ontological substrates—at least not in a manner we can determine empirically. Adhering to this map/ territory confusion leads to and perpetuates the division between the arts and sciences. In the attempt to overcome this Academic Dualism, we have presented a *Correspondence Theory of Truth,* which claims, essentially, that our notions of truth are derived, not from a correspondence between mental representations and material reality, but from the coherency of the phenomenal. But what is this phenomenal "stuff," and why is there coherency within it?

Some have already recognized this point and have addressed the issue of what this "stuff" might be. Jordan (1998a, 1998b, 1999) for example, proposes a neutral, monistic ontology in which the aspects of phenomenology we refer to as *objects* are not a priori material givens that need to be represented in the brain before they can enter phenomenology, but are, rather, system-relative transformation states that obtain their "objectivity" within a system's field of transformational influence. Having acknowledged the system's contribution to what it takes to constitute 'reality,' this ontology then proposes that within such fields of transformation, interactions among what we refer to as *parts* of the field, render every part of the field *self-referential*, or *about* every other *part* of the field. It is this self-referential nature of trans-formation—*transformed/transforming aboutness*—that is assume to constitute the one substance of the universe.[7] According to such an ontology, phenomenology and its inherent 'of-ness' is not something that emerges as a non-efficacious by-product of the dynamics of a material world. Rather, "aboutness" is the system's 'meaning,' and it is not to be found in a particular, material 'point,' of the system, but rather, within the entire field of transformation in which the system finds itself imbedded.

Another account of the coherency of phenomenal "stuff" and how it came to be is given by Vandervert (1995). He has developed a systems-theoretical, pattern-ontology he refers to as Neuropositivism. Within this chaos-theoretical account of phenomenology, Vandervert claims that the algorithms (i.e., "patterns") of phenomenology were driven into existence, over the course of evolution, via the struggle for available energy. Those thermodynamic energy-transformers (i.e., organisms) whose algorithms (i.e., dynamic structure) made them more capable of capturing available energy (i.e., predators capturing prey) passed on their algorithmic structure to their offspring. It was this thermodynamic struggle among algorithms (i.e., energy-information patterns) that brought about the coherency of the phenomenal.

The positions of Jordan and Vandervert are not being presented here in order to answer the question, "What is phenomenal stuff, and why is their coherency within it?" Rather, they are being presented because they represent attempts to address such issues. Such attempts are of pressing importance given the recent resurgence of consciousness as a topic of scientific investigation. This resurgence is perhaps best sym-bolized by the appearance of John Horgan's article entitled, *Can Science Explain Consciousness?* in the July 1994 edition of Scientific American. In this article, and others regarding the new science of consciousness, the predominant theory of truth and consciousness being presented constituted nothing more than a re-hashing of the theories presented the last time consciousness came around as a topic of scientific investigation: Consciousness was being modeled as an *effect*. Instead of being modeled as the effect of an environmental stimulus, as it had been at the turn of the century, it was now being modeled as an effect of brain activity. This simple cause-effect model of consciousness only serves to perpetuate Academic Dualism, for as soon as one asks, "But how do we know what is causing these brain events?" one is unavoidably drawn down the path of radical skepticism. The epistemological arguments presented in the present paper make it clear today, just as they did when they were first presented by their originators some hundreds of years ago;[8] correspondence theories of truth and consciousness are conceptually inadequate. They may serve as convenient fictions in the laboratory, but they are wholly inappropriate guides for liberal education. Liberal education must make the nature of truth and consciousness one of its more central issues, for it is only in addressing these issues that one comes to challenge the commonsensical notion that reality exists within "matter," and our experiences are simply "caused-effects" of that matter.

Interestingly enough, when psychology became disenfranchised with consciousness at the turn of the century, there were, by-in-large, two different reactions. American psychologists preferred the cause-effect model of classical physics and thus, turned from studying an unreliable effect such as consciousness to studying a reliable effect such as muscle movement (i.e., behaviorism). In Germany, however, some psychologists believed that a science of psychology should remain a science of consciousness. Thus, instead of giving up on consciousness, they gave up on the corpuscular, cause-effect notions of classical physics, and developed what is perhaps best known as Gestalt psychology. In this model of science, phenomena are taken as the basic datum of all knowledge, and the observer is irreducibly involved in every observation. The similarity between these Gestalt ideas and those presented in the present paper is, by no means, a coincidence. Both are dedicated to developing a model of knowledge that avoids radical skepticism, yet maintains our convictions regarding reality.

During a recent discussion regarding these different approaches to truth and consciousness, a colleague described the Gestalt transition from a correspondence theory of truth and consciousness to a theory based on coherence: "When the Germans made that shift in Gestalt psychology, it was like taking a kaleidoscope and giving the barrel a stiff twist. You end of having a lot of the same phenomena there, but they take on different colors, different hues, and different boundaries" (Colella, 1997).

It is time to bring about such a *stiff twist* in our thinking about liberal education. Bolstering the core, offering multidisciplinary courses, and devising Great Books curricula are excellent ideas, but such twists will not produce integration between the arts and sciences unless they have, at their core, the questioning of our assumptions regarding truth and consciousness. It is in the active maintenance of such ambiguity that the arts and sciences can share equal footing. Once we allow the ambiguity to collapse into matter and mental, we make it impossible for the arts and sciences to address the same issues. Such prolonged ambiguity may seem inappropriate in professionally-driven course work, and history reveals it to be very difficult to maintain.[9] But in liberal education, maintaining such ambiguity is not only appropriate, it is our very mission.

Acknowledgments: We would like to thank Richard Yanikoski, Judith Hiltner, Maire Mullins, and Cees van Leeuwen for their comments on earlier versions of this manuscript.

Notes

[1]See Vandervert (1999) for a review of the energy-information principles underlying the evolution of knowledge.

[2]See Colella (1999) for an in-depth comparison of the models of consciousness proposed by Rene Descartes and Giambattista Vico.

[3]Though some may argue that current forms of dualism are superior to those proposed by the British empiricists, these current forms nonetheless still posit the existence of two substances. Chalmers (1996), for example, proposes that since the phenomenal (i.e., consciousness) is only *naturally*-supervenient, and not *logically*-supervenient, upon the physical (i.e., the causally-closed material world), it constitutes a unique, fundamental property of the universe. He refers to this ontology as *natural dualism*. Alywn Scott (1995) bases his *emergent dualism* on the notion that that the dynamics maintaining a given level of organization within a hierarchy of self-organizing systems, are unique to that level, yet emergent from lower levels. Thus for Scott, consciousness is but one of these levels.

In both of these dualisms, it is clear the authors have incorporated the major advances in science that have been made since the time of the British empiricists. These technological breakthroughs however, still do not overcome the issue of radical skepticism. They do make it *appear*, however, as though we are getting closer to doing so.

[4]Even though this thought experiment reflects third-person description, it is written in a manner that invites the reader to imagine him- or her-self as being one of the characters. This affords an examination of both (1) the means by which we define reality in first-person phenomenology (i.e., between-instance coherence) and (2) the means by which we do so in groups (i.e., between-observer coherence). See Souder (1999) for a review of the manner in which the use of certain pronouns in thought experiments tends to constrain the debate regarding the nature of consciousness.

[5]See Bailey (1999) for an overview of James' struggle with the notions of reality and consciousness.

[6]Though some may find it odd to use words such as *lawful* and *order* to describe the work of artists, research regarding the process of creation (van Leeuwen, Verstijnen, & Hekkert, 1999) reveals it to be both lawful, and directed toward some form of solution—what one might refer to as a state of coherence. In addition, Charlotte Stokes states the following: "It is only through the force of their own personalities and talent that artists achieve a sense of order, albeit a very personal, even unique, sense of order" (1999, p. 241).

[7]See Kirchoff (1999) for a look at the impact one's accepted notion of reality has upon one's theory of consciousness.

[8]Though these argument may appear somewhat dated, there exists ample evidence that ontological/epistemological confusion still exists. In a recent publication, for example, Gold and Stoljar (in press) question the claims of some philosophers that disciplines such as psychology and linguistics will ulti-mately cease to exist as brain scientists create better and better models of mind via the techniques and terminology of neurobiology. According to this view, a mature cognitive science will turn out to be a mature neurobiology. While revealing this notion's scientifically untenable nature, Gold and Stoljor admit that most cognitive scientists do harbor a rather trivial adherence to a basic 'mind-is-brain' materialism. Their defense of such adherence, however, is based simply on convention. That is, most cognitive scientists are 'mind-is-brain' materialists because it seems to have been accepted by the cognitive scientific community as the most reasonable ontological position on which to base a science of mind and consciousness. Again, such a position reveals a confusion of ontological and epistemological issues. Jordan (in press), for example, makes the point that since science deals purely in the empirical; that

is, the epistemic, commitments to a particular ontological position can be maintained only via tenacity. Therefore, non-neutral ontologies such as materialism or dualism should be avoided in a science of mind and consciousness, for they prevent one, simply on the basis of non-testable assumption, from entertaining the rather provocative notion that 'mind' and 'brain' might someday come to be conceptualized within an ontological framework in which both are construed of the same substance.

[9]See Rabe (1999) for a review of the prolonged period of aniconic ambiguity that took place during the early days of Buddhist art.

References

Atmanspacher, H., and Kronz, F. 1999. Many realisms. In *Modeling consciousness across the disciplines*, edited by J. S. Jordan. New York: University Press of America (this volume).

Bailey, A. 1999. The strange attraction of Sciousness: William James on consciousness. In *Modeling consciousness across the disciplines*, edited by J. S. Jordan. New York: University Press of America (this volume).

Bennett, W. 1984. *To reclaim a legacy: A report on the humanities in higher education*. Washington: National Endowment for the Humanities.

Bloom, A. 1987. *The closing of the American mind: How higher education has failed democracy and impoverished the souls of today's students*. New York: Simon and Schuster.

Boorstin, D. 1983. *The discovers*. New York: Random House.

Boorstin, D. 1994. The cultures of pride and awe. In *Cleopatra's nose: Essays on the unexpected*, edited by R. F. Boorstin. New York: Random House.

Boring, E. 1950. *A history of experimental psychology*. New York: Appleton-Century-Crofts.

Carnegie Foundation for the Advancement of Teaching. 1977. *Missions of the college curriculum: A contemporary review*. San Francisco: Jossey-Bass.

Chalmers, D. 1996. *The conscious mind: In search of a fundamental theory*. New York: Oxford University Press.

Colella, E. P. 1997. Personal communication with the author, 25 April.

———. 1999. Modern philosophical culture, education and the fragmentation of consciousness: Giambattista Vico and the road not taken. In *Modeling consciousness across the disciplines*, edited by J. S. Jordan. New York: University Press of America (this volume).

Dennett, D. 1991. *Consciousness explained*. New York: Little, Brown, & Company.

Horgan, J. 1994. Can Science Explain Consciousness. *Scientific American* (July) 88-94.

Hayakawa, S. I. 1949. *Language in thought and action.* San Diego: Harcourt Brace.

Hume, D. [1748] 1977. *An inquiry concerning human understanding.* Reprint, Indianapolis: The Bobbs-Merrill Company.

Gold, I., and Stoljar, D. in press. A neuron doctrine in the philosophy of neuroscience. *Behavioral and Brain Sciences.*

James, W. [1906] 1970. *The meaning of truth.* Reprint, Michigan. Ann Arbor Paperbacks.

Jordan, J. S. 1997. Will the real fundamental theory of consciousness please move forward! [Review of D. Chalmers' The conscious Mind]. *Contemporary Psychology* 42(4):298-299.

———. 1998a. Recasting Dewey's critique of the reflex-are concept via a theory of anticipatory consciousness: Implications for theories of perception. *New Ideas in Psychology* 16:165-187.

———. 1998b. Intentionality, perception, and autocatalytic closure: A potential means of repaying psychology's conceptual debt. In *Systems theories and a priori aspects of perception,* edited by J. S. Jordan. Amsterdam: Elsevier.

———. 1999. Cognitive science, representation, and epiphenomenalsim: Beyond materialism. *Dialouges in Psychology* 5:1-7.

———. in-press. 'Mind is brain' is trivial and non-scientific in both neurobiology and cognitive science. *Behavioral and Brain Sciences.*

Kant, I. [1783] 1929. Critique of pure reason. Translated by N. K. Smith. Reprint, New York: St. Martin's Press.

Kimball, B. A. 1996. A historical perspective. In *Rethinking liberal education,* edited by N. H. Farnham and Yarmolinsky. New York: Oxford University Press.

Kirchoff, B. 1999. Consciousness, communities and the brain: Toward an ontology of being. In *Modeling consciousness across the disciplines,* edited by J. S. Jordan. New York: University Press of America (this volume).

Mather, K. F. 1951. Objectives and nature of integrative studies. *Main Currents in Modern Thought* 8:4-6.

Menicas, P. and Secord, P. 1983. Implications for psychology of the new philosophy of science. *American Psychologist* 38:399-413.

Rabe, M. 1999. "Not-Self" consciousness and the aniconic in early buddhism. In *Modeling consciousness across the disciplines,* edited by J. S. Jordan. New York: University Press of America (this volume)

Scott, A. 1995. *Stairway to the mind: The controversial new science of consciousness.* New York: Springer-Verlag.

Souder, L. 1999. Is the dialogue over the nature of consciousness limited by its own terms? In *Modeling consciousness across the disciplines,* edited by J. S. Jordan. New York: University Press of America (this volume).

Stapp. H. 1972. The Copenhagen interpretation. *American Journal of Physics* 40:1098-1116

Stokes, C. 1999. One model, diverse manifestations: A paradigm of consciousness in twentieth-century art. In *Modeling consciousness across the disciplines*, edited by J. S. Jordan. New York: University Press of America (this volume).

Tomcho,T., Norcross, J., and Correia, C. 1994. Great books curricula: What is being read. *JGE: The Journal of General Education* 43:90-101.

Vandervert, L. 1995. Chaos theory and the evolution of consciousness and mind: A thermodynamic—holographic resolution to the mind-body problem. *New Ideas in Psychology* 13:107-127.

———. 1999. Maximizing consciousness across the disciplines: Mechanisms of information growth in general education. In *Modeling consciousness across the disciplines*, edited by J. S. Jordan. New York: University Press of America (this volume).

van Leeuwen, C., Verstijnen, I., and Hekkert, P. 1999. Common unconscious dynamics underlie uncommon conscious effects: A case study in the iterative nature of perception and creation. In *Modeling consciousness across the disciplines*, edited by J. S. Jordan. New York: University Press of America (this volume).

Weigert, K. M. 1984. Sermonizing on the Great Books. *The Educational Forum* 49:155-64.

Zingg, P. 1980. The liberal arts student—A sphinx in the land of academe. *Liberal Education* 66: 321-26.

———. 1987. Quality in the curriculum: The renewed search for coherence and unity. *The Journal of General Education* 39:173-92.

Index

About the Authors

J. Scott Jordan

J. Scott Jordan conducted his Ph.D. research on spatial perception and saccadic eye-movements at Northern Illinois University, and obtained his degree in 1991. During the 1992-93 academic year he conducted post-doctoral studies on learning, memory, and event-related brain potentials at the University of Ulm via a post-doctoral fellowship from the Alexander von Humboldt Foundation. He has since been a faculty member in the Department of Psychology at Saint Xavier University in Chicago, and spent the 1998-1999  academic year as an Invited Scholar at the Max-Planck-Institute for Psychological Research in Munich. He has published multiple empirical and theoretical papers in such journals as *Perception & Psychophysics*; *Psychophysiology*; *NeuroReport*; and *New Ideas in Psychology*. He has also published multiple book chapters, and recently edited a volume of Elsevier's Advances in Psychology series entitled *Systems Theories and A Priori Aspects of Perception* (Elsevier, 1998).

Larry R. Vandervert

In the late 1980's Larry Vandervert began publishing journal articles on how the relationship between the brain and the external world evolved. In 1991, with Fred Abraham and Alan Combs, he led the founding of The Society for Chaos Theory in Psychology and the Life Sciences. Dr. Vandervert has been a Fellow of the American Psychological Association since 1992. In 1997 he completed his editorship of a special issue of *The Journal of Mind and Behavior* titled, "Understanding Tomorrow's Mind: Advances in Chaos Theory, Quantum Theory, and Consciousness in Psychology." Dr. Vandervert also led the founding of a second society, The Society for the Multidisciplinary Study of Consciousness, in 1998. The activities of the Society can be accessed on the internet at: http://www.geocities. com/ResearchTriangle/Facility/3451. A multi-disciplinary mapping of consciousness concepts constructed by Dr. Vandervert appears in the journal *New Ideas in Psychology* (1998) 16(3):159-164.

E. Paul Colella

E. Paul Colella is Professor of Philosophy at Xavier University in Cincinnati, Ohio. He received his doctorate from Fordham University in 1981 and has written on political philosophy and Italian philosophy. He currently directs the Honors Program at Xavier University.

Andrew Bailey

Andrew Bailey studied philosophy at Oxford University and The University of Calgary, completing his Ph.D. at Calgary in 1998. He is currently teaching in the Philosophy Department at the University of Calgary. He has published a number of articles related to the thoughts of William James and the metaphysics of consciousness in journals such as *Synthèse, The Journal of Consciousness Studies, Transactions of the C.S. Peirce Society*, and *Anthropology of Consciousness*, and in two edited collections of papers, *Toward A Science of Consciousness II* (MIT Press, 1998) and *Systems Theories and A Priori Aspects of Perception* (Elsevier, 1998).

Jochen Müsseler

Jochen Müsseler obtained his Ph.D. in 1986 at the University of Bielefeld for a thesis regarding the perception of space and time. His current research interests focus further on the interface of perception and action, the cognitive representations of actions, and attentional mechanisms. He completed his Habilitation in Psychology at the Ludwig Maximilians University of Munich in 1995. At present he is a senior scientist in the Department for Cognition and Action at the Max Planck Institute for Psychological Research in Munich. Among his recently published works is an edited book (together with G. Aschersleben and T. Bachman) entitled *Cognitive Contributions to the Perception of Spatial and Temporal Events* (Elsevier, 1999).

L. Andrew Coward

L. Andrew Coward was educated in England, graduating from Downing College, Cambridge in Natural Philosophy (Physics) in 1965. He was employed by Nortel Networks (Northern Telecom) for over 30 years until his retirement in 1999. At different times he was responsible for most of the different aspects of applying advanced technology to the design of systems to perform very complex combinations of telecommunications functions. He has performed silicon process and device design, software design, development tool design, and system architecture design including system reliability. He has contributed to the design of systems with billions of transistors and millions of lines of software which perform thousands of interacting real time functions. Since 1982 he has studied how the methods and constraints in the design of functionally complex systems can be applied to understanding biological brains. His book on this topic, "Pattern Thinking" was published by Praeger in 1990.

Cees van Leeuwen

Cees van Leeuwen did his Ph.D. in Nijmegen with Emmanuel Leeuwenberg and Hans Buffart and is currently a faculty member of graduate school EOPS, where he teaches visual perception and neuro-computation. His research interests are: visual perception of structures and shapes, attention and awareness, and neurocomputational modeling of visual and imagery processes.

Lawrence Souder

Currently at Drexel University in Philadelphia, and currently the editor of the journal of the Center for Frontier Sciences, *Frontier Perspectives*, Souder has written for a variety of academic and corporate settings. His primary interests are the epistemological and rhetorical issues of science. He has contributed to several encyclopedias of science including *Encyclopedia of the History of Science, Technology and Medicine in Non-Western Cultures* (Kluwer); *Notable Twentieth Century Scientists* (Gale Research); and *Reader's Guide to the History of Science* (Fitzroy Dearborn).

Charlotte Stokes

Charlotte Stokes was formerly Professor of Art History and Dean of the College of Liberal Arts and Education at the University Wisconsin-Platteville, and is now Vice President for Academic Affairs at Humboldt State University in California. Her teaching career began at Oakland University, located 30 miles north of Detroit. She came to Oakland in 1977 after receiving her Ph.D. in art history at the University of Washington, Seattle. She has served as a consultant and chief reader for the Advance Placement test administered by ETS. She has written a monograph on public art, reviews of contemporary art, and book reviews. Her major research interest is related to the subject of her dissertation, "La femme 100 têtes by Max Ernst." She has published more than twenty-five articles and given numerous papers on Surrealism, Dada and Max Ernst. Most recently, she has published a monograph on the Dada movement in Cologne for the series "Crisis and the Arts: A History of Dada."

Bruce K. Kirchoff

Bruce K. Kirchoff is an Associate Professor of Biology at the University of North Carolina at Greensboro. His research spans the areas of biology and the sociology of knowledge. His biological research is centered on questions of flower development and the evolution of development. His work in the sociology of knowledge deals with the relationship between scientific and artistic perception, and social influences on consciousness. He has spoken and written on the connections between art and science and the role of love as a holistic aesthetic for science. Address for correspondence: Department of Biology, P. O. Box 26174, University of North Carolina at Greensboro, Greensboro, NC 27401-6174, USA.

Michael D. Rabe

Michael D. Rabe is an Associate Professor of Art history, teaching surveys as a generalist at Saint Xavier University while serving as an Adjunct South Asianist for the School of the Art Institute of Chicago. Since completing his doctorate at the University of Minnesota in 1987 he has published numerous articles on Indian Art including nine entries for The Dictionary of Art (Macmillian, 1996), a decipherment of the Great Penance Relief, Mamallapuram in Artibus Asiae (vol. 57:3/4, 1997), and a state-of-the-question examination of erotic imagery on the temples of Khajuraho for an on-line journal at: www.asiatica.org. His is currently working on an Asian art history textbook.

Harald Atmanspacher

Harald Atmanspacher obtained his Ph.D. in physics in 1985 at the University of München for a thesis regarding the nonlinear dynamics of multimode laser systems. From 1986 to 1988 he was a Reimar Lüst fellow, and since then he has been a research scientist in the theory division at the Max-Planck-Institut für extraterrestrische Physik in Garching/München. He completed his Habilitation in theoretical physics (nonlinear dynamics and complex systems) at the University of Potsdam in 1995. Since 1998 he has been head of the theory division at the Institut für Grenzgebiete der Psychologie in Freiburg. He has also conducted research at Santa Fe Institute, and the study center of the Rockefeller Foundation in Bellagio, Italy. He has published many books, including "Die Vernunft der Metis" (1993), "Information Dynamics" (with H. Scheingraber, 1991), "Inside Versus Outside" (with G. J. Dalenoort, 1994), "Der Pauli-Jung-Dialog und seine Bedeutung für die moderne Wissenschaft" (with H. Primas and E. Wertenschlag, 1995), "Time, Temporality, Now" (with E. Ruhnau, 1997).

Frederick Kronz

Frederick Kronz is an associate professor in the Department of Philosophy at the University of Texas at Austin. His research interests include the philosophy of physics (especially quantum mechanics and chaos theory) and the methodology of science. He has publications in distinguished journals such as *Philosophy of Science* and *Synthese*, and has received a research grant from the National Science Foundation. He has served as a visiting researcher at the Center for Philosophy of Science at the University of Pittsburgh, the Max Planck Institute für extraterrestrische Physik, in Munich, and the Institute für Grenzgebiete der Psychologie, in Freiburg.

Wolfgang Prinz

Wolfgang Prinz studied Psychology, Philosophy and Zoology from 1962 to 1966 while working with Wolfgang Metzger at the University of Münster. He obtained his Diploma in Psychology in 1966. From 1966 to 1975 he was an Assistant Professor of Cognitive Psychology at the Psychological Institute of the Ruhr-University Bochum. In 1970 he obtained a Ph.D. from the Department of Philosophy, Pedagogics, and Psychology at the Ruhr-University Bochum. From 1975-1990 he was a Full Professor of Psychology at the University of Bielefeld, and from 1990-1998, a Full Professor and Chair of Psychology and Philosophy at the Ludwig-Maximilians-University Munich. Since 1990 he has been the director of the Max Planck Institute for Psychological Research in Munich. In 1971 he received a dissertation award from the "Gesellschaft der Freunde der Ruhr-Universität Bochum". And in 1993 he received the Gottfried-Wilhelm-Leibniz-Award of the Deutsche Forschungsgemeinschaft (German Science Foundation).